Adobe
Photoshop CC
2014 release

Bē
Kylli Sparre

CLASSROOM IN A BOOK®
The official training workbook from Adobe

Andrew Faulkner & Brie Gyncild

W9-BKF-872

Adobe® Photoshop® CC Classroom in a Book® (2014 release)

© 2015 Adobe Systems Incorporated and its licensors. All rights reserved.

If this guide is distributed with software that includes an end user agreement, this guide, as well as the software described in it, is furnished under license and may be used or copied only in accordance with the terms of such license. Except as permitted by any such license, no part of this guide may be reproduced, stored in a retrieval system, or transmitted, in any form or by any means, electronic, mechanical, recording, or otherwise, without the prior written permission of Adobe Systems Incorporated. Please note that the content in this guide is protected under copyright law even if it is not distributed with software that includes an end user license agreement.

The content of this guide is furnished for informational use only, is subject to change without notice, and should not be construed as a commitment by Adobe Systems Incorporated. Adobe Systems Incorporated assumes no responsibility or liability for any errors or inaccuracies that may appear in the informational content contained in this guide.

Please remember that existing artwork or images that you may want to include in your project may be protected under copyright law. The unauthorized incorporation of such material into your new work could be a violation of the rights of the copyright owner. Please be sure to obtain any permission required from the copyright owner.

Any references to company names in sample files are for demonstration purposes only and are not intended to refer to any actual organization.

Adobe, the Adobe logo, Acrobat, the Adobe PDF logo, After Effects, Behance, Classroom in a Book, Creative Suite, Dreamweaver, Flash, Illustrator, InDesign, Lightroom, Photoshop, PostScript, and Premiere are either registered trademarks or trademarks of Adobe Systems Incorporated in the United States and/or other countries.

Apple, Mac OS, Macintosh, and QuickTime are trademarks of Apple, registered in the U.S. and other countries. Microsoft, Windows, and Internet Explorer are either registered trademarks or trademarks of Microsoft Corporation in the U.S. and/or other countries. Autodesk, Google Earth, and all other trademarks are the property of their respective owners.

Adobe Systems Incorporated, 345 Park Avenue, San Jose, California 95110-2704, USA

Notice to U.S. Government End Users. The Software and Documentation are "Commercial Items," as that term is defined at 48 C.F.R. §2.101, consisting of "Commercial Computer Software" and "Commercial Computer Software Documentation," as such terms are used in 48 C.F.R. §12.212 or 48 C.F.R. §227.7202, as applicable. Consistent with 48 C.F.R. §12.212 or 48 C.F.R. §§227.7202-1 through 227.7202-4, as applicable, the Commercial Computer Software and Commercial Computer Software Documentation are being licensed to U.S. Government end users (a) only as Commercial Items and (b) with only those rights as are granted to all other end users pursuant to the terms and conditions herein. Unpublished-rights reserved under the copyright laws of the United States. Adobe Systems Incorporated, 345 Park Avenue, San Jose, CA 95110-2704, USA. For U.S. Government End Users, Adobe agrees to comply with all applicable equal opportunity laws including, if appropriate, the provisions of Executive Order 11246, as amended, Section 402 of the Vietnam Era Veterans Readjustment Assistance Act of 1974 (38 USC 4212), and Section 503 of the Rehabilitation Act of 1973, as amended, and the regulations at 41 CFR Parts 60-1 through 60-60, 60-250, and 60-741. The affirmative action clause and regulations contained in the preceding sentence shall be incorporated by reference.

Adobe Press books are published by Peachpit, a division of Pearson Education located in San Francisco, California. For the latest on Adobe Press books, go to www.adobepress.com. To report errors, please send a note to errata@peachpit.com. For information on getting permission for reprints and excerpts, contact permissions@peachpit.com.

Printed and bound in the United States of America

ISBN-13: 978-0-133-92444-2

ISBN-10:   0-133-92444-0

9 8 7 6 5 4

WHERE ARE THE LESSON FILES?

Purchasing this Classroom in a Book gives you access to the lesson files you'll need to complete the exercises in the book.

You'll find the files you need on your **Account** page at peachpit.com on the **Lesson & Update Files** tab.

For complete instructions, see "Accessing the Classroom in a Book files" in the Getting Started section of this book.

The example below shows how the files appear on your **Account** page. The files are packaged as ZIP archives, which you will need to expand after downloading. You can download the lessons individually or as a single large ZIP file if your network connection is fast enough.

CONTENTS

GETTING STARTED

Adobe® Photoshop® CC, the benchmark for digital imaging excellence, provides strong performance, powerful image editing features, and an intuitive interface. Adobe Camera Raw, included with Photoshop CC, offers flexibility and control as you work with raw images as well as TIFF and JPEG images. Photoshop CC gives you the digital-editing tools you need to transform images more easily than ever before.

About Classroom in a Book

Adobe Photoshop CC Classroom in a Book® (2014 release) is part of the official training series for Adobe graphics and publishing software, developed with the support of Adobe product experts. The lessons are designed to let you learn at your own pace. If you're new to Adobe Photoshop, you'll learn the fundamental concepts and features you'll need to master the program. And if you've been using Adobe Photoshop for a while, you'll find that Classroom in a Book teaches many advanced features, including tips and techniques for using the latest version of the application and preparing images for the web.

Although each lesson provides step-by-step instructions for creating a specific project, there's room for exploration and experimentation. You can follow the book from start to finish, or do only the lessons that match your interests and needs. Each lesson concludes with a review section summarizing what you've covered.

What's new in this edition

This edition covers new features in Adobe Photoshop CC, such as Adobe Generator, which quickly and easily generates image files from layers and layer groups; 3D printing, which lets you bring the 3D objects you design to reality; and Perspective Warp, which lets you adjust the perspective of a shot after it's taken or merge two images shot from different perspectives. In addition, these lessons introduce you to linked Smart Objects, new motion blurs in the Blur Gallery, easier ways to find the right font for your project, how to upload your work to share on your Behance portfolio, and more.

This edition is also chock-full of extra information on Photoshop features and how to work effectively with this robust application. You'll learn best practices for organizing, managing, and showcasing your photos, as well as how to optimize images for the web. And throughout this edition, look for tips and techniques from one of Adobe's own experts, Photoshop evangelist Julieanne Kost.

Prerequisites

Before you begin to use *Adobe Photoshop CC Classroom in a Book (2014 release)*, you should have a working knowledge of your computer and its operating system. Make sure that you know how to use the mouse and standard menus and commands, and also how to open, save, and close files. If you need to review these techniques, see the documentation included with your Microsoft® Windows® or Apple® Mac® OS X documentation.

To complete the lessons in this book, you'll need to have both Adobe Photoshop CC (2014 release) and Adobe Bridge CC installed.

Installing Adobe Photoshop and Adobe Bridge

Before you begin using *Adobe Photoshop CC Classroom in a Book (2014 release)*, make sure that your system is set up correctly and that you've installed the required software and hardware. You must license the Adobe Photoshop CC software separately. For system requirements and complete instructions on installing the software, visit www.adobe.com/support. Note that some Photoshop CC features, including all 3D features, require a video card that supports OpenGL 2.0 and that has at least 512MB of dedicated VRAM.

Many of the lessons in this book use Adobe Bridge. Photoshop and Bridge use separate installers. You must install these applications from Adobe Creative Cloud (creative.adobe.com) onto your hard disk. Follow the onscreen instructions.

Starting Adobe Photoshop

You start Photoshop just as you do most software applications.

To start Adobe Photoshop in Windows: Choose Start > All Programs > Adobe Photoshop CC.

To start Adobe Photoshop in Mac OS: Open the Applications/Adobe Photoshop CC folder, and double-click the Adobe Photoshop program icon.

Accessing the Classroom in a Book files

In order to work through the projects in this book, you will need to download the lesson files from peachpit.com. You can download the files for individual lessons, or download them all in a single file.

Your Account page is also where you'll find any updates to the chapters or to the lesson files. Look on the Lesson & Update Files tab to access the most current content.

To access the Classroom in a Book files, do the following:

1 On a desktop or laptop computer, go to www.peachpit.com/redeem, and enter the code found at the back of your book.

2 If you do not have a Peachpit.com account, create one when you're prompted to do so.

3 Click the Lesson & Update Files tab on your Account page. This tab lists downloadable files.

4 Click the lesson file links to download them to your computer.

5 Create a new folder on your hard disk, and name it **Lessons**. Then, drag the lesson files you downloaded into the Lessons folder on your hard disk.

Note: As you complete each lesson, you will preserve the start files. In case you overwrite them, you can restore the original files by downloading the corresponding lesson files from your Account page at peachpit.com.

Restoring default preferences

The preferences file stores information about panel and command settings. Each time you quit Adobe Photoshop, the positions of the panels and certain command settings are recorded in the preferences file. Any selections you make in the Preferences dialog box are also saved in the preferences file.

To ensure that what you see onscreen matches the images and instructions in this book, you should restore the default preferences as you begin each lesson. If you prefer to preserve your preferences, be aware that the tools, panels, and other settings in Photoshop CC may not match those described in this book.

If you have custom-calibrated your monitor, save the calibration settings before you start work in this book. To save your monitor-calibration settings, follow the simple procedure described on the next page.

To save your current color settings:

1   Start Adobe Photoshop.

2   Choose Edit > Color Settings.

3   Note what is selected in the Settings menu:

   • If it is anything other than Custom, write down the name of the settings file, and click OK to close the dialog box. You do not need to perform steps 4–6 of this procedure.

   • If Custom is selected in the Settings menu, click Save (*not* OK).

The Save dialog box opens. The default location is the Settings folder, which is where you want to save your file. The default file extension is .csf (color settings file).

4   In the File Name field (Windows) or Save As field (Mac OS), type a descriptive name for your color settings, preserving the .csf file extension. Then click Save.

5   In the Color Settings Comment dialog box, type any descriptive text that will help you identify the color settings later, such as the date, specific settings, or your workgroup.

6   Click OK to close the Color Settings Comment dialog box, and again to close the Color Settings dialog box.

To restore your color settings:

1   Start Adobe Photoshop.

2   Choose Edit > Color Settings.

3   In the Settings menu in the Color Settings dialog box, select the settings file you noted or saved in the previous procedure, and click OK.

Additional resources

Adobe Photoshop CC Classroom in a Book (2014 release) is not meant to replace documentation that comes with the program or to be a comprehensive reference for every feature. Only the commands and options used in the lessons are explained in this book. For comprehensive information about program features and tutorials, refer to these resources:

Adobe Photoshop Help and Support: www.adobe.com/support/photoshop is where you can find and browse Help and Support content on Adobe.com.

Adobe Creative Cloud Learn: helpx.adobe.com/creative-cloud/tutorials.html provides inspiration, key techniques, cross-product workflows, and updates on new features.

Adobe Forums: forums.adobe.com lets you tap into peer-to-peer discussions, questions, and answers on Adobe products.

Adobe TV: tv.adobe.com is an online video resource for expert instruction and inspiration about Adobe products, including a How To channel to get you started with your product.

Resources for educators: www.adobe.com/education and edex.adobe.com offer a treasure trove of information for instructors who teach classes on Adobe software. Find solutions for education at all levels, including free curricula that use an integrated approach to teaching Adobe software and can be used to prepare for the Adobe Certified Associate exams.

Also check out these useful links:

Adobe Add-ons: creative.adobe.com/addons is a central resource for finding tools, services, extensions, code samples, and more to supplement and extend your Adobe products.

Adobe Photoshop CC product home page: www.adobe.com/products/photoshop

Adobe Authorized Training Centers

Adobe Authorized Training Centers offer instructor-led courses and training on Adobe products. A directory of AATCs is available at http://partners.adobe.com.

1 GETTING TO KNOW THE WORK AREA

Lesson overview

In this lesson, you'll learn how to do the following:

- Open image files in Adobe Photoshop.

- Select and use tools in the Tools panel.

- Set options for a selected tool using the options bar.

- Use various methods to zoom in to and out from an image.

- Select, rearrange, and use panels.

- Choose commands in panel and context menus.

- Open and use a panel in the panel dock.

- Undo actions to correct mistakes or to make different choices.

This lesson will take about an hour to complete. Download the Lesson01 project files from the Lesson & Update Files tab on your Account page at www.peachpit.com, if you haven't already done so.

As you work on this lesson, you'll preserve the start files. If you need to restore the start files, download them from your Account page.

PROJECT: BIRTHDAY CARD DESIGN

As you work with Adobe Photoshop, you'll discover that you can often accomplish the same task in several ways. To make the best use of the extensive editing capabilities in Photoshop, you must first learn to navigate the work area.

Starting to work in Adobe Photoshop

The Adobe Photoshop work area includes menus, toolbars, and panels that give you quick access to a variety of tools and options for editing and adding elements to your image. You can also add commands and filters to the menus by installing third-party software known as plug-ins.

In Photoshop, you primarily work with bitmapped, digitized images (that is, continuous-tone images that have been converted into a series of small squares, or picture elements, called *pixels*). You can also work with vector graphics, which are drawings made of smooth lines that retain their crispness when scaled. You can create original artwork in Photoshop, or you can import images from many sources, such as:

- Photographs from a digital camera or mobile phone
- Stock photography
- Scans of photographs, transparencies, negatives, graphics, or other documents
- Captured video images
- Artwork created in drawing programs

Starting Photoshop and opening a file

Note: Typically, you won't need to reset defaults when you're working on your own projects. However, you'll reset the preferences before working on most lessons in this book to ensure that what you see onscreen matches the descriptions in the lessons. For more information, see "Restoring default preferences" on page 4.

To begin, you'll start Adobe Photoshop and reset the default preferences.

1 Double-click the Adobe Photoshop icon on your taskbar (Windows) or Dock (Mac OS), and then immediately hold down Ctrl+Alt+Shift (Windows) or Command+Option+Shift (Mac OS) to reset the default settings.

If you don't see the Photoshop icon in your taskbar or dock, choose Start > All Programs > Adobe Photoshop CC (Windows) or look in the Applications folder (Mac OS).

2 When prompted, click Yes to confirm that you want to delete the Adobe Photoshop Settings file.

The Photoshop work area appears as shown in the following illustration.

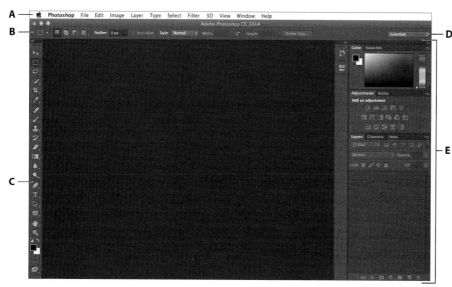

A. *Menu bar*
B. *Options bar*
C. *Tools panel*
D. *Workspaces menu*
E. *Panels*

● **Note:** This illustration shows the Mac OS version of Photoshop. The arrangement is similar on Windows, but operating system styles may vary.

On Mac OS, the application frame keeps the image, panels, and menu bar together.

The default workspace in Photoshop consists of the menu bar and options bar at the top of the screen, the Tools panel on the left, and several open panels in the panel dock on the right. When you have documents open, one or more image windows also appear, and you can display them at the same time using the tabbed interface. The Photoshop user interface is very similar to the one in Adobe Illustrator®, Adobe InDesign®, and Adobe Flash®—so learning how to use the tools and panels in one application means that you'll be familiar with them when you work in the others.

There is one main difference between the Photoshop work area on Windows and that on Mac OS: Windows always presents Photoshop in a contained window. On Mac OS, you can choose whether to work with an application frame, which contains the Photoshop application's windows and panels within a frame that is distinct from other applications you may have open; only the menu bar is outside the application frame. The application frame is enabled by default; to disable the application frame, choose Window > Application Frame.

3   Choose File > Open, and navigate to the Lessons/Lesson01 folder that you copied to your hard drive from the peachpit.com website. (If you haven't downloaded the files, see "Accessing the Classroom in a Book files" on page 3.)

4   Select the 01End.psd file, and click Open. Click OK if you see the Embedded Profile Mismatch dialog box.

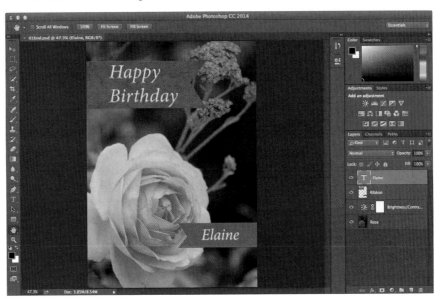

The 01End.psd file opens in its own window, called the *image window*. The end files in this book show you what you are creating in each project. In this project, you'll create a birthday card.

5   Choose File > Close, or click the close button (the x next to the file name) on the title bar of the image window. (Do not close Photoshop.)

Using the tools

Photoshop provides an integrated set of tools for producing sophisticated graphics for print, web, and mobile viewing. We could easily fill the entire book with details on the wealth of Photoshop tools and tool configurations. While that would certainly be a useful reference, it's not the goal of this book. Instead, you'll start gaining experience by configuring and using a few tools on a sample project. Every lesson will introduce you to more tools and ways to use them. By the time you finish all the lessons in this book, you'll have a solid foundation for further explorations of the Photoshop toolset.

Selecting and using a tool from the Tools panel

The Tools panel is the long, narrow panel on the far left side of the work area. It contains selection tools, painting and editing tools, foreground- and background-color selection boxes, and viewing tools.

● **Note:** For a complete list of the tools in the Tools panel, see the Appendix, "Tools panel overview."

You'll start by using the Zoom tool, which also appears in many other Adobe applications, including Illustrator, InDesign, and Acrobat.

1   Choose File > Open, navigate to the Lessons/Lesson01 folder, and double-click the 01Start.psd file to open it.

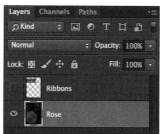

The 01Start.psd file contains the background image and a ribbon graphic that you'll use to create the birthday card that you viewed in the end file.

2   Click the double arrows just above the Tools panel to toggle to a double-column view. Click the double arrows again to return to a single-column Tools panel and use your screen space more efficiently.

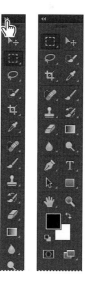

3 Examine the status bar at the bottom of the work area (Windows) or image window (Mac OS), and notice the percentage that appears on the far left. This represents the current enlargement view of the image, or zoom level.

4 Move the pointer over the Tools panel, and hover it over the magnifying-glass icon until a tool tip appears. The tool tip displays the tool's name (Zoom tool) and keyboard shortcut (Z).

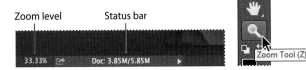

5 Click the Zoom tool (🔍) in the Tools panel, or press Z to select it.

6 Move the pointer over the image window. The pointer now looks like a tiny magnifying glass with a plus sign in the center of the glass (🔍).

7 Click anywhere in the image window.

The image enlarges to a preset percentage level, which replaces the previous value in the status bar. If you click again, the zoom advances to the next preset level, up to a maximum of 3200%.

8 Hold down the Alt key (Windows) or Option key (Mac OS) so that the Zoom tool pointer appears with a minus sign in the center of the magnifying glass (🔍), and then click anywhere in the image. Then release the Alt or Option key.

Now the view zooms out to a lower preset magnification, so that you can see more of the image, but in less detail.

Note: You can use other methods to zoom in and out. For example, when the Zoom tool is selected, you can select the Zoom In or Zoom Out mode on the options bar. You can choose View > Zoom In or View > Zoom Out. Or, you can type a new percentage in the status bar and press Enter or Return.

9 If Scrubby Zoom is selected in the options bar, click anywhere on the image and drag the Zoom tool to the right. The image enlarges. Drag the Zoom tool to the left to zoom out.

When Scrubby Zoom is selected, you can drag the Zoom tool across the image to zoom in and out.

10 Deselect Scrubby Zoom in the options bar if it's selected. Then, using the Zoom tool, drag a rectangle to enclose part of the rose blossom.

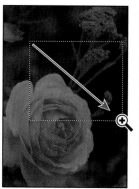 

The image enlarges so that the area you enclosed in your rectangle now fills the entire image window.

11 Click Fit Screen in the options bar to see the entire image again.

You have used the Zoom tool in four different ways to change the magnification in the image window: clicking, holding down a keyboard modifier while clicking, dragging to zoom in and out, and dragging to define a magnification area. Many of the other tools in the Tools panel can be used with keyboard combinations and options, as well. You'll have opportunities to use these techniques as you work through the lessons in this book.

Zooming and scrolling
with the Navigator panel

The Navigator panel is another speedy way to make large changes in the zoom level, especially when the exact percentage of magnification is unimportant. It's also a great way to scroll around in an image, because the thumbnail shows you exactly what part of the image appears in the image window. To open the Navigator panel, choose Window > Navigator.

The slider under the image thumbnail in the Navigator panel enlarges the image when you drag to the right (toward the large mountain icon) and reduces it when you drag to the left.

The red rectangular outline represents the area of the image that appears in the image window. When you zoom in far enough that the image window shows only part of the image, you can drag the red outline around the thumbnail area to see other areas of the image. This is also an excellent way to verify which part of an image you're working on when you work at very high zoom levels.

Brightening an image

One of the most common edits you're likely to make is to brighten an image taken with a digital camera or phone. You'll brighten this image by changing its brightness and contrast values.

1 In the Layers panel, on the right side of the workspace, make sure the Rose layer is selected.

2 In the Adjustments panel, which is above the Layers panel in the panel dock, click the Brightness/Contrast icon to add a Brightness/Contrast adjustment layer. The Properties panel opens, displaying the Brightness/Contrast settings.

3 In the Properties panel, move the Brightness slider to **98** and the Contrast slider to **18**.

The image of the rose brightens.

In these lessons, we'll often instruct you to enter specific numbers in panels and dialog boxes to achieve particular effects. When you're working on your own projects, experiment with different values to see how they affect your image. There is no right or wrong setting; the values you should use depend on the results you want.

4 In the Layers panel, examine the Brightness/Contrast adjustment layer.

Adjustment layers let you make changes to your image, such as adjusting the brightness of the rose, without affecting the actual pixels. Because you've used an adjustment layer, you can always return to the original image by hiding or deleting the adjustment layer—and you can edit the adjustment layer at any time. You'll use adjustment layers in several lessons in this book.

Layering is one of the fundamental and most powerful features in Photoshop. Photoshop includes many kinds of layers, some of which contain images, text, or solid colors, and others that simply interact with layers below them. You'll learn more about layers in Lesson 4, "Layer Basics," and throughout the book.

5 Click the double arrows at the top of the Properties panel to close it.

6 Choose File > Save As, name the file **01Working.psd**, and click OK or Save.

7 Click OK in the Photoshop Format Options dialog box.

Saving the file with a different name ensures that the original file (01Start.psd) remains unchanged. That way, you can return to it if you want to start over.

You've just completed your first task in Photoshop. Your image is bright and punchy and ready for a birthday card.

Sampling a color

By default, the foreground color in Photoshop is black and the background color is white. You can change the foreground and background colors in several ways. One way is to use the Eyedropper tool to sample a color from the image. You'll use the Eyedropper tool to sample the blue of one ribbon so that you can match that color when you create another ribbon.

First, you'll need to display the Ribbons layer so you can see the color you want to sample.

1 In the Layers panel, click the Visibility column for the Ribbons layer to make the layer visible. When a layer is visible, an eye icon (👁) appears in that column.

 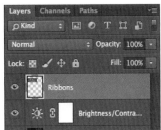

A ribbon with "Happy Birthday" written on it appears in the image window.

2 Select the Ribbons layer in the Layers panel so that it's the active layer.

3 Select the Eyedropper tool (🖊) in the Tools panel.

4 Click the blue area in the Happy Birthday ribbon to sample a blue color.

The foreground color changes in the Tools panel and the Color panel. Anything you draw will be this color until you change the foreground color again.

Working with tools and tool properties

When you selected the Zoom tool in the previous project, you saw that the options bar provided ways for you to change the view of the current image window. Now you'll learn more about setting tool properties using context menus, the options bar, panels, and panel menus. You'll use all of these methods as you work with tools to add the second ribbon to your birthday card.

Using context menus

Context menus are short menus that contain commands and options appropriate to specific elements in the work area. They are sometimes referred to as "right-click" or "shortcut" menus. Usually, the commands on a context menu are also available in some other area of the user interface, but using the context menu can save time.

1 Select the Zoom tool (🔍), and zoom in so you can clearly see the lower third of the card.

2 Select the Rectangular Marquee tool (⬚) in the Tools panel.

The Rectangular Marquee tool selects rectangular areas. You'll learn more about selection tools in Lesson 3, "Working with Selections."

3   Drag the Rectangular Marquee tool to create a selection about ½ inch tall and 2 inches wide, ending at the right edge of the card. (See the illustration below.) As you drag the tool, Photoshop displays the width and height of the selected area. It's okay if the size of your selection is a little different from ours.

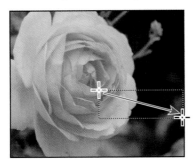 

Selection areas are shown by moving dotted lines, sometimes referred to as *marching ants*.

4   Select the Brush tool (✏) in the Tools panel.

5   In the image window, right-click (Windows) or Control-click (Mac OS) anywhere in the image to open the Brush tool context menu.

Context menus vary with their context, of course, so what appears can be a menu of commands or a panel-like set of options, which is what happens in this case.

6   Select the first brush (Soft Round), and change the size to **65** pixels.

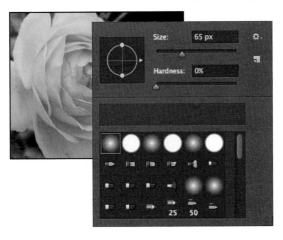

● **Note:** Clicking anywhere in the work area closes the context menu.

7   Click anywhere outside the selection to close the panel.

8   Drag the cursor across the selected area until it's fully painted blue. Don't worry about staying within the selection; you can't affect anything outside the selection as you paint.

9 When the bar is colored in, choose Select > Deselect so that nothing is selected.

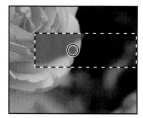  

The selection is gone, but the blue bar remains.

Selecting and using a hidden tool

Photoshop has many tools you can use to edit image files, but you will probably work with only a few of them at a time. The Tools panel arranges some of the tools in groups, with only one tool shown for each group. The other tools in the group are hidden behind that tool. You'll use the Polygonal Lasso tool to remove a triangular notch from the color bar so that it matches the ribbon at the top of the card.

A small triangle in the lower right corner of a button is your clue that other tools are available but hidden under that tool.

1 Position the pointer over the third tool from the top in the Tools panel until the tool tip appears. The tool tip identifies the Lasso tool (⌀), with the keyboard shortcut L. Select the Lasso tool.

2 Select the Polygonal Lasso tool (⌀), which is hidden behind the Lasso tool, using one of the following methods:

- Press and hold the mouse button over the Lasso tool to open the pop-up list of hidden tools, and select the Polygonal Lasso tool.

- Alt-click (Windows) or Option-click (Mac OS) the tool button in the Tools panel to cycle through the hidden lasso tools until the Polygonal Lasso tool is selected.

- Press Shift+L, which cycles between the Lasso, Polygonal Lasso, and Magnetic Lasso tools tools.

With the Lasso tool, you can draw free-form selections; the Polygonal Lasso tool makes it easier to draw straight-edged sections of a selection border. You'll learn more about selection tools, making selections, and adjusting the selection contents in Lesson 3, "Working with Selections."

3 Move the pointer over the left edge of the blue color bar that you just painted. Click just to the left of the upper left corner of the bar to start your selection. You should begin your selection just outside the colored area.

4 Move the cursor to the right about ¼ inch and click about halfway between the top and bottom of the bar. You're creating the first side of the triangle. It doesn't need to be perfect.

5 Click just to the left of the bottom left corner of the bar to create the second side of the triangle.

6 Click the point where you started to finish the triangle.

7 Press the Delete key on your keyboard to delete the selected area from the colored bar, creating a notch for your ribbon.

8 Choose Select > Deselect to deselect the area you deleted.

The ribbon is ready. Now you can add a name to your birthday card.

Setting tool properties in the options bar

Next you'll use the options bar to select the text properties and then to type the name.

1 In the Tools panel, select the Horizontal Type tool (T).

The buttons and menus in the options bar now relate to the Type tool.

2 In the options bar, select a font you like from the first pop-up menu. (We used Minion Pro Italic, but you can use another font if you prefer.)

3 Specify **32 pt** for the font size.

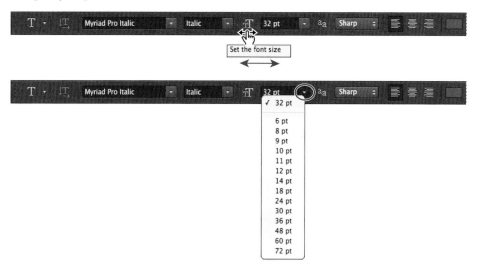

You can specify 32 points by typing directly in the font-size text box and pressing Enter or Return, or by scrubbing the font-size menu label. You can also choose a standard font size from the font-size pop-up menu.

4 Click once anywhere on the left side of the colored bar, and type **Elaine**. Or you can type a different name, if you like. Don't worry if the text isn't positioned well; you'll correct that later.

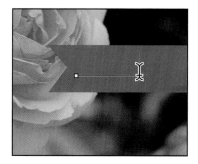
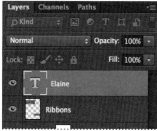

The text is the same color as the bar you typed it on. You'll fix that next.

▶ **Tip:** You can place the pointer over the labels of most numeric settings in the tool options bar, in panels, and in dialog boxes in Photoshop to display a "scrubby slider." Dragging the pointing-finger slider to the right increases the value; dragging to the left decreases the value. Alt-dragging (Windows) or Option-dragging (Mac OS) changes the values in smaller increments; Shift-dragging changes them in larger increments.

Using panels and panel menus

The text color is the same as the Foreground Color swatch in the Tools panel, which is the blue color you used to paint the bar. You'll select the text and choose another color from the Swatches panel.

1 Make sure the Horizontal Type tool (T) is selected in the Tools panel.

2 Drag the Horizontal Type tool across the text to select the full name.

3 Click the Swatches tab to bring that panel forward, if it's not already visible.

● **Note:** When you move the pointer over the swatches, it temporarily changes into an eyedropper. Set the tip of the eyedropper on the swatch you want, and click to select it.

4 Select any light-colored swatch. (We chose pastel yellow.)

 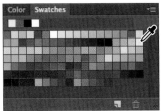

The color you select appears in three places: as the Foreground Color in the Tools panel, in the text color swatch in the options bar, and in the text you selected in the image window.

5 Select another tool in the Tools panel, such as the Move tool (✥), to deselect the text so that you can see the text color.

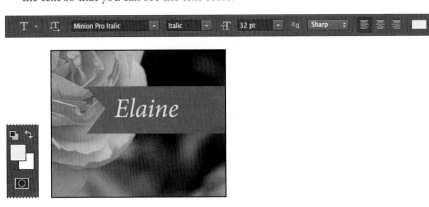

That's how easy it is to select a color, although there are other methods in Photoshop. However, you'll use a specific color for this project so that it matches the text in the other ribbon. It's easier to find it if you change the Swatches panel display.

6 Click the menu button (⁃≣) on the Swatches panel to open the panel menu, and choose Small List.

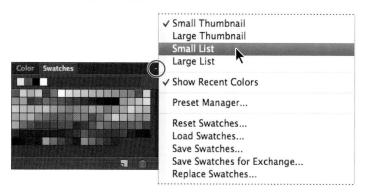

7 Select the Type tool and reselect the text, as you did in steps 1 and 2.

8 In the Swatches panel, scroll about halfway down the list to find the Light Yellow Orange swatch, and then select it.

9 Select the Move tool (⊹) again to deselect the text.

Now the text appears in the orange color.

Undoing actions in Photoshop

In a perfect world, you'd never make a mistake. You'd never click the wrong object. You'd always correctly anticipate how specific actions would bring your design ideas to life exactly as you imagined them. You'd never have to backtrack.

For the real world, Photoshop gives you the power to step back and undo actions so that you can try other options. You can experiment freely, knowing that you can reverse the process.

Even beginning computer users quickly come to appreciate the familiar Undo command. You'll use it to move back one step, and then step further backward. In this case, you'll go back to the light color that you originally chose for the name.

● **Note:** Don't select the Move tool using the V keyboard shortcut, because you're in text-entry mode. Typing V will add the letter to your text in the image window.

● **Note:** The Undo command isn't available if you've already saved your changes. However, you can still use the Step Backward command and the History panel (covered in Lesson 9), as long as you haven't closed the project since you made the changes.

1 Choose Edit > Undo Edit Type Layer, or press Ctrl+Z (Windows) or Command+Z (Mac OS) to undo your last action.

The name returns to its previous color.

2 Choose Edit > Redo Edit Type Layer, or press Ctrl+Z (Windows) or Command+Z (Mac OS) to reapply the orange color to the name.

Undo reverses the last step.   Redo restores the undone step.

The Undo command in Photoshop reverses only one step. This is a practicality, because Photoshop files can be very large, and maintaining multiple Undo steps can tie up a lot of memory, which tends to degrade performance. If you press Ctrl+Z or Command+Z again, Photoshop restores the step you removed initially.

However, you can often use the Step Backward and Step Forward commands (in the Edit menu) to move through multiple steps.

3 Once the name is back to the color you'd like it to be, use the Move tool to drag the name so it's centered in the blue bar.

4 Save the file. Your birthday card is done!

More about panels and panel locations

Photoshop panels are powerful and varied. Rarely would you need to see all panels simultaneously. That's why they're in panel groups, and why the default configurations leave many panels unopened.

The complete list of panels appears in the Window menu. Check marks appear next to the names of the panels that are open and active in their panel groups. You can open a closed panel or close an open one by selecting the panel name in the Window menu.

You can hide all panels at once—including the options bar and Tools panel—by pressing the Tab key. To reopen them, press Tab again.

You already used panels in the panel dock when you used the Layers and Swatches panels. You can drag panels to or from the panel dock. This is convenient for bulky panels or ones that you use only occasionally but want to keep handy.

You can arrange panels in other ways, as well:

- To move an entire panel group, drag the title bar to another location in the work area.

- To move a panel to another group, drag the panel tab into that panel group so that a blue highlight appears inside the group, and then release the mouse button.

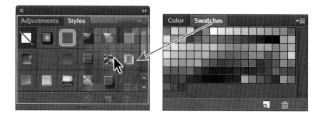
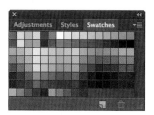

- To dock a panel or panel group, drag the title bar or panel tab onto the top of the dock.

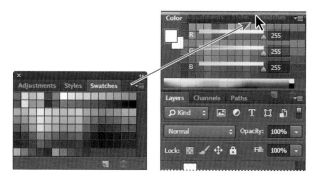
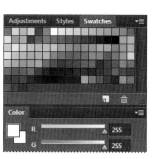

- To undock a panel or panel group so that it becomes a floating panel or panel group, drag its title bar or panel tab away from the dock.

Note: When panels are hidden, a thin, semitransparent strip is visible at the edge of the document. Hovering the pointer over the strip displays its contents.

Expanding and collapsing panels

You can resize panels to use screen space more efficiently and to see fewer or more panel options, either by dragging or clicking to toggle between preset sizes:

- To collapse open panels to icons, click the double arrow in the title bar of the dock or panel group. To expand a panel, click its icon or the double arrow.

- To change the height of a panel, drag its lower right corner.

- To change the width of the dock, position the pointer on the left edge of the dock until it becomes a double-headed arrow, and then drag to the left to widen the dock, or to the right to narrow it.

- To resize a floating panel, move the pointer over the right, left, or bottom edge of the panel until it becomes a double-headed arrow, and then drag the edge in or out. You can also pull the lower right corner in or out.

Note: You can collapse, but not resize, the Character and Paragraph panels.

- To collapse a panel group so that only the dock header bar and tabs are visible, double-click a panel tab or panel title bar. Double-click again to restore it to the expanded view. You can open the panel menu even when the panel is collapsed.

Notice that the tabs for the panels in the panel group and the button for the panel menu remain visible after you collapse a panel.

Special notes about the Tools panel and options bar

The Tools panel and the options bar share some characteristics with other panels:

- You can drag the Tools panel by its title bar to a different location in the work area. You can move the options bar to another location by dragging the grab bar at the far left end of the panel.

- You can hide the Tools panel and options bar.

However, some panel features are not available or don't apply to the Tools panel or options bar:

- You cannot group the Tools panel or options bar with other panels.

- You cannot resize the Tools panel or options bar.

- You cannot stack the Tools panel or options bar in the panel dock.

- The Tools panel and options bar do not have panel menus.

Finding resources for using Photoshop

The following resources can help you take your explorations even further, answer questions you have, and help you resolve any issues you encounter as you work on your own projects.

Adobe Photoshop Help and Support: www.adobe.com/support/photoshop is where you can find and browse Help and Support content on Adobe.com.

Adobe Creative Cloud Learn: helpx.adobe.com/creative-cloud/tutorials.html provides inspiration, key techniques, cross-product workflows, and updates on new features.

Adobe Forums: forums.adobe.com lets you tap into peer-to-peer discussions, questions, and answers on Adobe products.

Changing interface settings

By default, the panels, dialog boxes, and background in Photoshop are dark. You can lighten the interface or make other changes in the Photoshop Preferences dialog box:

1   Choose Edit > Preferences > Interface (Windows) or Photoshop > Preferences > Interface (Mac OS).

2   Select a different color theme, or make other changes.

When you select a different theme, you can see the changes immediately. You can also select specific colors for different screen modes and change other interface settings in this dialog box.

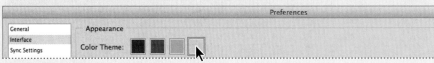

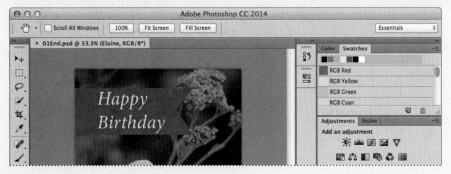

3   When you're satisfied with the changes, click OK.

Review questions

1 Describe two types of images you can open in Photoshop.

2 How do you select tools in Photoshop?

3 Describe two ways to zoom in to or out from an image.

4 What are two ways to get more information about Photoshop?

Review answers

1 You can scan a photograph, transparency, negative, or graphic into the program; capture a digital video image; or import artwork created in a drawing program. You can also import digital photos.

2 To select a tool in Photoshop, click its icon in the Tools panel, or press the tool's keyboard shortcut. A selected tool remains active until you select a different tool. To select a hidden tool, either use a keyboard shortcut to toggle through the tools, or click and hold the tool in the Tools panel to open a pop-up menu of the hidden tools.

3 Choose commands from the View menu to zoom in on or out from an image, or to fit it onscreen, or use the zoom tools and click or drag over an image to enlarge or reduce the view. You can also use keyboard shortcuts or the Navigator panel to control the display of an image.

4 The Photoshop Help system includes full information about Photoshop features plus keyboard shortcuts, task-based topics, and illustrations. Creative Cloud Learn provides inspiration, key techniques, cross-product workflows, and updates on new features.

2 BASIC PHOTO CORRECTIONS

Lesson overview

In this lesson, you'll learn how to do the following:

- Understand image resolution and size.

- View and access files in Adobe Bridge.

- Straighten and crop an image.

- Adjust the tonal range of an image.

- Use the Spot Healing Brush tool to repair part of an image.

- Use the content-aware Patch tool to remove or replace objects.

- Use the Clone Stamp tool to touch up areas.

- Remove digital artifacts from an image.

- Apply the Smart Sharpen filter to finish retouching photos.

 This lesson will take about an hour to complete. Download the Lesson02 project files from the Lesson & Update Files tab on your Account page at www.peachpit.com, if you haven't already done so. As you work on this lesson, you'll preserve the start files. If you need to restore the start files, download them from your Account page.

PROJECT: VINTAGE PHOTOGRAPH RESTORATION

Photoshop includes a variety of tools and commands for improving the quality of a photographic image. This lesson steps you through the process of acquiring, resizing, and retouching a vintage photograph.

Strategy for retouching

● **Note:** In this lesson, you retouch an image using only Photoshop. For other images, it may be more efficient to work in Adobe Camera Raw, which is installed with Photoshop. You'll learn about the tools Camera Raw has to offer in Lesson 12, "Working with Camera Raw."

How much retouching you do depends on the image you're working on and your goals for it. For many images, you may need only to change the resolution, lighten the image, or repair a minor blemish. For others, you may need to perform several tasks and employ more advanced filters.

Organizing an efficient sequence of tasks

Most retouching procedures follow these general steps, though not every task may be necessary for all projects:

- Duplicating the original image or scan; working in a copy of the image file makes it easy to recover the original later if necessary
- Ensuring that the resolution is appropriate for the way you'll use the image
- Cropping the image to its final size and orientation
- Removing any color casts
- Adjusting the overall contrast or tonal range of the image
- Repairing flaws in scans of damaged photographs (such as rips, dust, or stains)
- Adjusting the color and tone in specific parts of the image to bring out highlights, midtones, shadows, and desaturated colors
- Sharpening the overall focus of the image

The order of the tasks may vary depending on the project, though you should always start by duplicating the image and adjusting its resolution. Likewise, sharpening should usually be your final step. For the other tasks, consider your project and plan accordingly, so that the results of one process do not cause unintended changes to other aspects of the image, making it necessary for you to redo some of your work.

Adjusting your process for different intended uses

The retouching techniques you apply to an image depend in part on how you'll use the image. Whether an image is intended for black-and-white publication on newsprint or for full-color online distribution affects everything from the resolution of the initial scan to the type of tonal range and color correction that the image requires. Photoshop supports the CMYK color mode for preparing an image to be printed using process colors, as well as RGB and other color modes for web and mobile authoring.

Resolution and image size

The first step in retouching a photograph in Photoshop is to make sure that the image has an appropriate resolution. The term *resolution* refers to the number of small squares, known as *pixels,* that describe an image and establish its detail. Resolution is determined by *pixel dimensions*, or the number of pixels along the width and height of an image.

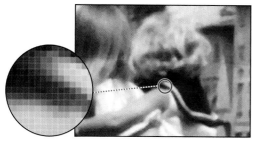

Pixels in a photographic image

In computer graphics, there are different types of resolution:

The number of pixels per unit of length in an image is called the *image resolution,* usually measured in pixels per inch (ppi). An image with a high resolution has more pixels (and therefore a larger file size) than an image of the same dimensions with a low resolution. Images in Photoshop can vary from high resolution (300 ppi or higher) to low resolution (72 ppi or 96 ppi).

The number of pixels per unit of length on a monitor is the *monitor resolution,* also usually measured in pixels per inch (ppi). Image pixels are translated directly into monitor pixels. In Photoshop, if the image resolution is higher than the monitor resolution, the image appears larger onscreen than its specified print dimensions. For example, when you display a 1x1-inch, 144-ppi image on a 72-ppi monitor, the image fills a 2x2-inch area of the screen.

7x7 inches at 72 ppi; file size 744.2KB
100% onscreen view

7x7 inches at 200 ppi; file size 5.61MB
100% onscreen view

Note: To determine the image resolution for a photograph you plan to print, follow the computer-graphics rule of thumb for color or grayscale images intended for print on large commercial printers: Scan at a resolution 1.5 to 2 times the screen frequency used by the printer. If the image will be printed using a screen frequency of 133 lpi, scan the image at 200 ppi (133x1.5).

Note: It's important to understand what "100% view" means when you work onscreen. At 100%, one image pixel = one monitor pixel. Unless the resolution of your image is exactly the same as the resolution of the monitor, the image size (in inches, for example) onscreen may be larger or smaller than the image size will be when printed.

The number of ink dots per inch (dpi) produced by a platesetter or laser printer is the printer, or output, resolution. Higher resolution images output to higher resolution printers generally produce the best quality. The appropriate resolution for a printed image is determined both by the printer resolution and by the screen frequency, or lines per inch (lpi), of the halftone screens used to reproduce images.

Keep in mind that the higher the image resolution, the larger the file size, and the longer the file will take to print or to download from the web.

For more information on resolution and image size, see Photoshop Help.

Opening a file with Adobe Bridge

In this book, you'll work with different start files in each lesson. You may make copies of these files and save them under different names or locations, or you may work from the original start files and then download them from the peachpit.com website again if you want a fresh start.

In this lesson, you'll retouch a scan of a damaged and discolored vintage photograph so it can be shared or printed. The final image size will be 7x7 inches.

● **Note:** If Bridge isn't installed, you'll need to install it from Adobe Creative Cloud. For more information, see page 3.

In Lesson 1, you used the Open command to open a file. You'll start this lesson by comparing the original scan to the finished image in Adobe Bridge, a visual file browser that helps take the guesswork out of finding the image file that you need.

1   Start Photoshop, and then immediately hold down Ctrl+Alt+Shift (Windows) or Command+Option+Shift (Mac OS) to reset the default settings.

2   When prompted, click Yes to confirm that you want to delete the Adobe Photoshop Settings file.

3   Choose File > Browse In Bridge. If you're prompted to enable the Photoshop extension in Bridge, click OK.

Adobe Bridge opens, displaying a collection of panels, menus, and buttons.

4   Select the Folders tab in the upper left corner, and then browse to the Lessons folder you downloaded onto your hard disk, so that the lesssons in the Lessons folder appear in the Content panel.

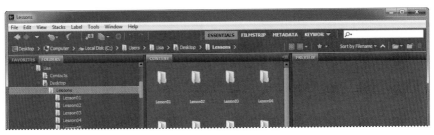

5 With the Lessons folder still selected in the Folders panel, choose File > Add To Favorites.

Adding files, folders, application icons, and other assets that you use often to the Favorites panel lets you access them quickly.

6 Select the Favorites tab to open the panel, and click the Lessons folder to open it. Then, in the Content panel, double-click the Lesson02 folder.

Thumbnail previews of the folder contents appear in the Content panel.

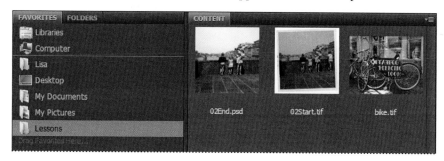

7 Compare the 02Start.tif and 02End.psd files. To enlarge the thumbnails in the Content panel, drag the Thumbnail slider at the bottom of the Bridge window to the right.

In the 02Start.tif file, notice that the image is crooked, the colors are relatively dull, and the image has a green color cast and a distracting crease. You'll fix all of these problems in this lesson, and a few others. You'll start by cropping and straightening the image.

8 Double-click the 02Start.tif thumbnail to open the file in Photoshop. Click OK if you see the Embedded Profile Mismatch dialog box.

9 In Photoshop, choose File > Save As. Choose Photoshop from the Format menu, and name the file **02Working.psd**. Then click Save.

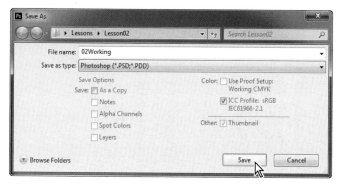

Straightening and cropping the image in Photoshop

► **Tip:** Deselect the Delete Cropped Pixels option if you want to crop nondestructively, so that you can revise the crop later.

You'll use the Crop tool to straighten, trim, and scale the photograph. You can use either the Crop tool or the Crop command to crop an image. By default, cropping deletes the cropped pixels.

1   In the Tools panel, select the Crop tool (⊣).

Crop handles appear, and a *cropping shield* covers the area outside the cropping selection.

2   In the options bar, choose W x H x Resolution from the Preset Aspect Ratio menu. (Ratio is the default value.)

3   In the options bar, type **7 in** for the width, **7 in** for the height, and **200** px/in for the resolution. A crop grid appears.

First, you'll straighten the image.

4   Click Straighten in the options bar. The pointer changes to the Straighten tool.

5   Click at the top corner of the photo, press the mouse button as you drag a straight line across the top edge of the photo, and then release.

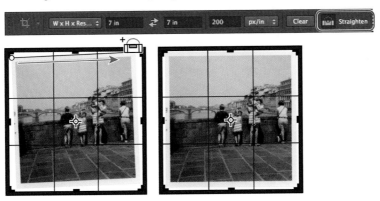

Photoshop straightens the image, so that the line you drew is parallel with the top of the image area. You drew a line across the top of the photo, but any line that defines either the vertical or horizontal axis of the image will work.

Now, you'll trim the white border and scale the image.

6 Drag the corners of the crop grid in to the corners of the photo itself to crop out the white border. If you need to adjust the position of the photo, click and drag it within the crop grid.

Tip: You can choose Image > Trim to discard a border area around the edge of the image, based on transparency or edge color.

7 Press Enter or Return to accept the crop.

The image is now cropped, and the cropped image fills the image window, straightened, sized, and positioned according to your specifications.

Tip: To quickly straighten a photo and crop out the scanned background, choose File > Automate > Crop And Straighten Photos.

8 To see the image dimensions, choose Document Dimensions from the pop-up menu at the bottom of the application window.

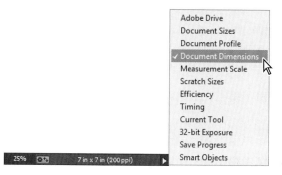

9 Choose File > Save to save your work. Click OK if you see the Photoshop Format Options dialog box.

Adjusting the color and tone

You'll use Curves and Levels adjustment layers to remove the color cast and adjust the color and tone in the image. Don't let the Curves or Levels options intimidate you. You'll work with them more in later lessons; for now, you'll take advantage of their tools to quickly brighten and adjust the tone of the image.

1 Click Curves in the Adjustments panel to add a Curves adjustment layer.

2 Select the White Point tool on the left side of the Properties panel.

Specifying a white point changes all the colors in the image. The white point is the color that Photoshop defines as pure white, and it adjusts all other colors accordingly. To set an accurate white point, select a white area in the image.

3 Click a white stripe on the girl's dress.

The color tone of the image changes dramatically. You can click different white areas, such as the child's sailor dress, a stripe on the woman's dress, or the girl's sock, to see how each selection changes the color.

In some images, adjusting the white point is enough to remove a color cast and correct the tone of the image. Here, selecting a white point is a good start. You'll use a Levels adjustment layer to fine-tune the tone.

4 Click Levels in the Adjustments panel to add a Levels adjustment layer.

The Levels histogram in the Properties panel displays the range of dark and light values in the image. You'll learn more about working with levels in later lessons. Right now, you just need to know that the left triangle represents the black point (the point Photoshop defines as the darkest in the image), the right triangle represents the white point (the lightest in the image), and the middle triangle represents the midtones.

5 Drag the left triangle (blacks) under the histogram to the right, where the blacks are more pronounced. Our value was 15.

6 Drag the middle triangle a little to the right to adjust the midtones. Our value was .90.

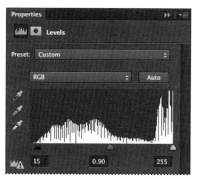

Now that you've adjusted the color, you'll flatten the image so it's easier to work with while you touch it up. Flattening an image merges its layers. After you flatten an image, you can no longer edit layers individually, but the file is smaller, and you can easily make changes to the entire image at once.

7 Choose Layer > Flatten Image.

The adjustment layers merge with the Background layer.

As owner of Gawain Weaver Art Conservation, Gawain Weaver has conserved and restored original works by artists ranging from Eadward Muybridge to Man Ray, and from Ansel Adams to Cindy Sherman. He teaches workshops internationally as well as online on the care and identification of photographs.

Find out more at gawainweaver.com.

Real-world photo restoration

The tools in Photoshop make restoration of old or damaged photographs seem like magic, giving virtually anyone the power to scan, retouch, print, and frame their photo collections.

However, when dealing with works by famous artists, museums, galleries, and collectors need to preserve original objects to the greatest degree possible despite deterioration or accidental damage. Professional art conservators are called upon to clean dust and soiling from print surfaces, remove discoloration and staining, repair tears, stabilize prints to prevent future damage, and even paint in missing areas of a work.

*Carleton E. Watkins, Nevada Fall, 700 FT, Yosemite Valley, CA, mammoth albumen print, 15⅝"x20¾".
This print was removed from its mount to remove the stains and then remounted.*

"Photograph conservation is both a science and an art," says Weaver. "We must apply what we know about the chemistry of the photograph, its mount, and any varnishes or other coatings in order to safely clean, preserve, and enhance the image. Since we cannot quickly 'undo' a step in a conservation treatment, we must always proceed with great caution and a healthy respect for the fragility of the photographic object whether it's a 160-year-old salt print of Notre Dame or gelatin silver print of Half Dome from the 1970s."

Many of the manual tools of an art conservator have analogous digital versions in Photoshop:

 An art conservator might wash a photograph to remove the discolored components of the paper, or even use a mild bleaching process known as light-bleaching to oxidize and remove the colored components of a stain or overall discoloration. In Photoshop, you can use a Curves adjustment layer to remove the color cast from an image.

 A conservator working on a fine-art photograph might use special paints and fine brushes to manually "in-paint" damaged areas of a photograph. Likewise, you can use the Spot Healing Brush in Photoshop to spot out specks of dust or dirt on a scanned image.

 A conservator might use Japanese papers and wheat-starch paste to carefully repair and rebuild torn paper before finalizing the repair with some skillful in-painting. In Photoshop, you can remove a crease or repair a tear in a scanned image with a few clicks of the Clone tool.

A fixative was applied to the artist's signature with a small brush to protect it when the mount was washed.

"Although our work has always been first and foremost about the preservation and restoration of the original photographic object, there are instances, especially with family photographs, where the use of Photoshop is more appropriate," says Weaver. "More dramatic results can be achieved in far less time. After digitization the original print can be safely stored away, while the digital version can be copied or printed for many family members. Often, we first clean or unfold family photographs to safely reveal as much of the original image as possible, and then we repair the remaining discoloration, stains, and tears on the computer after digitization."

AFTER

Using the Spot Healing Brush tool

Note: The Healing Brush tool works similarly to the Spot Healing Brush tool, except that it requires you to sample source pixels before retouching an area.

The next task is to remove the crease in the photo. You'll use the Spot Healing Brush to erase the crease. While you're at it, you'll use it to address a few other issues.

The Spot Healing Brush tool quickly removes blemishes and other imperfections. It samples pixels around the retouched area and matches the texture, lighting, transparency, and shading of the sampled pixels to the pixels being healed.

The Spot Healing Brush is excellent for retouching blemishes in portraits, but also works nicely wherever there's a uniform appearance near the areas you want to retouch.

1   Zoom in to see the crease clearly.

2   In the Tools panel, select the Spot Healing Brush tool (🖌).

3   In the options bar, open the Brush pop-up panel, and specify a **100%** hard brush about 25 px in diameter. Make sure Content-Aware is selected in the options bar.

4   In the image window, drag the Spot Healing Brush down from the top of the crease. You can probably repair the entire crease with four to six neat downward strokes. As you drag, the stroke at first appears black, but when you release the mouse, the painted area is "healed."

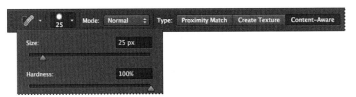

5   Zoom in to see the white hair in the upper right area of the image. Then select the Spot Healing Brush again, and paint over the hair.

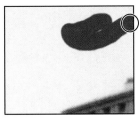

6   Zoom out, if necessary, to see the full sky. Then click the Spot Healing Brush wherever there are dark areas you want to heal.

7   Save your work so far.

Applying a content-aware patch

Use the Patch tool to remove unwanted elements from an image. You'll use a content-aware patch to remove an unrelated person from the right side of the photo. In Content-Aware mode, the Patch tool creates nearly seamless blending with the nearby content.

1   In the Tools panel, select the Patch tool (⬚), hidden beneath the Spot Healing Brush tool (✐).

2   In the options bar, choose Content-Aware from the Patch menu, and make sure that Sample All Layers is selected. Then click the Adaptation gear icon, and choose 5 from the Structure menu.

The Structure menu determines how closely the patch reflects the existing image patterns. You can choose from 1 to 5, with 1 allowing the loosest adherence to the source structure and 5 requiring the strictest.

3   Drag the Patch tool around the boy and his shadow, as closely as possible. You may want to zoom in to see him more clearly.

4   Click within the area you've just selected, and drag it to the left. Photoshop displays a preview of the content that will replace the boy. Keep dragging to the left until the preview area no longer overlaps the area occupied by the boy, but without overlapping the woman or the girl she's holding. Release the mouse button when the patch is positioned where you want it.

The selection changes to match the area around it. The boy is gone, and where he stood is a section of the bridge wall, and a building.

5 Choose Select > Deselect.

The effect was pretty impressive, but not quite perfect. You'll touch up the results next.

Repairing areas with the Clone Stamp tool

The Clone Stamp tool uses pixels from one area of an image to replace the pixels in another part of the image. Using this tool, you can not only remove unwanted objects from your images, but you can also fill in missing areas in photographs you scan from damaged originals.

You'll use the Clone Stamp tool to smooth out some irregularities in the height of the bridge wall and the windows on the building.

1 Select the Clone Stamp tool (🔖) in the Tools panel, and select a **60 px** brush with **30%** hardness. Make sure that the Aligned option is selected.

2 Move the Clone Stamp tool to an area where the top of the bridge wall is smooth. That's the area you want to copy to smooth out the area that was patched.

3 Alt-click (Windows) or Option-click (Mac OS) to start sampling that part of the image. (When you press Alt or Option, the pointer appears as target cross-hairs.)

4 Drag the Clone Stamp tool across the top of the bridge wall in the patched area to even it out, and then release the mouse button.

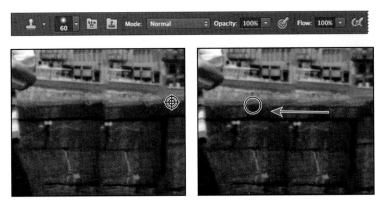

Each time you click the Clone Stamp tool, it begins again with a new source point, in the same relationship to the tool as the first stroke you made. That is, if you begin painting further right, it samples from stone that is further right than the original source point. That's because Aligned is selected in the options bar. Deselect Aligned if you want to start from the same source point each time.

5 Select a source point where the bottom of the bridge wall is even, and then drag the Clone Stamp tool across the bottom of the wall where you patched it.

6 Select a smaller brush size, and deselect Aligned. Then select a source point over the rightmost windows in the lowest row on the building you patched. Click across to create accurate windows there.

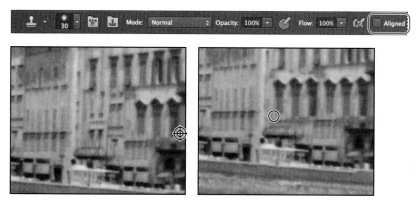

7 Repeat step 6 to make any adjustments you want to make to the lowest area of the building and the wall that runs in front of it.

8 If you like, you can use a smaller brush size to touch up the stones in the patched portion of the wall.

9 Save your work.

Sharpening the image

The last task you might want to do when retouching a photo is to sharpen the image. There are several ways to sharpen an image in Photoshop, but the Smart Sharpen filter gives you the most control. Because sharpening can emphasize artifacts, you'll remove those first.

1   Zoom in to about 400% to see the boy's shirt clearly. The colored dots you see are artifacts of the scanning process.

2   Choose Filter > Noise > Dust & Scratches.

3   In the Dust & Scratches dialog box, leave the default settings with a Radius of 1 pixel and Threshold at 0, and click OK.

The Threshold value determines how dissimilar the pixels should be before they are eliminated. The Radius value determines the size of the area searched for dissimilar pixels. The default values are great for tiny dots of color like the ones in this image.

Now that the artifacts are gone, you can sharpen the image.

4   Choose Filter > Sharpen > Smart Sharpen.

5   In the Smart Sharpen dialog box, make sure that Preview is selected, so you can see the effect of settings you adjust in the image window.

You can drag inside the preview window in the dialog box to see different parts of the image, or use the plus and minus buttons below the thumbnail to zoom in and out.

6   Make sure Lens Blur is chosen in the Remove menu.

You can choose to remove Lens Blur, Gaussian Blur, or Motion Blur in the Smart Sharpen dialog box. Lens Blur provides finer sharpening of detail and reduced sharpening halos. Gaussian Blur increases contrast along the edges in an image.

Motion Blur reduces the effects of blur that resulted from the camera or the subject moving when the photo was taken.

7 Drag the Amount slider to about **60%** to sharpen the image.

8 Drag the Radius slider to about **1.5**.

The Radius value determines the number of pixels surrounding the edge pixels that affect the sharpening. The higher the resolution, the higher the Radius setting should usually be.

9 When you're satisfied with the results, click OK to apply the Smart Sharpen filter.

10 Choose File > Save, and then close the project file.

Your image is ready to share or print!

Extra credit

Converting a color image to black and white

You can get great results converting a color image to black and white (with or without a tint) in Photoshop.

1   Choose File > Open, and navigate to the bike.tif file in the Lesson02 folder. Click Open.

2   In the Adjustments panel, click the Black & White button to add a Black & White adjustment layer.

3   Adjust the color sliders to change the saturation of color channels. You can also experiment with options from the preset menu, such as Darker or Infrared. Or, select the tool in the upper left corner of the Adjustments panel, and then drag it across the image to adjust the colors associated with that area. (We darkened the bike itself and made the background areas lighter.)

4   If you want to add a tint to the photo, select Tint. Then, click the color swatch and select a tint color (we used R=227, G=209, B=198).

Review questions

1 What does *resolution* mean?

2 What does the Crop tool do?

3 How can you adjust the tone and color of an image in Photoshop?

4 What tools can you use to remove blemishes in an image?

5 How can you remove digital artifacts such as colored pixels from an image?

Review answers

1 The term *resolution* refers to the number of pixels that describe an image and establish its detail. *Image resolution* and *monitor resolution* are measured in pixels per inch (ppi). *Printer,* or *output, resolution* is measured in ink dots per inch (dpi).

2 You can use the Crop tool to trim, scale, or straighten an image.

3 To adjust the tone and color of an image in Photoshop, first use the White Point tool in a Curves adjustment layer. Then refine the tone using a Levels adjustment layer.

4 The Healing Brush, Spot Healing Brush, Patch tool, and Clone Stamp tools let you replace unwanted portions of an image with other areas of the image. The Clone Stamp tool copies the source area exactly; the Healing Brush and Spot Healing Brush tools blend the area with the surrounding pixels. The Spot Healing Brush tool doesn't require a source area at all; it "heals" areas to match the surrounding pixels. In Content-Aware mode, the Patch tool replaces a selection with content that matches the surrounding area.

5 The Dust & Scratches filter removes digital artifacts from an image.

3 WORKING WITH SELECTIONS

Lesson overview

In this lesson, you'll learn how to do the following:

- Make specific areas of an image active using selection tools.
- Reposition a selection marquee.
- Move and duplicate the contents of a selection.
- Use keyboard-mouse combinations that save time and hand motions.
- Deselect a selection.
- Constrain the movement of a selected area.
- Adjust the position of a selected area using the arrow keys.
- Add to and subtract from a selection.
- Rotate a selection.
- Use multiple selection tools to make a complex selection.

 This lesson will take about an hour to complete. Download the Lesson03 project files from the Lesson & Update Files tab on your Account page at www.peachpit.com, if you haven't already done so. As you work on this lesson, you'll preserve the start files. If you need to restore the start files, download them from your Account page.

PROJECT: SHADOWBOX COLLAGE

Learning how to select areas of an image is of primary importance—you must first select what you want to affect. Once you've made a selection, only the area within the selection can be edited.

About selecting and selection tools

● **Note:** You'll learn how to select vector areas using the pen tools in Lesson 8, "Vector Drawing Techniques."

Making changes to an area within an image in Photoshop is a two-step process. You first use one of the selection tools to select the part of an image you want to change. Then you use another tool, filter, or other feature to make changes, such as moving the selected pixels to another location or applying a filter to the selected area. You can make selections based on size, shape, and color. When a selection is active, changes you make apply only to the selected area; other areas are unaffected.

The best selection tool for a specific area often depends on the characteristics of that area, such as shape or color. There are four primary types of selections:

Geometric selections The Rectangular Marquee tool ([]) selects a rectangular area in an image. The Elliptical Marquee tool (○), which is hidden behind the Rectangular Marquee tool, selects elliptical areas. The Single Row Marquee tool (╍) and Single Column Marquee tool (ᵇ) select either a 1-pixel-high row or a 1-pixel-wide column, respectively.

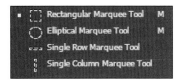

Freehand selections The Lasso tool (○) traces a freehand selection around an area. The Polygonal Lasso tool (◹) sets anchor points in straight-line segments around an area. The Magnetic Lasso tool (◳) works something like a combination of the other two lasso tools, and gives the best results when good contrast exists between the area you want to select and its surroundings.

Edge-based selections The Quick Selection tool (◔) quickly "paints" a selection by automatically finding and following defined edges in the image.

Color-based selections The Magic Wand tool (✹) selects parts of an image based on the similarity in pixel color. It is useful for selecting odd-shaped areas that share a specific range of colors.

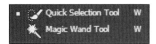

Getting started

First, you'll look at the image you will create as you explore the selection tools in Photoshop.

1   Start Photoshop, and then immediately hold down Ctrl+Alt+Shift (Windows) or Command+Option+Shift (Mac OS) to restore the default preferences. (See "Restoring default preferences" on page 4.)

2   When prompted, click Yes to confirm that you want to delete the Adobe Photoshop Settings file.

3   Choose File > Browse In Bridge to open Adobe Bridge.

Note: If Bridge isn't installed, you'll be prompted to install it when you choose Browse In Bridge. For more information, see page 3.

4   In the Favorites panel, click the Lessons folder. Then double-click the Lesson03 folder in the Content panel to see its contents.

5   Study the 03End.psd file. Move the thumbnail slider to the right if you want to see the image in more detail.

The project is a shadowbox that includes a piece of coral, a sand dollar, a mussel, a nautilus, and a plate of small shells. The challenge in this lesson is to arrange these elements, which were scanned together on the single page you see in the 03Start.psd file.

6   Double-click the 03Start.psd thumbnail to open the image file in Photoshop.

7   Choose File > Save As, rename the file **03Working.psd**, and click Save.

By saving another version of the start file, you don't have to worry about overwriting the original.

Using the Quick Selection tool

The Quick Selection tool provides one of the easiest ways to make a selection. You simply paint an area of an image, and the tool automatically finds the edges. You can add or subtract areas of the selection until you have exactly the area you want.

The image of the sand dollar in the 03Working.psd file has clearly defined edges, making it an ideal candidate for the Quick Selection tool. You'll select just the sand dollar, not the background behind it.

1 Select the Zoom tool in the Tools panel, and then zoom in so that you can see the sand dollar well.

2 Select the Quick Selection tool (✐) in the Tools panel.

3 Select Auto Enhance in the options bar.

When Auto Enhance is selected, the Quick Selection tool creates better quality selections, with edges that are truer to the object. The selection process is a little slower than using the Quick Selection tool without Auto Enhance, but the results are superior.

4 Click on an off-white area near the outside edge of the sand dollar.

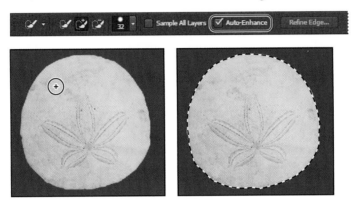

The Quick Selection tool finds the full edge automatically, selecting the entire sand dollar. Leave the selection active so that you can use it in the next exercise.

Moving a selected area

Once you've made a selection, any changes you make apply exclusively to the pixels within the selection. The rest of the image is not affected by those changes.

To move the selected area to another part of the composition, you use the Move tool. This image has only one layer, so the pixels you move will replace the pixels beneath them. This change is not permanent until you deselect the moved pixels, so you can try different locations for the selection you're moving before you make a commitment.

1 If the sand dollar is not still selected, repeat the previous exercise to select it.

2 Zoom out so you can see both the shadowbox and the sand dollar.

3   Select the Move tool (⯈⊹). Notice that the sand dollar remains selected.

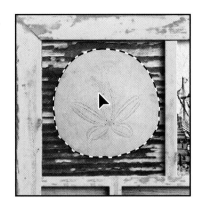

4   Drag the selected area (the sand dollar) up to the upper left area of the frame, which is labeled "A." Position it over the silhouette in the frame, leaving the lower left part of the silhouette showing as a shadow.

5   Choose Select > Deselect, and then choose File > Save.

In Photoshop, it's not easy to lose a selection. Unless a selection tool is active, clicking elsewhere in the image will not deselect the active area. To deliberately deselect a selection, you can choose Select > Deselect, press Ctrl+D (Windows) or Command+D (Mac OS), or click outside the selection with any selection tool to start a different selection.

Julieanne Kost is an official Adobe Photoshop evangelist.

Tool tips from the Photoshop evangelist

Move tool tip

If you're moving objects in a multilayer file with the Move tool and you suddenly need to select one of the layers, try this: With the Move tool selected, move the pointer over any area of an image and right-click (Windows) or Control-click (Mac OS). The layers that are under the pointer appear in the context menu. Choose the one you'd like to make active.

Manipulating selections

You can move selections, reposition them as you create them, and even duplicate them. In this section, you'll learn several ways to manipulate selections. Most of these methods work with any selection, but you'll use them here with the Elliptical Marquee tool, which lets you select ovals or perfect circles.

One of the best things about this section is the introduction of keyboard shortcuts that can save you time and arm motions.

Repositioning a selection marquee while creating it

Selecting ovals and circles can be tricky. It's not always obvious where you should start dragging, so sometimes the selection will be off-center, or the ratio of width to height won't match what you need. In this exercise, you'll learn techniques for managing those problems, including two important keyboard-mouse combinations that can make your Photoshop work much easier.

As you perform this exercise, be very careful to follow the directions about keeping the mouse button or specific keys pressed. If you accidentally release the mouse button at the wrong time, simply start the exercise again from step 1.

1   Select the Zoom tool (🔍), and click the plate of shells at the bottom of the image window to zoom in to at least 100% view (use 200% view if the entire plate of shells will still fit in the image window on your screen).

2   Select the Elliptical Marquee tool (○), hidden under the Rectangular Marquee tool (▭).

3   Move the pointer over the plate of shells, and drag diagonally across the oval bowl to create a selection, but *do not release the mouse button*. It's OK if your selection does not match the plate shape yet.

If you accidentally release the mouse button, draw the selection again. In most cases—including this one—the new selection replaces the previous one.

4   Still holding down the mouse button, press the spacebar, and continue to drag the selection. Instead of resizing the selection, now you're moving it. Position it so that it more closely aligns with the plate.

● **Note:** You don't have to include every pixel in the bowl of shells, but the selection should be the shape of the bowl, and should contain the shells comfortably.

5   Carefully release the spacebar (but not the mouse button) and continue to drag, trying to make the size and shape of the selection match the oval plate of shells as closely as possible. If necessary, hold down the spacebar again and drag to move the selection marquee into position around the plate of shells.

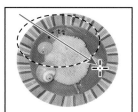 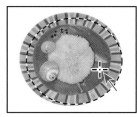 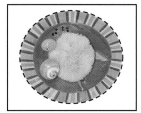

Begin dragging a selection.   *Press the spacebar to move it.*   *Complete the selection.*

6   When the selection border is positioned appropriately, release the mouse button.

7   Choose View > Fit On Screen or use the slider in the Navigator panel to reduce the zoom view so that you can see all of the objects in the image window.

Leave the Elliptical Marquee tool and the selection active for the next exercise.

Moving selected pixels with a keyboard shortcut

Now you'll use a keyboard shortcut to move the selected pixels onto the shadowbox. The shortcut temporarily switches the active tool to the Move tool, so you don't need to select it from the Tools panel.

1   If the plate of shells is not still selected, repeat the previous exercise to select it.

2   With the Elliptical Marquee tool (○) selected in the Tools panel, press Ctrl (Windows) or Command (Mac OS), and move the pointer within the selection.

The pointer icon now includes a pair of scissors (✂) to indicate that the selection will be cut from its current location.

3   Drag the plate of shells onto the area of the shadowbox labeled "B." (You'll use another technique to nudge the oval plate into the exact position in a minute.)

4   Release the mouse button, but don't deselect the plate of shells.

Note: You can release the Ctrl or Command key after you start dragging, and the Move tool remains active. Photoshop reverts to the previously selected tool when you deselect, whether you click outside the selection or use the Deselect command.

Moving a selection with the arrow keys

You can make minor adjustments to the position of selected pixels by using the arrow keys. You can nudge the selection in increments of either one pixel or ten pixels.

When a selection tool is active in the Tools panel, the arrow keys nudge the selection border, but not the contents. When the Move tool is active, the arrow keys move both the selection border and its contents.

You'll use the arrow keys to nudge the plate of shells. Before you begin, make sure that the plate of shells is still selected in the image window.

1   Press the Up Arrow key (⬆) on your keyboard a few times to move the oval upward.

Notice that each time you press the arrow key, the plate of shells moves one pixel. Experiment by pressing the other arrow keys to see how they affect the selection.

2   Hold down the Shift key as you press an arrow key.

When you hold down the Shift key, the selection moves ten pixels every time you press an arrow key.

Sometimes the border around a selected area can distract you as you make adjustments. You can hide the edges of a selection temporarily without actually deselecting, and then display the selection border once you've completed the adjustments.

3   Choose View > Show > Selection Edges or View > Extras.

Either command hides the selection border around the plate of shells.

4   Use the arrow keys to nudge the plate of shells until it's positioned over the silhouette, so that there's a shadow on the left and bottom of the plate. Then choose View > Show > Selection Edges to reveal the selection border again.

Hidden selection edges   *Visible selection edges*

5   Choose Select > Deselect, or press Ctrl+D (Windows) or Command+D (Mac OS).

6   Choose File > Save to save your work so far.

Using the Magic Wand tool

The Magic Wand tool selects all the pixels of a particular color or color range. It's most useful for selecting an area of similar colors surrounded by areas of very different colors. As with many of the selection tools, after you make the initial selection, you can add or subtract areas of the selection.

The Tolerance option sets the sensitivity of the Magic Wand tool. This value limits or extends the range of pixel similarity. The default tolerance value of 32 selects the color you click plus 32 lighter and 32 darker tones of that color. You may need to adjust the tolerance level up or down depending on the color ranges and variations in the image.

If a multicolored area that you want to select is set against a background of a different color, it can be much easier to select the background than the area itself. In this procedure, you'll use the Rectangular Marquee tool to select a larger area, and then use the Magic Wand tool to subtract the background from the selection.

1 Select the Rectangular Marquee tool (⬚), hidden behind the Elliptical Marquee tool (◯).

2 Drag a selection around the piece of coral. Make sure that your selection is large enough so that a margin of white appears between the coral and the edges of the marquee.

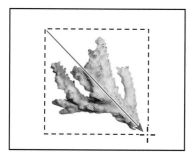

At this point, the coral and the white background area are selected. You'll subtract the white area from the selection so that only the coral remains in the selection.

3 Select the Magic Wand tool (🪄), hidden under the Quick Selection tool (✎).

4 In the options bar, confirm that the Tolerance value is **32**. This value determines the range of colors the wand selects.

5 Select the Subtract From Selection button (🗗) in the options bar.

A minus sign appears next to the wand in the pointer icon. Anything you select now will be subtracted from the initial selection.

6 Click in the white background area within the selection marquee.

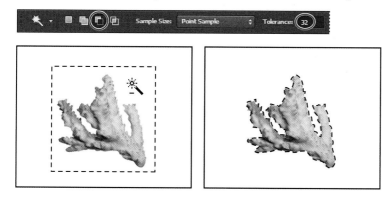

The Magic Wand tool selects the entire background, subtracting it from the selection. Now all the white pixels are deselected, leaving the coral perfectly selected.

7   Select the Move tool (▶✛), and drag the coral to the area of the shadowbox labeled "C," positioning it so that a shadow appears to the left and below the coral.

8   Choose Select > Deselect, and then save your work.

Softening the edges of a selection

To smooth the hard edges of a selection, you can apply anti-aliasing or feathering, or use the Refine Edge option.

Anti-aliasing smooths the jagged edges of a selection by softening the color transition between edge pixels and background pixels. Since only the edge pixels change, no detail is lost. Anti-aliasing is useful when cutting, copying, and pasting selections to create composite images.

Anti-aliasing is available for the Lasso, Polygonal Lasso, Magnetic Lasso, Elliptical Marquee, and Magic Wand tools. (Select the tool to display its options in the options bar.) To apply anti-aliasing, you must select the option before making the selection. Once a selection is made, you cannot add anti-aliasing to it.

Feathering blurs edges by building a transition boundary between the selection and its surrounding pixels. This blurring can cause some loss of detail at the edge of the selection.

You can define feathering for the marquee and lasso tools as you use them, or you can add feathering to an existing selection. Feathering effects become apparent when you move, cut, or copy the selection.

*   To use the Refine Edge option, first make a selection, and then click Refine Edge in the options bar to open its dialog box. You can use the Refine Edge option to smooth the outline, feather it, or contract or expand it.

*   To use anti-aliasing, select a lasso tool, or the Elliptical Marquee or Magic Wand tool, and select Anti-alias in the options bar.

*   To define a feathered edge for a selection tool, select any of the lasso or marquee tools. Enter a Feather value in the options bar. This value defines the width of the feathered edge and can range from 1 to 250 pixels.

*   To define a feathered edge for an existing selection, choose Select > Modify > Feather. Enter a value for the Feather Radius, and click OK.

Selecting with the lasso tools

As we mentioned earlier, Photoshop includes three lasso tools: the Lasso tool, the Polygonal Lasso tool, and the Magnetic Lasso tool. You can use the Lasso tool to make selections that require both freehand and straight lines, using keyboard short-cuts to move back and forth between the Lasso tool and the Polygonal Lasso tool. You'll use the Lasso tool to select the mussel. It takes a bit of practice to alternate between straight-line and freehand selections—if you make a mistake while you're selecting the mussel, simply deselect and start again.

1 Select the Zoom tool ($\mathcal{Q}$), and click the mussel until the view enlarges to 100%. Make sure you can see the entire mussel in the window.

2 Select the Lasso tool ($\wp$). Starting at the lower left section of the mussel, drag around the rounded end of the mussel, tracing the shape as accurately as possible. *Do not release the mouse button.*

3 Press the Alt (Windows) or Option (Mac OS) key, and then release the mouse button so that the lasso pointer changes to the polygonal lasso shape ($\bowtie$). *Do not release the Alt or Option key.*

4 Begin clicking along the end of the mussel to place anchor points, following the contours of the mussel. Be sure to hold down the Alt or Option key throughout this process.

Drag with the Lasso tool.

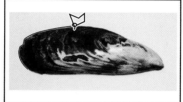
Click with the Polygonal Lasso tool.

The selection border automatically stretches like a rubber band between anchor points.

5 When you reach the tip of the mussel, hold down the mouse button as you release the Alt or Option key. The pointer again appears as the lasso icon.

6 Carefully drag around the tip of the mussel, holding down the mouse button.

7 When you finish tracing the tip and reach the lower side of the mussel, first press Alt or Option again, and then release the mouse button. Click along the lower side of the mussel with the Polygonal Lasso tool as you did on the top. Continue to trace the mussel until you arrive back at the starting point of your selection near the left end of the image.

Note: To make sure that the selection is the shape you want when you use the Lasso tool, end the selection by dragging across the starting point of the selection. If you start and stop the selection at different points, Photoshop draws a straight line between the start point of the selection and the end point of the selection.

8 Click the starting point of the selection, and then release Alt or Option. The mussel is now entirely selected. Leave the mussel selected for the next exercise.

Rotating a selection

Now you'll rotate the mussel.

Before you begin, make sure that the mussel is still selected.

1 Choose View > Fit On Screen to resize the image window to fit on your screen.

2 Press Ctrl (Windows) or Command (Mac OS) as you drag the selected mussel to the section of the shadowbox labeled "D."

The pointer changes to the Move tool icon when you press Ctrl or Command.

3 Choose Edit > Transform > Rotate.

The mussel and selection marquee are enclosed in a bounding box.

4 Move the pointer outside the bounding box so that it becomes a curved, double-headed arrow (↰). Drag to rotate the mussel to a 90-degree angle. You can verify the angle in the Rotate box in the options bar. Press Enter or Return to commit the transformation.

5 If necessary, select the Move tool (▶⊹) and drag to reposition the mussel, leaving a shadow to match the others. When you're satisfied, choose Select > Deselect.

6 Choose File > Save.

Selecting with the Magnetic Lasso tool

You can use the Magnetic Lasso tool to make freehand selections of areas with high-contrast edges. When you draw with the Magnetic Lasso tool, the selection border automatically snaps to the edge between areas of contrast. You can also control the selection path by occasionally clicking the mouse to place anchor points in the selection border.

You'll use the Magnetic Lasso tool to select the nautilus so that you can move it to the shadowbox.

1 Select the Zoom tool (🔍), and click the nautilus to zoom in to at least 100%.

2 Select the Magnetic Lasso tool (🅿️), hidden under the Lasso tool (◯).

3 Click once along the left edge of the nautilus, and then move the Magnetic Lasso tool along the edge to trace its outline.

▶ **Tip:** In low-contrast areas, you may want to click to place your own fastening points. You can add as many as you need. To remove the most recent fastening point, press Delete, and then move the mouse back to the remaining fastening point and continue selecting.

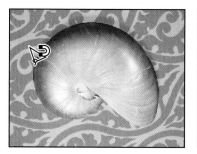 

Even though you're not holding down the mouse button, the tool snaps to the edge of the nautilus and automatically adds fastening points.

4 When you reach the left side of the nautilus again, double-click to return the Magnetic Lasso tool to the starting point, closing the selection. Or you can move the Magnetic Lasso tool over the starting point and click once.

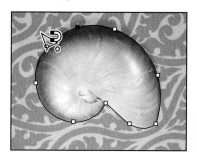 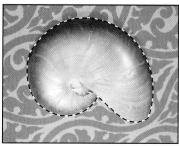

5 Double-click the Hand tool (✋) to fit the image in the image window.

6 Select the Move tool (✛), and drag the nautilus onto its silhouette in the section of the frame labeled "E," leaving a shadow below it and on the left side.

7 Choose Select > Deselect, and then choose File > Save.

Selecting from a center point

In some cases, it's easier to make elliptical or rectangular selections by drawing a selection from an object's center point. You'll use this technique to select the head of the screw for the shadowbox corners.

1 Select the Zoom tool (🔍), and zoom in on the screw to a magnification of about 300%. Make sure that you can see the entire screw head in your image window.

2 Select the Elliptical Marquee tool (◯) in the Tools panel.

3 Move the pointer to the approximate center of the screw.

4 Click and begin dragging. Then, without releasing the mouse button, press Alt (Windows) or Option (Mac OS) as you continue dragging the selection to the outer edge of the screw.

The selection is centered over its starting point.

▶ **Tip:** To select a perfect circle, press Shift as you drag. Hold down Shift while dragging the Rectangular Marquee tool to select a perfect square.

5 When you have the entire screw head selected, release the mouse button first, and then release Alt or Option (and the Shift key if you used it). Do not deselect, because you'll use this selection in the next exercise.

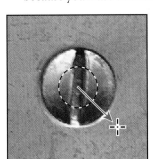

6 If necessary, reposition the selection border using one of the methods you learned earlier. If you accidentally released the Alt or Option key before you released the mouse button, select the screw again.

Resizing and copying a selection

Now you'll move the screw to the lower right corner of the wooden shadowbox, and then duplicate it for the other corners.

Resizing the contents of a selection

You'll start by moving the screw, but it's too large for the space. You'll need to resize it as well.

Before you begin, make sure that the screw is still selected. If it's not, reselect it by completing the previous exercise.

1   Choose View > Fit On Screen so that the entire image fits within the image window.

2   Select the Move tool (⊹) in the Tools panel.

3   Position the pointer within the screw selection.

The pointer becomes an arrow with a pair of scissors (✂), indicating that dragging the selection will cut it from its current location and move it to the new location.

4   Drag the screw onto the lower right corner of the shadowbox.

5   Choose Edit > Transform > Scale. A bounding box appears around the selection.

6   Press Shift as you drag one of the corner points inward to reduce the screw to about 40% of its original size, or until it is small enough to sit on the shadowbox frame. Then press Enter or Return to commit the change and remove the transformation bounding box.

As you resize the object, the selection marquee resizes, too. Pressing the Shift key as you resize the selection constrains the proportions so that the reduced object isn't distorted.

7   Use the Move tool to reposition the screw after resizing it, so that it is centered in the corner of the shadowbox frame.

8   Leaving the screw selected, choose File > Save to save your work.

Moving and duplicating a selection simultaneously

You can move and duplicate a selection at the same time. You'll copy the screw for the other three corners of the frame. If the screw is no longer selected, reselect it now, using the techniques you learned earlier.

1 With the Move tool (⊕) selected, press Alt (Windows) or Option (Mac OS) as you position the pointer inside the screw selection.

The pointer changes, displaying the usual black arrow and an additional white arrow, which indicates that a duplicate will be made when you move the selection.

2 Continue holding down the Alt or Option key as you drag a duplicate of the screw straight up to the top right corner of the frame. Release the mouse button and the Alt or Option key, but don't deselect the duplicate image.

3 Hold down Alt+Shift (Windows) or Option+Shift (Mac OS), and drag a new copy of the screw straight left to the upper left corner of the frame.

Pressing the Shift key as you move a selection constrains the movement horizontally or vertically in 45-degree increments.

4 Repeat step 3 to drag a fourth screw to the lower left corner of the frame.

5 When you're satisfied with the position of the fourth screw, choose Select > Deselect, and then choose File > Save.

Copying selections

You can use the Move tool to copy selections as you drag them within or between images, or you can copy and move selections using the Copy, Copy Merged, Paste, and Paste Into commands. Dragging with the Move tool saves memory, because the clipboard is not used as it is with the commands.

Photoshop has several copy and paste commands:

- **Copy** copies the selected area on the active layer.
- **Copy Merged** creates a merged copy of all the visible layers in the selected area.
- **Paste** pastes a cut or copied selection into another part of the image or into another image as a new layer.
- **Paste Into** pastes a cut or copied selection inside another selection in the same or a different image. The source selection is pasted onto a new layer, and the destination selection border is converted into a layer mask.

Keep in mind that when a selection is pasted between images with different resolutions, the pasted data retains its pixel dimensions. This can make the pasted portion appear out of proportion to the new image. Use the Image Size command to make the source and destination images the same resolution before copying and pasting.

Cropping an image

Now that your composition is in place, you'll crop the image to a final size. You can use either the Crop tool or the Crop command to crop an image.

1 Select the Crop tool (⊟), or press C to switch from the current tool to the Crop tool. Photoshop displays a crop boundary around the entire image.

2 In the options bar, make sure Ratio is selected in the Preset pop-up menu and that there are no ratio values specified. Then confirm that Delete Cropped Pixels is selected.

When Ratio is selected but no ratio values are specified, you can crop the image with any proportions.

Tip: To crop an image with its original proportions intact, choose Original Ratio from the Preset pop-up menu in the options bar.

3 Drag the crop handles so that the shadowbox is in the highlighted area, omitting the backgrounds from the original objects at the bottom of the image. Crop the frame so that there's an even area of white around it.

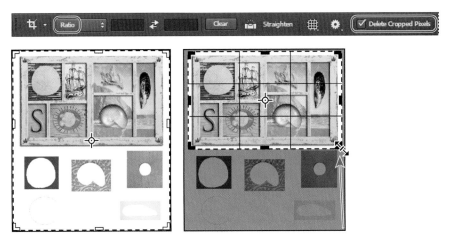

4 When you're satisfied with the position of the crop area, click the Commit Current Crop Operation button (✔) in the options bar.

5 Choose File > Save to save your work.

You've used several different selection tools to move all the seashells into place. The shadowbox is complete!

Review questions

1   Once you've made a selection, what area of the image can be edited?

2   How do you add to and subtract from a selection?

3   How can you move a selection while you're drawing it?

4   What does the Quick Selection tool do?

5   How does the Magic Wand tool determine which areas of an image to select? What is tolerance, and how does it affect a selection?

Review answers

1   Only the area within an active selection can be edited.

2   To add to a selection, click the Add To Selection button in the options bar, and then click the area you want to add. To subtract from a selection, click the Subtract From Selection button in the options bar, and then click the area you want to subtract. You can also add to a selection by pressing Shift as you drag or click; to subtract, press Alt (Windows) or Option (Mac OS) as you drag or click.

3   To reposition a selection while you're drawing it, continue to press the mouse button as you hold down the spacebar and drag.

4   The Quick Selection tool expands outward from where you click to automatically find and follow defined edges in the image.

5   The Magic Wand tool selects adjacent pixels based on their similarity in color. The Tolerance value determines how many color tones the Magic Wand tool will select. The higher the tolerance setting, the more tones are selected.

4 LAYER BASICS

Lesson overview

In this lesson, you'll learn how to do the following:

- Organize artwork on layers.

- Create, view, hide, and select layers.

- Rearrange layers to change the stacking order of artwork.

- Apply blending modes to layers.

- Resize and rotate layers.

- Apply a gradient to a layer.

- Apply a filter to a layer.

- Add text and layer effects to a layer.

- Add an adjustment layer.

- Save a copy of the file with the layers flattened.

 This lesson will take less than an hour to complete. Download the Lesson04 project files from the Lesson & Update Files tab on your Account page at www.peachpit.com, if you haven't already done so. As you work on this lesson, you'll preserve the start files. If you need to restore the start files, download them from your Account page.

PROJECT: TRAVEL POSTCARD

Pineapple and flower photography © Image Source, www.imagesource.com

In Photoshop, you can isolate different parts of an image on layers. Each layer can then be edited as discrete artwork, giving you tremendous flexibility as you compose and revise an image.

About layers

Every Photoshop file contains one or more *layers*. New files are generally created with a *background layer,* which contains a color or an image that shows through the transparent areas of subsequent layers. All new layers in an image are transparent until you add text or artwork (pixel values).

Working with layers is analogous to placing portions of a drawing on clear sheets of film, such as those viewed with an overhead projector: Individual sheets may be edited, repositioned, and deleted without affecting the other sheets. When the sheets are stacked, the entire composition is visible.

Getting started

You'll start the lesson by viewing an image of the final composition.

1   Start Photoshop, and then immediately hold down Ctrl+Alt+Shift (Windows) or Command+Option+Shift (Mac OS) to restore the default preferences. (See "Restoring default preferences" on page 4.)

2   When prompted, click Yes to delete the Adobe Photoshop Settings file.

3   Choose File > Browse In Bridge to open Adobe Bridge.

● **Note:** If Bridge isn't installed, you'll be prompted to install it. For more information, see page 3.

4   In the Favorites panel, click the Lessons folder. Then double-click the Lesson04 folder in the Content panel to see its contents.

5   Study the 04End.psd file. Move the thumbnail slider to the right if you want to see the image in more detail.

This layered composite represents a postcard. You will create it in this lesson as you learn how to create, edit, and manage layers.

6   Double-click the 04Start.psd file to open it in Photoshop.

7   Choose File > Save As, rename the file **04Working.psd**, and click Save. Click OK if you see the Photoshop Format Options dialog box.

Saving another version of the start file frees you to make changes without worrying about overwriting the original.

Using the Layers panel

The Layers panel lists all the layers in an image, displaying the layer names and thumbnails of the content on each layer. You can use the Layers panel to hide, view, reposition, delete, rename, and merge layers. The layer thumbnails are automatically updated as you edit the layers.

1 If the Layers panel is not visible in the work area, choose Window > Layers.

The Layers panel lists five layers for the 04Working.psd file (from top to bottom): Postage, HAWAII, Flower, Pineapple, and Background.

2 Select the Background layer to make it active (if it's not already selected). Notice the layer thumbnail and the icons shown for the Background layer:

- The lock icon (🔒) indicates that the layer is protected.

- The eye icon (👁) indicates that the layer is visible in the image window. If you click the eye, the image window no longer displays that layer.

▶ **Tip:** Use the context menu to hide or resize the layer thumbnail. Right-click (Windows) or Control-click (Mac OS) a thumbnail in the Layers panel to open the context menu, and then choose a thumbnail size.

The first task for this project is to add a photo of the beach to the postcard. First, you'll open the beach image in Photoshop.

3   In Photoshop, choose File > Open, navigate to the Lesson04 folder, and then double-click the Beach.psd file to open it in Photoshop.

The Layers panel changes to display the layer information for the active Beach.psd file. Notice that only one layer appears in the Beach.psd image: Layer 1, not Background. (For more information, see the sidebar "About the background layer.")

About the background layer

When you create a new image with a white or colored background, the bottom layer in the Layers panel is named Background. An image can have only one background layer. You cannot change the stacking order of a background layer, its blending mode, or its opacity. You can, however, convert a background layer to a regular layer.

When you create a new image with transparent content, the image doesn't have a background layer. The bottom layer isn't constrained like the background layer; you can move it anywhere in the Layers panel, and change its opacity and blending mode.

To convert a background layer into a regular layer:

1   Click the lock icon next to the layer name.

2   Rename the layer.

To convert a regular layer into a background layer:

1   Select a layer in the Layers panel.

2   Choose Layer > New > Background From Layer.

Renaming and copying a layer

To add content to an image and simultaneously create a new layer for it, drag an object or layer from one file into the image window of another file. Whether you drag from the image window of the original file or from its Layers panel, only the active layer is reproduced in the destination file.

You'll drag the Beach.psd image onto the 04Working.psd file. Before you begin, make sure that both the 04Working.psd and Beach.psd files are open, and that the Beach.psd file is selected.

First, you'll give Layer 1 a more descriptive name.

1 In the Layers panel, double-click the name Layer 1, type **Beach**, and then press Enter or Return. Keep the layer selected.

2 Choose Window > Arrange > 2-Up Vertical. Photoshop displays both of the open image files. Select the Beach.psd image so that it is the active file.

3 Select the Move tool (⊹), and use it to drag the Beach.psd image onto the 04Working.psd image window.

▶ **Tip:** If you hold down Shift as you drag an image from one file into another, the dragged image automatically centers itself in the target image window.

The Beach layer now appears in the 04Working.psd file image window and its Layers panel, between the Background and Pineapple layers. Photoshop always adds new layers directly above the selected layer; you selected the Background layer earlier.

4 Close the Beach.psd file without saving changes to it.

Viewing individual layers

The 04Working.psd file now contains six layers. Some of the layers are visible and some are hidden. The eye icon (👁) next to a layer thumbnail in the Layers panel indicates that the layer is visible.

1 Click the eye icon (👁) next to the Pineapple layer to hide the image of the pineapple.

You can hide or show a layer by clicking this icon or clicking in its column— also called the Show/Hide Visibility column.

2   Click again in the Show/Hide Visibility column to display the pineapple.

Adding a border to a layer

Now you'll add a white border around the Beach layer to create the impression that it's an old photograph.

1   Select the Beach layer. (To select the layer, click the layer name in the Layers panel.)

The layer is highlighted, indicating that it is active. Changes you make in the image window affect the active layer.

2   To make the opaque areas on this layer more obvious, hide all layers except the Beach layer: Press Alt (Windows) or Option (Mac OS) as you click the eye icon (👁) next to the Beach layer.

The white background and other objects in the image disappear, leaving only the beach image against a checkerboard background. The checkerboard indicates transparent areas of the active layer.

3   Choose Layer > Layer Style > Stroke.

The Layer Style dialog box opens. Now you'll select the options for the white stroke around the beach image.

4 Specify the following settings:

- Size: **5** px
- Position: Inside
- Blend Mode: Normal
- Opacity: **100**%
- Color: White (Click the Color box, and select white in the Color Picker.)

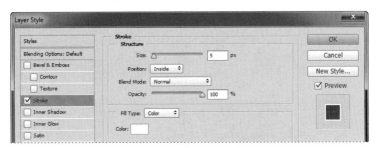

5 Click OK. A white border appears around the beach photo.

Rearranging layers

The order in which the layers of an image are organized is called the *stacking order*. The stacking order determines how the image is viewed—you can change the order to make certain parts of the image appear in front of or behind other layers.

You'll rearrange the layers so that the beach image is in front of another image that is currently hidden in the file.

1. Make the Postage, HAWAII, Flower, Pineapple, and Background layers visible by clicking the Show/Hide Visibility column next to their layer names.

The beach image is almost entirely blocked by images on other layers.

2. In the Layers panel, drag the Beach layer up so that it is positioned between the Pineapple and Flower layers—when you've positioned it correctly, you'll see a thick line between the layers in the panel—and then release the mouse button.

The Beach layer moves up one level in the stacking order, and the beach image appears on top of the pineapple and background images, but under the postage, flower, and the word "HAWAII."

▶ **Tip:** You can also control the stacking order of layered images by selecting them in the Layers panel and choosing Layer > Arrange, and then choosing Bring To Front, Bring Forward, Send To Back, or Send Backward.

Changing the opacity of a layer

You can reduce the opacity of any layer to reveal the layers below it. In this case, the postmark is too dark on the flower. You'll edit the opacity of the Postage layer to let the flower and other images show through.

1 Select the Postage layer, and then click the arrow next to the Opacity field to display the Opacity slider. Drag the slider to 25%. You can also type **25** in the Opacity box or scrub the Opacity label.

The Postage layer becomes partially transparent, so you can see the other layers underneath. Notice that the change in opacity affects only the image area of the Postage layer. The Pineapple, Beach, Flower, and HAWAII layers remain opaque.

2 Choose File > Save to save your work.

Duplicating a layer and changing the blending mode

You can apply different blending modes to a layer. *Blending modes* affect how the color pixels on one layer blend with pixels on the layers underneath. First you'll use blending modes to increase the intensity of the image on the Pineapple layer so that it doesn't look so dull. Then you'll change the blending mode on the Postage layer. (Currently, the blending mode for both layers is Normal.)

1 Click the eye icons next to the HAWAII, Flower, and Beach layers to hide them.

2 Right-click or Control-click the Pineapple layer, and choose Duplicate Layer from the context menu. (Make sure you click the layer name, not its thumbnail, or you'll see the wrong context menu.) Click OK in the Duplicate Layer dialog box.

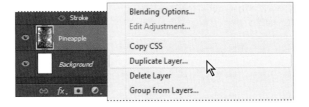

A layer called "Pineapple copy" appears above the Pineapple layer in the Layers panel.

Blending modes

Blending modes affect how the color pixels on one layer blend with pixels on the layers beneath them. The default blending mode, Normal, hides pixels beneath the top layer unless the top layer is partially or completely transparent. Each of the other blending modes let you control the way the pixels in the layers interact with each other.

Often, the best way to see how a blending mode affects your image is simply to try it. You can easily experiment with different blending modes in the Layers panel, applying one after another to compare the effects. As you begin experimenting, keep in mind how different groups of blending modes affect an image. Generally, if you want to:

- Darken your image, try Darken, Multiply, Color Burn, or Linear Burn.

- Lighten your image, try Lighten, Screen, Color Dodge, or Linear Dodge.

- Increase the contrast in the image, try Overlay, Soft Light, Hard Light, Vivid Light, Linear Light, Pin Light, or Hard Mix.

- Change the actual color values of the image, try Hue, Saturation, Color, or Luminosity.

- Create an inversion effect, try Difference or Exclusion.

The following blending modes often come in handy, and can be a good place to start your experimentation:

- **Multiply** does just what the name implies: it multiplies the color in the underlying colors with the color in the top layer.

- **Lighten** replaces pixels in the underlying layers with those in the top layer whenever the pixels in the top layer are lighter.

Multiply

Lighten

- **Overlay** multiplies either the colors or the inverse of the colors, depending on the colors in the underlying layers. Patterns or colors overlay the existing pixels while preserving the highlights and shadows of the underlying layers.

 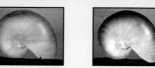

Overlay   Luminosity   Difference

- **Luminosity** replaces only the luminance of the underlying colors with that of the top layer.

- **Difference** subtracts darker colors from lighter ones.

3 With the Pineapple copy layer selected, choose Overlay from the Blending Modes menu in the Layers panel.

The Overlay blending mode blends the Pineapple copy layer with the Pineapple layer beneath it to create a vibrant, more colorful pineapple with deeper shadows and brighter highlights.

4 Select the Postage layer, and choose Multiply from the Blending Modes menu.

The Multiply blending mode multiplies the colors in the underlying layers with the color in the top layer. In this case, the postmark becomes a little stronger.

5 Choose File > Save to save your work.

Resizing and rotating layers

You can resize and transform layers.

1 Click the Visibility column on the Beach layer to make the layer visible.

2 Select the Beach layer in the Layers panel, and choose Edit > Free Transform.

A Transform bounding box appears around the beach image. The bounding box has handles on each corner and each side.

First, you'll resize and angle the layer.

3 Press Shift as you drag a corner handle inward to scale the beach photo down by about 50%. (Watch the Width and Height percentages in the options bar.)

4 With the bounding box still active, position the pointer just outside one of the corner handles until it becomes a curved double arrow. Drag clockwise to rotate the beach image approximately 15 degrees. You can also enter **15** in the Set Rotation box in the options bar.

5 Click the Commit Transform button (✔) in the options bar.

6 Make the Flower layer visible. Then, select the Move tool (▶✛), and drag the beach photo so that its corner is tucked neatly beneath the flower, as in the illustration.

7 Choose File > Save.

Using a filter to create artwork

Next, you'll create a new layer with no artwork on it. (Adding empty layers to a file is comparable to adding blank sheets of film to a stack of images.) You'll use this layer to add realistic-looking clouds to the sky with a Photoshop filter.

1   In the Layers panel, select the Background layer to make it active, and then click the Create A New Layer button (🗐) at the bottom of the Layers panel.

● **Note:** You can also create a new layer by choosing Layer > New > Layer, or by choosing New Layer from the Layers panel menu.

A new layer, named Layer 1, appears between the Background and Pineapple layers. The layer has no content, so it has no effect on the image.

2   Double-click the name Layer 1, type **Clouds**, and press Enter or Return to rename the layer.

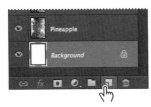 

3   In the Tools panel, click the foreground color swatch, select a sky blue color from the Color Picker, and click OK. We selected a color with the following values: R=48, G=138, B=174. The Background Color remains white.

4   With the Clouds layer still active, choose Filter > Render > Clouds.

Realistic-looking clouds appear behind the image.

5   Choose File > Save.

Dragging to add a new layer

You can add a layer to an image by dragging an image file from the desktop, Bridge, or Explorer (Windows) or the Finder (Mac OS). You'll add another flower to the postcard now.

1   If Photoshop fills your monitor, reduce the size of the Photoshop window:

   • In Windows, click the Restore button (▣) in the upper right corner, and then drag the lower right corner of the Photoshop window to make it smaller.

   • In Mac OS, click the green Maximize/Restore button (◉) in the upper left corner of the image window.

2   In Photoshop, select the Pineapple copy layer in the Layers panel to make it the active layer.

3   In Explorer (Windows) or the Finder (Mac OS), navigate to the Lessons folder you downloaded from the peachpit.com website. Then navigate to the Lesson04 folder.

4   Select Flower2.psd, and drag it from Explorer or the Finder onto your image.

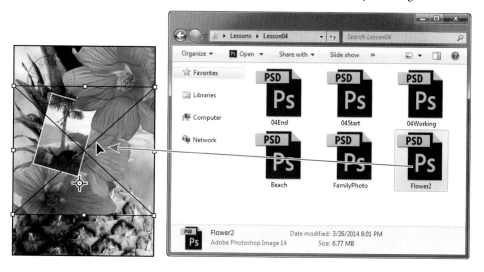

The Flower2 layer appears in the Layers panel, directly above the Pineapple copy layer. Photoshop places the image as a Smart Object, which is a layer you can edit without making permanent changes. You'll work more extensively with Smart Objects in Lesson 8.

5 Position the Flower2 layer in the lower left corner of the postcard, so that about half of the top flower is visible.

6 Click the Commit Transform button (✔) in the options bar to accept the layer.

Adding text

Now you're ready to create some type using the Horizontal Type tool, which places the text on its own type layer. You'll then edit the text and apply a special effect.

1 Make the HAWAII layer visible. You'll add text just below this layer, and apply special effects to both layers.

2 Choose Select > Deselect Layers, so that no layers are selected.

3 In the Tools panel, select the Horizontal Type tool (T). Then, choose Window > Character to open the Character panel. Do the following in the Character panel:

- Select a serif font (we used Birch Std; if you use a different font, adjust other settings accordingly).

- Select a font style (we used Regular).

- Select a large font size (we used 36 points).

- Select a large tracking value (⟨ᴠᴀ⟩) (we used 250).

- Click the color swatch, select a shade of grassy green in the Color Picker, and click OK to close the Color Picker.

- Click the Faux Bold button (ᴛ).

- Click the All Caps button (ᴛᴛ).

- Select Crisp from the Anti-aliasing menu (ᵃa).

4 Click just below the "H" in the word "HAWAII," and type **Island Paradise**.
   Then click the Commit Any Current Edits button (✔) in the options bar.

● **Note:** If you make a mistake when you click to set the type, simply click away from the type and repeat step 4.

The Layers panel now includes a layer named Island Paradise with a "T" thumbnail, indicating that it is a type layer. This layer is at the top of the layer stack.

 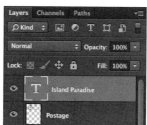

The text appears where you clicked, which probably isn't exactly where you want it to be positioned.

5 Select the Move tool (▸⊹), and drag the "Island Paradise" text so that it is centered below "HAWAII."

Applying a gradient to a layer

You can apply a color gradient to all or part of a layer. In this example, you'll apply a gradient to the word "HAWAII" to make it more colorful. First you'll select the letters, and then you'll apply the gradient.

1 Select the HAWAII layer in the Layers panel to make it active.

Note: Make sure you click the thumbnail, rather than the layer name, or you'll see the wrong context menu.

2   Right-click or Control-click the thumbnail in the HAWAII layer, and choose Select Pixels.

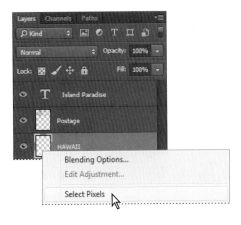

Note: Though the layer contains the word "HAWAII," it is not a type layer. The text has been rasterized.

Everything on the HAWAII layer (the white lettering) is selected. Now that you've selected the area to fill, you'll apply a gradient.

3   In the Tools panel, select the Gradient tool (■).

4   Click the Foreground Color swatch in the Tools panel, select a bright shade of orange in the Color Picker, and click OK. The Background Color should still be white.

5   In the options bar, make sure that Linear Gradient (■) is selected.

Tip: To list the gradient options by name rather than by sample, click the menu button in the gradient picker, and choose either Small List or Large List. Or, hover the pointer over a thumbnail until a tool tip appears, showing the gradient name.

6   In the options bar, click the arrow next to the Gradient Editor box to open the Gradient Picker. Select the Foreground To Background swatch (it's the first one), and then click anywhere outside the gradient picker to close it.

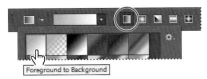

7   With the selection still active, drag the Gradient tool from the bottom to the top of the letters. If you want to be sure you drag straight up, press the Shift key as you drag.

The gradient extends across the type, starting with orange at the bottom and gradually blending to white at the top.

8   Choose Select > Deselect to deselect the HAWAII type.

9   Save the work you've done so far.

Applying a layer style

You can enhance a layer by adding a shadow, stroke, satin sheen, or other special effect from a collection of automated and editable layer styles. These styles are easy to apply, and they link directly to the layer you specify.

Like layers, layer styles can be hidden by clicking eye icons (👁) in the Layers panel. Layer styles are nondestructive, so you can edit or remove them at any time. You can apply a copy of a layer style to a different layer by dragging the effect onto the destination layer.

Earlier, you used a layer style to add a stroke to the beach photo. Now, you'll add drop shadows to the text to make it stand out.

1. Select the Island Paradise layer, and then choose Layer > Layer Style > Drop Shadow.

2. In the Layer Style dialog box, make sure that the Preview option is selected, and then, if necessary, move the dialog box so that you can see the Island Paradise text in the image window.

3. In the Structure area, select Use Global Light, and then specify the following settings:

   - Blend Mode: Multiply
   - Opacity: **75**%
   - Angle: **78** degrees
   - Distance: **5** px
   - Spread: **30**%
   - Size: **10** px

▶ **Tip:** You can also open the Layer Style dialog box by clicking the Add A Layer Style button at the bottom of the Layers panel and then choosing a layer style, such as Bevel And Emboss, from the pop-up menu.

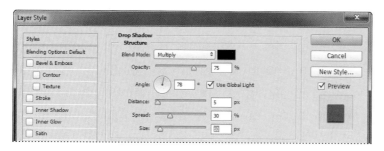

When Use Global Light is selected, one "master" lighting angle is available in all the layer effects that use shading. If you set a lighting angle in one of these effects, every other effect with Use Global Light selected inherits the same angle setting.

Angle determines the lighting angle at which the effect is applied to the layer. Distance determines the offset distance for a shadow or satin effect. Spread determines how gradually the shadow fades toward the edges. Size determines how far the shadow extends.

Photoshop adds a drop shadow to the "Island Paradise" text in the image.

4   Click OK to accept the settings and close the Layer Style dialog box.

Photoshop nests the layer style in the Island Paradise layer. First it lists Effects, and then the layer styles applied to the layer. An eye icon (👁) appears next to the effect category and next to each effect. To turn off an effect, click its eye icon. Click the visibility column again to restore the effect. To hide all layer styles, click the eye icon next to Effects. To collapse the list of effects, click the arrow next to the layer.

5   Make sure that eye icons appear for both items nested in the Island Paradise layer.

6   Press Alt (Windows) or Option (Mac OS) and drag the Effects line or the fx symbol (fx) onto the HAWAII layer.

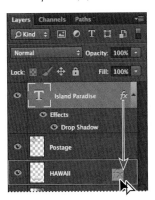

The Drop Shadow layer style is applied to the HAWAII layer, copying the settings you applied to the Island Paradise layer. Now you'll add a green stroke around the word HAWAII.

Julieanne Kost is an official Adobe Photoshop evangelist.

Tool tips from the Photoshop evangelist

Blending effects

Blending layers in a different order or on different groups changes the effect. You can apply a blending mode to an entire layer group and get a very different result than if you apply the same blending mode to each of the layers individually. When a blending mode is applied to a group, Photoshop treats the group as a single merged object and then applies the blending mode. Experiment with blending modes to get the effect you want.

7 Select the HAWAII layer in the Layers panel, click the Add A Layer Style button (*fx*) at the bottom of the panel, and then choose Stroke from the pop-up menu.

8 In the Structure area of the Layer Styles dialog box, specify the following settings:

- Size: **4** px

- Position: Outside

- Blend Mode: Normal

- Opacity: **100**%

- Color: Green (Select a shade that goes well with the one you used for the "Island Paradise" text.)

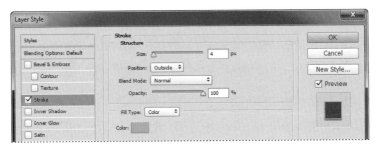

9 Click OK to apply the stroke.

Now you'll add a drop shadow and a satin sheen to the flower.

10 Select the Flower layer, and choose Layer > Layer Style > Drop Shadow. Then change the following settings in the Structure area:

- Opacity: **60**%

- Distance: **13** px

- Spread: **9**%.

- Make sure Use Global Light is selected, and that the Blend Mode is Multiply. Do not click OK.

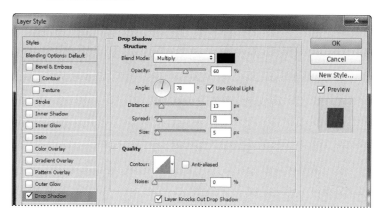

11 With the Layer Style dialog box still open, click the word Satin on the left to select it and display its options. Then make sure Invert is selected, and apply the following settings:

- Color (next to Blend Mode): Fuchsia (choose a color that complements the flower color)

- Opacity: **20**%

- Distance: **22** px

The Satin layer effect applies interior shading to create a satiny finish. The contour controls the shape of the effect; Invert flips the contour curve.

Note: Be sure to click the word Satin. If you click only the check box, Photoshop applies the layer style with its default settings but you won't see the options.

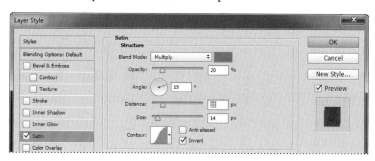

12 Click OK to apply both layer styles.

Before applying layer styles

The flower with the drop shadow and satin layer styles applied

Adding an adjustment layer

Adjustment layers can be added to an image to apply color and tonal adjustments without permanently changing the pixel values in the image. For example, if you add a Color Balance adjustment layer to an image, you can experiment with different colors repeatedly, because the change occurs only on the adjustment layer. If you decide to return to the original pixel values, you can hide or delete the adjustment layer.

You've used adjustment layers in other lessons. Here, you'll add a Hue/Saturation adjustment layer to change the color of the purple flower. An adjustment layer affects all layers below it in the image's stacking order unless a selection is active when you create it or you create a clipping mask.

1 Select the Flower2 layer in the Layers panel.

2 Click the Hue/Saturation icon in the Adjustments panel to add a Hue/Saturation adjustment layer.

3 In the Properties panel, apply the following settings:

- Hue: **43**

- Saturation: **19**

- Lightness: **0**

The changes affect the Flower2, Pineapple Copy, Pineapple, Clouds, and Background layers. The effect is interesting, but you only want to change the Flower2 layer.

4 Right-click (Windows) or Control-click (Mac OS) the layer name on the Hue/Saturation adjustment layer, and choose Create Clipping Mask.

● **Note:** Be sure to click the layer name, not the thumbnail, to see the appropriate context menu.

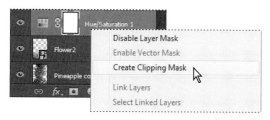

An arrow appears in the Layers panel, indicating that the adjustment layer applies only to the Flower2 layer. You'll learn more about clipping masks in Lessons 6 and 7.

Updating layer effects

Layer effects are automatically updated when you make changes to a layer. You can edit the text and watch how the layer effect tracks the change.

▶ **Tip:** You can search for layers in the Layers panel by layer type, layer name, effect, mode, attribute, and color. You can also display only the selected layers: choose Select > Isolate Layers, or choose Selected from the Kind menu in the Layers panel to enter Isolation mode.

1   Select the Island Paradise layer in the Layers panel.

2   In the Tools panel, select the Horizontal Type tool (T).

3   In the options bar, set the font size to **32** points, and press Enter or Return.

Although you didn't select the text by dragging the Type tool (as you would have to do in a word processing program), "Island Paradise" now appears in 32-point type.

4   Using the Horizontal Type tool, click between "Island" and "Paradise," and type **of**.

As you edit the text, the layer styles are applied to the new text.

5   You don't actually need the word "of," so delete it.

6   Select the Move tool (✛), and drag "Island Paradise" to center it beneath the word "HAWAII."

● **Note:** You don't have to click the Commit Any Current Edits button after making the text edits, because selecting the Move tool has the same effect.

When you add text, layer effects are automatically applied.

Center the text beneath the word "Hawaii."

7   Choose File > Save.

Adding a border

The Hawaii postcard is nearly done. The elements are almost all arranged correctly in the composition. You'll finish up by positioning the postmark and then adding a white postcard border.

1   Select the Postage layer, and then use the Move tool (✛) to drag it to the middle right of the image, as in the illustration.

2 Select the Island Paradise layer in the Layers panel, and then click the Create
A New Layer button (🗐) at the bottom of the panel.

3 Choose Select > All.

4 Choose Select > Modify > Border. In the Border Selection dialog box, type **10** pixels
for the Width, and click OK.

A 10-pixel border is selected around the entire image. Now, you'll fill it with white.

5 Select white for the Foreground Color, and then choose Edit > Fill.

6 In the Fill dialog box, choose Foreground Color from the Use menu, and click OK.

7 Choose Select > Deselect.

8 Double-click the Layer 1 name in the Layers panel, and rename the layer **Border.**

Flattening and saving files

When you finish editing all the layers in your image, you can merge or *flatten* layers to reduce the file size. Flattening combines all the layers into a single background layer. However, you cannot edit layers once you've flattened them, so you shouldn't flatten an image until you are certain that you're satisfied with all your design decisions. Rather than flattening your original PSD files, it's a good idea to save a copy of the file with its layers intact, in case you need to edit a layer later.

● **Note:** If the sizes do not appear in the status bar, click the status bar pop-up menu arrow, and choose Show > Document Sizes.

To appreciate what flattening does, notice the two numbers for the file size in the status bar at the bottom of the image window. The first number represents what the file size would be if you flattened the image. The second number represents the file size without flattening. This lesson file, if flattened, would be 2–3MB, but the current file is much larger. So flattening is well worth it in this case.

1 Select any tool but the Type tool (T), to be sure that you're not in text-editing mode. Then choose File > Save (if it is available) to be sure that all your changes have been saved in the file.

2 Choose Image > Duplicate.

3 In the Duplicate Image dialog box, name the file **04Flat.psd**, and click OK.

4 Leave the 04Flat.psd file open, but close the 04Working.psd file.

5 Choose Flatten Image from the Layers panel menu.

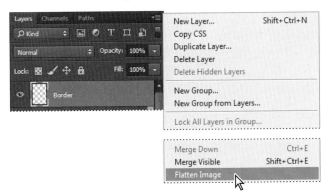

Only one layer, named Background, remains in the Layers panel.

6   Choose File > Save. Even though you chose Save rather than Save As, the Save As dialog box appears.

7   Make sure the location is the Lessons/Lesson04 folder, and then click Save to accept the default settings and save the flattened file.

You have saved two versions of the file: a one-layer, flattened copy as well as the original file, in which all the layers remain intact.

You've created a colorful, attractive postcard. This lesson only begins to explore the vast possibilities and the flexibility you gain when you master the art of using Photoshop layers. You'll get more experience and try out different techniques for layers in almost every chapter as you move forward in this book.

▶ **Tip:** If you want to flatten only some of the layers in a file, click the eye icons to hide the layers you don't want to flatten, and then choose Merge Visible from the Layers panel menu.

About layer comps

Layer comps provide one-click flexibility in switching between different views of a multilayered image file. A layer comp is simply a definition of the settings in the Layers panel. Once you've defined a layer comp, you can change as many settings as you please in the Layers panel and then create another layer comp to preserve that configuration of layer properties. Then, by switching from one layer comp to another, you can quickly review the two designs. The beauty of layer comps becomes apparent when you want to demonstrate a number of possible design arrangements. When you've created a few layer comps, you can review the design variations without having to tediously select and deselect eye icons or change settings in the Layers panel.

Say, for example, that you are designing a brochure, and you're producing a version in English as well as in French. You might have the French text on one layer, and the English text on another in the same image file. To create two different layer comps, you would simply turn on visibility for the French layer and turn off visibility for the English layer, and then click the Create New Layer Comp button on the Layer Comps panel. Then you'd do the inverse—turn on visibility for the English layer and turn off visibility for the French layer, and click the Create New Layer Comp button— to create an English layer comp. To view the different layer comps, click the Apply Layer Comp box for each comp in the Layer Comps panel in turn.

Layer comps can be an especially valuable feature when the design is in flux or when you need to create multiple versions of the same image file. If some aspects need to stay consistent among Layer Comps, you can change the visibility, position, or appearance of one layer in a Layer Comp and then sync it to see that change reflected in all the other Layer Comps.

Extra credit

Merging photos

Take the blinking and bad poses out of an otherwise great family portrait with the Auto-Align Layers feature.

1   Open FamilyPhoto.psd in your Lesson04 folder.

2   In the Layers panel, turn Layer 2 on and off to see the two similar photos. When both layers are visible, Layer 2 shows the tall man in the center blinking, and the two girls in the front looking away.

You'll align the two photos, and then use the Eraser tool to brush out the parts of the photo on Layer 2 that you want to improve.

3   Make both layers visible, and Shift-click to select them. Choose Edit > Auto-Align Layers; click OK to accept the default Auto position. Toggle the eye icon next to Layer 2 off and on to see that the layers are perfectly aligned.

Now for the fun part! You'll brush out the photo where you want to improve it.

4   Select the Eraser tool in the Tools panel, and pick a soft, 45-pixel brush in the options bar. Select Layer 2, and start brushing in the center of the blinking man's head to reveal the smiling face below.

5   Use the Eraser tool on the two girls looking away, revealing the image below, where they look into the camera.

You've created a natural family snapshot.

Review questions

1   What is the advantage of using layers?

2   When you create a new layer, where does it appear in the Layers panel stack?

3   How can you make artwork on one layer appear in front of artwork on another layer?

4   How can you apply a layer style?

5   When you've completed your artwork, what can you do to minimize the file size without changing the quality or dimensions?

Review answers

1   Layers let you move and edit different parts of an image as discrete objects. You can also hide individual layers as you work on other layers.

2   A new layer always appears immediately above the active layer.

3   You can make artwork on one layer appear in front of artwork on another layer by dragging layers up or down the stacking order in the Layers panel, or by using the Layer > Arrange subcommands—Bring To Front, Bring Forward, Send To Back, and Send Backward. However, you can't change the layer position of a background layer.

4   To apply a layer style, select the layer, and then click the Add A Layer Style button in the Layers panel, or choose Layer > Layer Style > [style].

5   To minimize file size, you can flatten the image, which merges all the layers onto a single background. It's a good idea to duplicate image files with layers intact before you flatten them, in case you have to make changes to a layer later.

5 QUICK FIXES

Lesson overview

In this lesson, you'll learn how to do the following:

- Remove red eye.

- Brighten an image.

- Combine images to create a panorama.

- Blur the background of an image using Iris Blur.

- Merge two images to extend depth of field.

- Apply optical lens correction to a distorted image.

- Move an object seamlessly.

- Use Perspective Warp to place an object into an image with a different perspective.

 This lesson will take about an hour to complete. Download the Lesson05 project files from the Lesson & Update Files tab on your Account page at www.peachpit.com, if you haven't already done so. As you work on this lesson, you'll preserve the start files. If you need to restore the start files, download them from your Account page.

PROJECT: RED EYE REDUCTION

PROJECT: CORRECTING
IMAGE DISTORTION

PROJECT: PANORAMA FROM MULTIPLE IMAGES

Sometimes just one or two clicks in Photoshop can
turn an image from so-so (or worse) to awesome.
Quick fixes get you the results you want without a lot
of fuss.

Getting started

Not every image requires a complicated makeover using advanced features in Photoshop. In fact, once you're familiar with Photoshop, you can often improve an image quickly. The trick is to know what's possible and how to find what you need.

In this lesson, you'll make quick fixes to several images using a variety of tools and techniques. You can use these techniques individually, or team them up when you're working with an image that needs just a little more help.

1   Start Photoshop, and then immediately hold down Ctrl+Alt+Shift (Windows) or Command+Option+Shift (Mac OS) to restore the default preferences. (See "Restoring default preferences" on page 4.)

2   When prompted, click Yes to delete the Adobe Photoshop Settings file.

Improving a snapshot

If you're sharing a snapshot with family and friends, you may not need it to look professional. But you probably don't want glowing eyes, and it would be good if the picture isn't too dark to show important detail. Photoshop gives you the tools to make quick changes to a snapshot.

Correcting red eye

Red eye occurs when the retina of a subject's eye is reflected by the camera flash. It commonly occurs in photographs taken in a dark room, because the subject's irises are wide open. Fortunately, red eye is easy to fix in Photoshop. In this exercise, you will remove the red eye from the boy's eyes in the portrait.

You'll start by viewing the before and after images in Adobe Bridge.

Note: If you haven't installed Bridge, you'll be prompted to do so when you choose Browse In Bridge. For more information, see page 3.

1   Choose File > Browse In Bridge to open Adobe Bridge.

2   In the Favorites panel in Bridge, click the Lessons folder. Then, in the Content panel, double-click the Lesson05 folder to open it.

3   Adjust the thumbnail slider, if necessary, so that you can see the thumbnail previews clearly. Then look at the Boy_Start.jpg and Boy_End.psd files.

Boy_Start.jpg

Boy_End.psd

Not only does red eye make an ordinary person or animal appear sinister, but it can distract from the subject of the image. It's easy to correct red eye in Photoshop, and you'll quickly lighten this image too.

4   Double-click the Boy_start.jpg file to open it in Photoshop.

5   Choose File > Save As, choose Photoshop for the Format, name the file **Boy_ Working.psd**, and click Save.

6   Select the Zoom tool (🔍), and then drag to zoom in to see the boy's eyes. If Scrubby Zoom isn't selected, drag a marquee around the eyes to zoom in.

7   Select the Red Eye tool (⁺👁), hidden under the Spot Healing Brush tool (🩹).

8   In the options bar, reduce the Pupil Size to **23%**, and the Darken Amount to **30%**.

The Darken Amount specifies how dark the pupil should be.

9   Click on the pupil in the boy's left eye. The red reflection disappears.

10 Click on the pupil in the boy's right eye to remove the red reflection there, too.

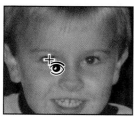
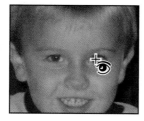

If the red reflection is directly over the pupil, clicking the pupil removes it. However, if the red reflection is slightly off the pupil, try clicking the highlight in the eye first. You may need to try a few different spots, but it's easy to undo and try again.

11 Choose View > Fit On Screen to see the entire image.

12 Choose File > Save to save your work so far.

Brightening an image

The eyes no longer glow, but the image is a bit dark. In Photoshop, you can brighten an image in several different ways, as you've already seen. Choosing only from adjustment layers, you can try modifying Brightness/Contrast, Levels, Curves, and Exposure. Sometimes the best option is to try them all and see which one you like best. That's easy to do with adjustment layers. But when you're really looking for a quick fix, a Curves adjustment layer is a great way to go.

1 Click Curves in the Adjustments panel.

2 Click Auto to see what Photoshop applies. The image brightens.

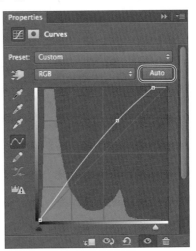

3 Choose Lighter from the Preset menu. Photoshop applies some subtle changes.

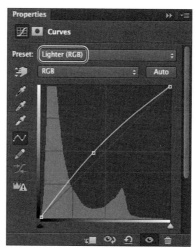

4 Select the White Point eyedropper in the Curves panel, and then click in the white area of the decal on the child's shirt. That brightens the image nicely, and also improves the contrast.

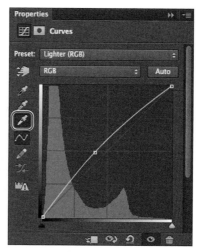

5 If you'd like to continue tweaking the settings, you can move the curve manually, or choose a black or gray point. To see how you've brightened the image, hide the Curves layer and then show it again.

6 Save the file, and then close it. The snapshot is ready to share.

Blurring a background

The interactive blurs in the Blur Gallery let you customize a blur as you preview it on your image. You'll use an iris blur to blur the background in an image, focusing the viewer's attention on the egret. You'll apply the blur as a Smart Filter so that you can modify it later if you want to.

You'll start by looking at the start and end files in Bridge.

1 Choose File > Browse In Bridge to open Adobe Bridge.

2 In the Favorites panel in Bridge, click the Lessons folder. Then, in the Content panel, double-click the Lesson05 folder to open it.

3 Compare the Egret_Start.jpg and Egret_End.psd thumbnail previews.

Egret_Start.jpg

Egret_End.psd

In the final image, the egret appears sharper, as its reflection and the grass around it have been blurred. Iris Blur, one of the interactive blurs in the Blur Gallery, makes the task an easy one—no masking required.

4 Return to Photoshop, and choose File > Open As Smart Object.

5 Select the Egret_Start.jpg file in the Lesson05 folder, and click OK or Open.

Photoshop opens the image. There is one layer in the Layers panel, and it's a Smart Object.

6 Choose File > Save As, choose Photoshop for the Format, name the file **Egret_Working.psd**, and click Save. Click OK in the Photoshop Format Options dialog box.

7 Choose Filter > Blur Gallery > Iris Blur.

A blur ellipse is centered on your image. You can adjust the location and scope of the blur by moving the center pin, feather handles, and ellipse handles. Photoshop also opens the Blur Gallery, which includes the Blur Tools, Blur Effects, and Motion Blur Effects panels.

8 Drag the center pin so that it's at the bottom of the bird's body.

9 Click the ellipse, and drag inward to tighten the focus around the bird.

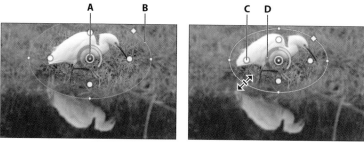

A. Center Pin **B.** Ellipse **C.** Feather handle **D.** Focus Ring

10 Press Alt (Windows) or Option (Mac OS) as you click and drag the feather handles to match those in the first image below. Pressing Alt or Option lets you drag each handle separately.

11 Click and drag on the focus ring to reduce the amount of blur to **5** px, creating a gradual but noticeable blur. You can also change the amount of blur by moving the Blur slider in the Iris Blur area of the Blur Tools panel.

12 Click OK in the options bar to apply the blur.

The blur may be a little too subtle. You'll edit the blur to increase it slightly.

13 Double-click the Blur Gallery in the Egret layer in the Layers panel to open it again. Adjust the blur to **6** px, and click OK in the options bar to apply it.

Because you applied the filter to a Smart Object, you can hide it or edit it without affecting the original image.

14 Save the file and close it.

The egret is accentuated by the blur.

Blur Gallery

The Blur Gallery includes five interactive blurs: Field Blur, Iris Blur, Tilt-Shift, Path Blur, and Spin Blur. Each gives you on-image selective motion blur tools, with an initial blur pin. You can create additional blur pins by clicking on the image. You can apply one or a combination of blurs, and you can create a strobe effect for path and spin blurs.

Before   *After*

Before   *After*

Field Blur applies a gradient blur to areas of the image, defined by pins you create and settings you specify for each. When you first apply Field Blur, a pin is placed in the center of the image. You can adjust the blur relative to that point by dragging the blur handle or specifying a value in the Blur Tools panel; you can also drag the pin to a different location.

Iris Blur simulates a shallow depth-of-field effect, gradually blurring everything outside the focus ring. Adjust the ellipse handles, feather handles, and blur amount to customize the iris blur.

Before   *After*

 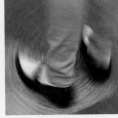

Before   *After*

Tilt-Shift simulates an image taken with a tilt-shift lens. This blur defines areas of sharpness and then fades to a blur at the edges. You can use this effect to simulate photos of miniature objects.

Spin Blur is a radial-style blur measured in degrees. You can change the size and shape of the ellipse, re-center the rotation point by pressing Alt or Option as you click and drag, and adjust the blur angle. You can also specify the blur angle in the Blur Tools panel. Multiple spin blurs can overlap.

Before   *After*

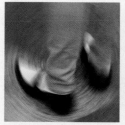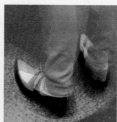

Before   *After*

Path Blur creates motion blurs along paths you draw. You control the shape and amount of the blur.

When you first apply a Path Blur, a default path appears. Drag the end point to reposition it. Click the center point and drag to change the curve. Click to add additional curve points. The arrow on the path indicates the blur's direction.

You can also create a multiple-point path or a shape. Blur shapes describe the local motion blurs, similar to camera shake (see "Camera Shake Reduction" on page 132). The Speed slider in the Blur Tools panel determines the speed for all the path blurs. The Centered Blur option ensures that the blur shape for any pixel is centered on that pixel, resulting in more stable-feeling motion blurs; to make the motion appear more fluid, deselect this option.

You can add a **strobe effect** to spin and path blurs. Select the **Motion Blur Effects** tab to bring its panel forward. The Strobe Strength slider determines how much blur shows between flash exposures (0% gives no strobe effect; 100% gives full strobe effect with little blur between exposures). Strobe Flashes determines the number of exposures.

In the Blur Effects panel, you specify the bokeh parameters to control the appearance of blurred areas. Light Bokeh brightens the blurred areas; Bokeh Color adds more vivid colors to lightened areas that aren't blown out to white; Light Range determines the range of tones that the settings affect.

Creating a panorama

Sometimes a vista is just too large for a single shot. Photoshop makes it easy to combine multiple images into a panorama so that your viewers can get the full effect.

Once again, you'll take a look at the end file first, to see where you're going.

1   Choose File > Browse In Bridge.

2   Navigate to the Lesson05 folder, if you're not there already. Then, look at the Skyline_End.psd thumbnail preview.

Skyline_End.psd

You'll combine four shots of the Seattle skyline into a single wide panorama image so that viewers get a sense of the whole scene. Creating a panorama from multiple images requires only a few clicks. Photoshop does the rest.

3   Return to Photoshop.

4   With no files open in Photoshop, choose File > Automate > Photomerge.

5   In the Source Files area, click Browse, and navigate to the Lesson05/Files For Panorama folder.

6   Shift-select all the images in the folder, and click OK or Open.

7   In the Layout area of the Photomerge dialog box, select Perspective.

8   At the bottom of the Photomerge dialog box, select Blend Images Together, Vignette Removal, and Geometric Distortion Correction. Then click OK.

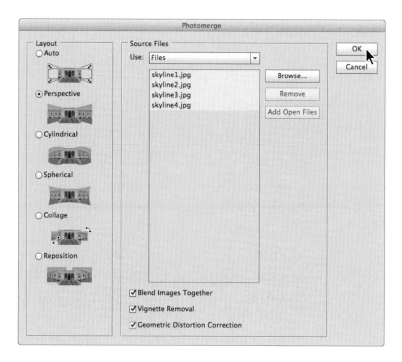

Blend Images Together blends images based on the optimal borders between them, instead of just creating a simple rectangular blend. Vignette Removal performs exposure compensation in images with darkened edges. Geometric Distortion Correction compensates for barrel, pincushion, or fisheye distortion.

Photoshop creates the panorama image. It's a complex process, so you may have to wait a few minutes while Photoshop works. When it's finished, you'll see the full vista in the image window, with four layers in the Layers panel—one for each of the images you selected. Photoshop has identified the overlapping areas of the images and matched them, correcting any angular discrepancies. In the process, it left some areas empty. You'll make the panorama tidy by adding a little sky to fill in some of the empty area, and by cropping the image.

Getting the best results with Photomerge

If you know you're going to create a panorama when you take your shots, keep the following guidelines in mind to get the best result.

Overlap images approximately 40%. You want enough overlap that Photomerge can assemble the panorama but not so much that it can't blend the images.

Use a consistent focal length. If you use a zoom lens, keep the focal length the same for all the pictures in the panorama.

Use a tripod if possible. You'll get the best results if the camera is at the same level when you take each of the shots. A tripod with a rotating head makes that easier.

Take the photos from the same position. If you're not using a tripod with a rotating head, try to stay in the same position as you take the photos so that they are taken from the same viewpoint.

Avoid distortion lenses. They can interfere with Photomerge. (The Auto option does adjust for images you take with fish-eye lenses, though.)

Use the same exposure. The images will blend more gracefully if they all have the same exposure. For example, either use flash for all the images or none of them.

Try different layout options. If you don't like the results you get when you create the panorama, try again using a different layout option. Often, Auto selects the appropriate option, but sometimes you'll get a better image with one of the other options.

9   Select all the layers in the Layers panel, and then choose Layer > Merge Layers.

 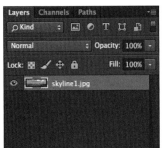

10 Choose File > Save As. Choose Photoshop for the Format, and name the file **Skyline_Working.psd**. Save the file in the Lesson05 folder. Click Save, and then click OK in the Photoshop Format Options dialog box.

11 Select the Crop tool. Drag the bottom edge of the crop boundary up so that there is no transparent area at the bottom. Crop on each side to omit the transparent areas. Then press Enter or Return to commit the crop.

12 Select the Magic Wand tool (🪄), hidden behind the Quick Selection tool (🖌) in the Tools panel. Then, click in the transparent area at the top of the image to select it.

13 Choose Edit > Fill.

14 In the Fill dialog box, choose Content-Aware from the Use menu, and click OK.

Photoshop fills the transparent area with color that blends with the existing sky.

15 Choose Select > Deselect.

The panorama looks great, but it's a little dark. You'll add a Levels adjustment layer to brighten it a little bit.

16 Click the Levels icon in the Adjustments panel to add a Levels adjustment layer.

17 Select the White Point eyedropper, and then click on a white area of the clouds.

The sky gets bluer and the entire image brightens.

18 Save your work and close the file.

It's that easy to create a panorama!

Correcting image distortion

The Lens Correction filter fixes common camera lens flaws, such as barrel and pincushion distortion, chromatic aberration, and vignetting. *Barrel distortion* is a lens defect that causes straight lines to bow out toward the edges of the image. *Pincushion distortion* is the opposite effect, causing straight lines to bend inward. *Chromatic aberration* appears as a color fringe along the edges of image objects. *Vignetting* occurs when the edges of an image, especially the corners, are darker than the center.

Some lenses exhibit these defects depending on the focal length or the f-stop used. The Lens Correction filter can apply settings based on the camera, lens, and focal length that were used to make the image. The filter can also rotate an image or fix image perspective caused by tilting a camera vertically or horizontally. The filter's image grid makes it easier and more accurate to make these adjustments than using the Transform command.

1 Choose File > Browse In Bridge.

2 Navigate to the Lesson05 folder if you're not already there, and then look at the Columns_Start.psd and Columns_End.psd thumbnail previews.

Columns_Start.psd   *Columns_End.psd*

In this case, the original image of a Greek temple is distorted, with the columns appearing to be bowed. This photo was shot at a range that was too close with a wide-angle lens. You'll quickly correct the lens barrel distortion.

3 Double-click the Columns_Start.psd file to open it in Photoshop.

4 Choose File > Save As. In the Save As dialog box, name the file **Columns_ Working.psd**, and save it in the Lesson05 folder. Click OK if the Photoshop Format Options dialog box appears.

5 Choose Filter > Lens Correction. The Lens Correction dialog box opens.

6 Select Show Grid at the bottom of the dialog box, if it's not already selected.

An alignment grid overlays the image, next to options for removing distortion, correcting chromatic aberration, removing vignettes, and transforming perspective.

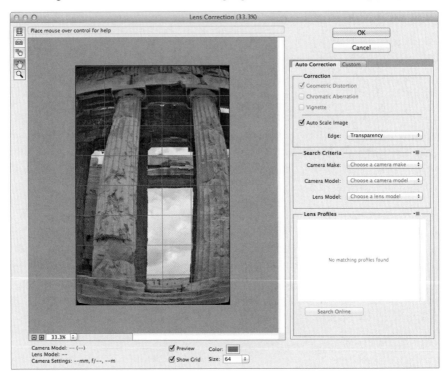

The Lens Correction dialog box includes auto-correction options. You'll adjust one setting in the Auto Correction tab and then customize the settings.

7 In the Correction area of the Auto Correction tab, make sure Auto Scale Image is selected, and that Transparency is selected from the Edge menu.

8 Select the Custom tab.

9 In the Custom tab, drag the Remove Distortion slider to about **+52.00** to remove the barrel distortion in the image. Alternatively, you could select the Remove Distortion tool (▣) and drag in the image preview area until the columns are straight. The adjustment causes the image borders to bow inward. However, because you selected Auto Scale Image, the Lens Correction filter automatically scales the image to adjust the borders.

▶ Tip: Watch the alignment grid as you make these changes so that you can see when the vertical columns are straightened in the image.

10 Click OK to apply your changes and close the Lens Correction dialog box.

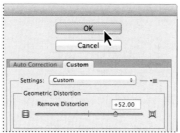

The curving distortion caused by the wide-angle lens and low shooting angle is eliminated.

11 (Optional) To see the effect of your change in the main image window, press Ctrl+Z (Windows) or Command+Z (Mac OS) twice to undo and redo the filter.

12 Choose File > Save to save your changes, click OK if the Photoshop Format Options dialog box appears, and then close the image.

The temple looks much more stable now!

Adding depth of field

When you're shooting a photo, you often have to choose to focus either the background or the foreground. If you want the entire image to be in focus, you can take two photos—one with the background in focus and one with the foreground in focus—and then merge the two in Photoshop.

Because you'll need to align the images exactly, it's helpful to use a tripod to keep the camera steady. Even with a handheld camera, though, you can get some amazing results. You'll add depth of field to an image of a wine glass in front of a beach.

1 Choose File > Browse In Bridge.

2 Navigate to the Lesson05 folder, if you're not there already, and then look at the Glass_Start.psd and Glass_End.psd thumbnail previews.

Glass_Start.psd   Glass_End.psd

The first image has two layers. Depending on which layer is visible, either the glass in the foreground or the beach in the background is in focus. You'll extend the depth of field to make both clear.

3 Double-click the Glass_Start.psd file to open it.

4 Choose File > Save As. Name the file **Glass_Working.psd**, and save it in the Lesson05 folder. Click OK if the Photoshop Format Options dialog box appears.

5 In the Layers panel, hide the Beach layer, so that only the Glass layer is visible. The glass is in focus, but the background is blurred. Then, show the Beach layer and hide the Glass layer. Now the beach is in focus, but the glass is blurred.

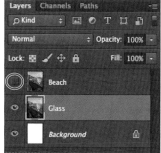

You'll merge the layers, using the part of each layer that is in focus. First, you need to align the layers.

6   Show both layers again, and then Shift-click to select both of them.

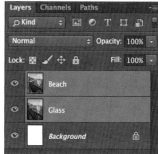

7 Choose Edit > Auto-Align Layers.

Because these images were shot from the same angle, Auto will work just fine.

8 Select Auto, if it isn't already selected. Make sure neither Vignette Removal nor Geometric Distortion is selected. Then click OK to align the layers.

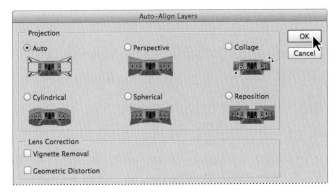

Now that the layers are perfectly aligned, you're ready to blend them.

9 Make sure both layers are still selected in the Layers panel. Then choose Edit > Auto-Blend Layers.

10 Select Stack Images and Seamless Tones And Colors, and then click OK.

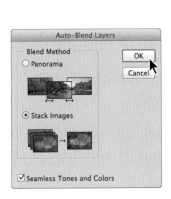 

11 Save your work, and close the file.

Both the wine glass and the beach behind it are in focus.

Moving objects with the Content-Aware Move tool

You've used the content-aware features in some pretty impressive ways in earlier lessons, and to fill in the sky in the panorama project in this lesson. Now you'll use the Content-Aware Move tool to move something in an image (in this case, a duck) and have Photoshop convincingly fill in the area where the item you moved used to be. You can also use the Content-Aware Move tool to extend a portion of an image, such as a stand of trees or fenceposts, seamlessly.

1 Choose File > Browse In Bridge.

2 Navigate to the Lesson05 folder, if you're not there already, and then look at the Ducks_Start.jpg and Ducks_End.psd thumbnail previews.

Ducks_Start.jpg

Ducks_End.psd

You'll use the Content-Aware Move tool to nudge the last duck into a cluster with its companions.

3 Double-click the Ducks_Start.jpg file to open it in Photoshop.

4 Choose File > Save As, choose Photoshop for the format type, and name the new file **Ducks_Working.psd**. Click Save.

5 Select the Content-Aware Move tool (⨯), which is hidden beneath the Red Eye Removal tool (⁺☉).

6 In the options bar, choose Move from the Mode menu. Then click the Settings button next to Adaptation, and enter **3** in the Structure field.

7 Draw a marquee around the third duck, with a margin large enough to include the grass and dirt around it.

8 Drag the selection to the left, slightly above the second duck, so that the ducks are clustered.

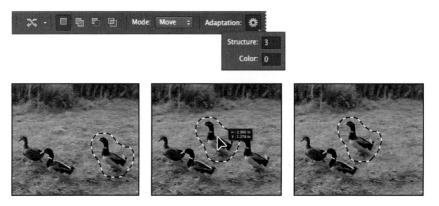

When you release the mouse, Photoshop fills in the area the duck left behind. How it creates the area depends on the Adaptation option you chose. You can try different options while the selection remains active.

9 Change the Structure setting to **5**, which requires stricter adherence to the pattern, and observe how the image changes. Then change the Structure setting to **1**, which results in a much looser adaptation. You can also experiment with different Color settings, from 0 to 10.

10 Choose the Adaptation options you think look best. Then choose Select > Deselect. Save the file and close it.

The three ducks are in a tighter formation now, and you can't tell that the third duck used to be in a different position.

More on the Content-Aware Move tool

The Content-Aware Move tool is very impressive when you're working with some images, and less impressive with others. For best results, use it when the background is consistent enough that Photoshop will be able to recognize and replicate a pattern. In the image of ducks, the grass and dirt are fairly consistent and repetitive. You can also try moving objects with backgrounds such as meadows, solid-colored walls, sky, wood grains, or water.

It's best to extend architectural objects in photos that have been shot on a parallel plane, rather than at an angle. If you're working with an image that has multiple layers, select Sample All Layers in the options bar to include them all in the selection.

The Adaptation options define how closely the results reflect the existing image patterns. In the Structure settings, 1 is the loosest and 5 is the strictest. The Color settings range from 0 (no color adaptation) to 10 (matching the color as closely as possible). Experiment with the options while the object is still selected to see which give you the best results in a particular image. You may want to hide the selection edges (choose View > Show > Selection Edges or View > Extras) to see how the object is integrated into its new position.

Adjusting perspective in an image

The Perspective Warp feature lets you adjust the way objects in your image relate to the scene. You can correct distortions, change the angle from which an object appears to be viewed, or shift the perspective of an object so that it merges smoothly with a new background.

Using the Perspective Warp feature is a two-step process: defining the planes and adjusting them. You start in Layout mode, drawing *quads* to define two or more planes; it's a good idea to align the edges of the quads so that they are parallel with the lines of the original object. Then you switch to Warp mode, and manipulate the planes you defined.

You'll use Perspective Warp to merge images with different perspectives.

1   Choose File > Browse In Bridge.

2   Navigate to the Lesson05 folder, if you're not there already, and then look
     at the Bridge_Start.psd and Bridge_End.psd thumbnail previews.

Bridge_Start.psd   Bridge_End.psd

In the Bridge_Start.psd file, the image of the train has been combined with the
image of a trestle bridge, but their perspectives don't match. If you're illustrating
a story about a flying train that is making a landing on a trestle bridge, this might
be perfect. But if you want a more realistic image, you'll need to adjust the perspective
of the train to put it firmly on the tracks. You'll use Perspective Warp to do just that.

3   Double-click the Bridge_Start.psd file to open it in Photoshop.

4   Choose File > Save As, and rename the file **Bridge_Working.psd**. Click OK in
     the Photoshop Format Options dialog box.

5   Select the Train layer.

The tracks are on the Background layer. The train is on the Train layer. Because the
Train layer is a Smart Object, you can apply Perspective Warp and then modify the
results if you're not satisfied.

6 Choose Edit > Perspective Warp.

A small animated tutorial appears, showing you how to draw a quad, which defines a plane.

7 Watch the animation, and then close it.

In the first step of the process, you want to enclose the object in quads that represent the current planes of the object.

8 Draw the quad for the side of the train: Click above the top of the smokestack, drag down to the railroad tie below the front wheel, and then drag across to the end of the caboose. The plane is currently a rectangle.

9 Drag a second quad for the front of the train, dragging across the cowcatcher at the bottom and into the trees at the top. Drag it to the right until it attaches to the left edge of the first quad.

10 Drag the corners of the planes to match the angles of the train. The bottom line of the side plane should run along the bottom of the train wheels; the top edge should border the top of the caboose. The front plane should mirror the lines of the cowcatcher and the top of the light.

Now that the quads are drawn, you're ready for the second step in the process: warping.

11 Click Warp in the options bar. Close the tutorial box that shows you how to warp the plane.

12 Click the Automatically Straighten Near Vertical Lines button, next to Warp in the options bar.

This makes the train appear properly vertical, making it easier to adjust the perspective accurately.

13 Drag the handles to manipulate the planes, moving the back end of the train down and into perspecive with the tracks. Exaggerate the perspective toward the caboose for a more dramatic result.

14 Warp other parts of the train as needed. You may need to adjust the front of the train. Pay attention to the wheels; make sure you don't distort them as you warp the perspective.

There is no precise right or wrong way to adjust perspective. Trust your eyes to tell you when it looks right. Remember you can return to tweak it again later, because you're applying Perspective Warp as a Smart Filter.

15 When you're satisfied with the perspective, click the Commit Perspective Warp button in the options bar.

16 To compare the changed image with the original, hide the Perspective Warp filter in the Layers panel. Then show the filter again.

If you want to make further adjustments, double-click the Perspective Warp filter in the Layers panel. You can continue to adjust the existing planes, or click Layout in the options bar to reshape them.

Changing the perspective of a building

In the exercise, you applied Perspective Warp to one layer to change its relationship with another. But you can also use Perspective Warp to change the perspective of an object in relationship to others in the same layer. For example, you can shift the angle from which you view a building.

In this case, you apply Perspective Warp the same way: In Layout mode, draw the planes of the object you want to affect. In Warp mode, manipulate those planes. Of course, because you're shifting angles within a layer, other objects on the layer will move, too, so you need to watch for any irregularities.

In this image, as the perspective of the building shifted, so did the perspective of the trees surrounding it.

Camera Shake Reduction

Even with a steady hand, unintended camera motion can occur with slow shutter speeds or long focal lengths. The Camera Shake Reduction filter reduces the resulting camera shake, giving you a sharper image.

Before applying the Camera Shake Reduction filter

You'll get the best results if you apply the filter to a particular part of an image, rather than the entire image. It can be especially useful if text has become illegible due to camera shake.

To use the Camera Shake Reduction filter, open the image, and choose Filter > Sharpen > Shake Reduction. The filter automatically analyzes the image, selects a region of interest, and corrects the blur. Use the Detail loupe to examine the preview. That may be all you need to do. If so, click OK to close the Shake Reduction dialog box and apply the filter.

After applying the Camera Shake Reduction filter

If you want to make further adjustments, expand the Advanced area of the dialog box. You can change the region of interest or adjust its size; view and resize the blur trace, which is the shape and size of the camera shake that Photoshop identified; and adjust the Smoothing and Artifact Suppression values to correct noise and artifacts. You can even save the blur trace to use the settings on another image. For full information about the Camera Shake Reduction filter, see Photoshop Help.

Review questions

1   What is red eye, and how do you correct it in Photoshop?

2   How can you create a panorama from multiple images?

3   Describe how to fix common camera lens flaws in Photoshop. What causes these defects?

4   What conditions provide the best results when using the Content-Aware Move tool?

Review answers

1   Red eye occurs when the retinas of a subject's eyes are reflected by the camera flash. To correct red eye in Photoshop, zoom in to the subject's eyes, select the Red Eye tool, and then click the eye.

2   To blend multiple images into a panorama, choose File > Automate > Photomerge, select the files you want to combine, and click OK.

3   The Lens Correction filter fixes common camera lens flaws, such as barrel and pincushion distortion, in which straight lines bow out towards the edges of the image (barrel) or bend inward (pincushion); chromatic aberration, where a color fringe appears along the edges of image objects; and vignetting at the edges of an image, especially corners, that are darker than the center. Defects can occur from incorrectly setting the lens's focal length or f-stop, or by tilting the camera vertically or horizontally.

4   The Content-Aware Move tool works best in images that have consistent backgrounds so that Photoshop can seamlessly replicate the patterns.

6 MASKS AND CHANNELS

Lesson overview

In this lesson, you'll learn how to do the following:

- Create a mask to remove a subject from a background.

- Refine a mask to include complex edges.

- Create a quick mask to make changes to a selected area.

- Edit a mask using the Properties panel.

- Manipulate an image using Puppet Warp.

- Save a selection as an alpha channel.

- View a mask using the Channels panel.

- Load a channel as a selection.

- Isolate a channel to make specific image changes.

 This lesson will take about an hour to complete. Download the Lesson06 project files from the Lesson & Update Files tab on your Account page at www.peachpit.com, if you haven't already done so. As you work on this lesson, you'll preserve the start files. If you need to restore the start files, download them from your Account page.

PROJECT: MAGAZINE COVER IMAGE

Photography © Image Source, www.imagesource.com

Use masks to isolate and manipulate specific parts of an image. The cutout portion of a mask can be altered, but the area surrounding the cutout is protected from change. You can create a temporary mask to use once, or you can save masks for repeated use.

Working with masks and channels

In Photoshop, masks isolate and protect parts of an image, just as masking tape protects window panes or trim from paint when a house is painted. When you create a mask based on a selection, the area you haven't selected is *masked,* or protected from editing. With masks, you can create and save time-consuming selections and then use them again. In addition, you can use masks for other complex editing tasks—for example, to apply color changes or filter effects to an image.

In Photoshop, you can make temporary masks, called *quick masks,* or you can create permanent masks and store them as special grayscale channels called *alpha channels.* Photoshop also uses channels to store an image's color information. Unlike layers, channels do not print. You use the Channels panel to view and work with alpha channels.

A key concept in masking is that black hides and white reveals. As in life, rarely is anything black and white. Shades of gray partially hide, depending on the gray levels (255 is the value for black, hiding artwork completely; 0 is the value for white, revealing artwork completely).

Getting started

First, you'll view the image that you'll create using masks and channels.

1   Start Photoshop, and then immediately hold down Ctrl+Alt+Shift (Windows) or Command+Option+Shift (Mac OS) to restore the default preferences. (See "Restoring default preferences" on page 4.)

2   When prompted, click Yes to delete the Adobe Photoshop Settings file.

● **Note:** If Bridge isn't installed, you'll be prompted to install it when you choose Browse In Bridge. For more information, see page 3.

3   Choose File > Browse In Bridge to open Adobe Bridge.

4   Click the Favorites tab on the left side of the Bridge window. Select the Lessons folder, and then double-click the Lesson06 folder in the Content panel.

5   Study the 06End.psd file. To enlarge the thumbnail so that you can see it more clearly, move the thumbnail slider at the bottom of the Bridge window to the right.

In this lesson, you'll create a magazine cover. The model for the cover was photographed in front of a different background. You'll use masking and the Refine Mask feature to place the model on the appropriate background.

6   Double-click the 06Start.psd thumbnail to open it in Photoshop. Click OK if you see an Embedded Profile Mismatch dialog box.

Creating a mask

You'll use the Quick Selection tool to create the initial mask in order to separate the model from the background.

1 Choose File > Save As, rename the file **06Working.psd**, and click Save. Click OK if the Photoshop Format Options dialog box appears.

Saving a working version of the file lets you return to the original if you need it.

2 Select the Quick Selection tool (✒). In the options bar, set up a brush with a size of **15** px and hardness of **100%**.

3 Drag to select the man. It's fairly easy to select his shirt and face, but the hair is trickier. Don't worry if the selection isn't perfect. You'll refine the mask in the next exercise.

▶ **Tip:** For help making selections, refer to Lesson 3, "Working with Selections."

4 At the bottom of the Layers panel, click the Add Layer Mask button (▣) to create a layer mask.

About masks and masking

Alpha channels, channel masks, clipping masks, layer masks, vector masks—what's the difference? In some cases, they're interchangeable: A channel mask can be converted to a layer mask, a layer mask can be converted to a vector mask, and vice versa.

Here's a brief description to help you keep them all straight. What they have in common is that they all store selections, and they all let you edit an image nondestructively, so you can return at any time to your original.

- An **alpha channel**—also called a *mask* or *selection*—is an extra channel added to an image; it stores selections as grayscale images. You can add alpha channels to create and store masks.

- A **layer mask** is like an alpha channel, but it's attached to a specific layer. A layer mask controls which part of a layer is revealed or hidden. It appears as a blank thumbnail next to the layer thumbnail in the Layers panel until you add content to it; a black outline indicates that it's selected.

- A **vector mask** is essentially a layer mask made up of vectors, not pixels. Resolution-independent, vector masks have crisp edges and are created with the pen or shape tools. They don't support transparency, so their edges can't be feathered. Their thumbnails appear the same as layer mask thumbnails.

- A **clipping mask** applies to a layer. It confines the influence of an effect to specific layers, rather than to everything below the layer in the layer stack. Using a clipping mask clips layers to a base layer; only that base layer is affected. Thumbnails of a clipped layer are indented with a right-angle arrow pointing to the layer below. The name of the clipped base layer is underlined.

- A **channel mask** restricts editing to a specific channel (for example, a Cyan channel in a CMYK image). Channel masks are useful for making intricate, fringed, or wispy-edged selections. You can create a channel mask based on a dominant color in an image or a pronounced contrast in an isolated channel, for example, between the subject and the background.

The selection becomes a pixel mask, and it appears as part of Layer 0 in the Layers panel. Everything outside the selection is transparent, represented by a checkerboard pattern.

Refining a mask

The mask is pretty good, but the Quick Selection tool couldn't quite capture all of the model's hair. The mask is also a little choppy around the contours of the shirt and face. You'll smooth the mask, and then fine-tune the area around the hair.

1   Choose Window > Properties to open the Properties panel.

2   If it isn't already selected, click the mask on Layer 0 in the Layers panel.

3   In the Properties panel, click Mask Edge. The Refine Mask dialog box opens.

4   In the View Mode area of the dialog box, click the arrow next to the preview window. Choose On Black from the pop-up menu.

The mask appears against a black background, which makes it easier to see the edge of the white shirt and the face.

5   In the Adjust Edge area of the dialog box, move the sliders to create a smooth, unfeathered edge along the shirt and face. The optimal settings depend on the selection you created, but they'll probably be similar to ours. We moved the Smooth slider to 15 to create a smoother outline, Contrast to 40% to make the transitions along the selection border more abrupt, and Shift Edge to -8% to move the selection border inward and help remove unwanted background colors from selection edges. (Adjusting Shift Edge to a positive number would move the border outward.)

6   In the Output area of the dialog box, select Decontaminate Colors. Choose New Layer With Layer Mask from the Output To menu.

Decontaminate Colors replaces color fringes with the color of fully selected pixels nearby. Because it changes pixel color, this option requires you to output to a new layer or document.

7   Select the Zoom tool in the Refine Mask dialog box, and then click the face to zoom in so you can see its edges more clearly.

8   Select the Refine Radius tool (✎) in the Refine Mask dialog box. Use it to paint out any white background that remains around the lips and the nose. Press the left bracket ([) to decrease the brush size and the right bracket (]) to increase it.

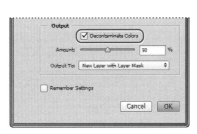

Julieanne Kost is an official Adobe Photoshop evangelist.

Tool tips from the Photoshop evangelist

Zoom tool shortcuts

Often when editing an image, you'll need to zoom in to work on a detail and then zoom out again to see the changes in context. Here are several keyboard shortcuts that make zooming even faster and easier.

*   With any tool selected, press Ctrl (Windows) or Command (Mac OS) with the plus sign (+) to zoom in, or with the minus sign (-) to zoom out.

*   Double-click the Zoom tool in the Tools panel to return the image to 100% view.

*   When Scrubby Zoom is selected in the options bar, just drag the Zoom tool to the left to zoom out or drag it to the right to zoom in.

*   Press Alt (Windows) or Option (Mac OS) to change the Zoom In tool to the Zoom Out tool, and click the area of the image you want to reduce. Each Alt/Option-click reduces the image by the next preset increment.

9 When you're satisfied with the mask around the face, click OK.

A new layer, named Layer 0 copy, appears in the Layers panel. You'll use this layer to add the spikes to the mask of the hair.

10 With Layer 0 copy active, click Mask Edge in the Properties panel to open the Refine Mask dialog box again.

11 From the View pop-up menu, choose On White. The black hair shows up well against the white matte. If necessary, zoom out or use the Hand tool to reposition the image so that you can see all of the hair.

12 Select the Refine Radius tool in the Refine Mask dialog box. Press the] key to increase the size of the brush. (The options bar displays the brush size; we used 300 px at first.) Then, begin brushing along the top of the hair, high enough to include the spikes.

13 Press the [key a few times to decrease the brush size by about half. Then, paint along the right side of the head, where the hair is a solid color, to pick up any small, fine hairs that protrude.

As you paint, Photoshop refines the mask edge, including the hair, but eliminating most of the background. If you were painting on a layer mask, the background would be included. The Refine Mask feature is good, but it's not perfect. You'll clean up any areas of background that are included with the hair.

14 Select the Erase Refinements tool (🖌️), hidden behind the Refine Radius tool in the Refine Mask dialog box. Click once or twice in each area where background color shows. When you erase an area, the Refine Mask feature erases similar colors, cleaning up more of the mask for you. Be careful not to erase the refinements you made to the hair edge. You can undo a step or use the Refine Radius tool to restore the edge if necessary.

15 Select Decontaminate Colors, and move the Amount slider to 85%. Choose New Layer With Layer Mask from the Output To menu. Then click OK.

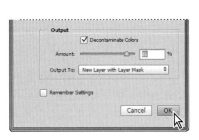 

16 In the Layers panel, make the Magazine Background layer visible. The model appears in front of an orange patterned background.

 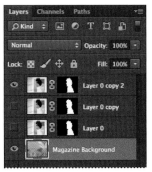

Creating a quick mask

You'll create a quick mask to change the color of the glasses frames. First, you'll clean up the Layers panel.

1. Hide the Magazine Background layer so you can focus on the model. Then delete the Layer 0 and Layer 0 copy layers. Click Yes or Delete to confirm deletion of the layers or their masks, if prompted; you do not need to apply the mask to the current layer because Layer 0 copy 2 already has the mask applied.

2. Double-click the Layer 0 copy 2 layer name, and rename it **Model**.

3. Click the Edit In Quick Mask Mode button in the Tools panel. (By default, you have been working in Standard mode.)

In Quick Mask mode, a red overlay appears as you make a selection, masking the area outside the selection the way a rubylith, or red acetate, was used to mask images in traditional print shops. You can apply changes only to the unprotected area that is visible and selected. Notice that the highlight for the selected layer in the Layers panel appears gray instead of blue, indicating you're in Quick Mask mode.

4. In the Tools panel, select the Brush tool ( ).

5. In the options bar, make sure that the mode is Normal. Open the Brush pop-up panel, and select a small brush with a diameter of **13** px. Click outside the panel to close it.

6. Paint the earpiece of the glasses frames. The area you paint will appear red, creating a mask.

7. Continue painting with the Brush tool to mask the earpiece of the frames and the frame around the lenses. Reduce the brush size to paint around the lenses. Don't worry about the hair overlapping the earpiece; go ahead and paint over it.

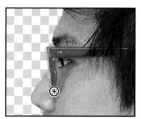
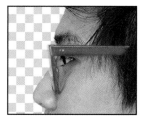

In Quick Mask mode, Photoshop automatically defaults to Grayscale mode, with a foreground color of black and a background color of white. When using a painting or editing tool in Quick Mask mode, keep these principles in mind:

- Painting with black adds to the mask (the red overlay) and decreases the selected area.

- Painting with white erases the mask (the red overlay) and increases the selected area.

- Painting with gray partially adds to the mask.

8 Click the Edit In Standard Mode button to exit Quick Mask Mode.

The unmasked area is selected. Unless you save a quick mask as a more permanent alpha-channel mask, Photoshop discards the temporary mask once it is converted to a selection.

9 Choose Select > Inverse to select the area you originally masked.

10 Choose Image > Adjustments > Hue/Saturation.

11 In the Hue/Saturation dialog box, change the Hue to **70**. The new green color fills the glasses frame. Click OK.

12 Choose Select > Deselect.

13 Save your work so far.

Manipulating an image with Puppet Warp

The Puppet Warp feature gives you flexibility in manipulating an image. You can reposition areas, such as hair or an arm, just as you might pull the strings on a puppet. Place pins wherever you want to control movement. You'll use Puppet Warp to tilt the model's head back, so he appears to be looking up.

1   Zoom out so you can see the entire model.

2   With the Model layer selected in the Layers panel, choose Edit > Puppet Warp.

A mesh appears over the visible areas in the layer—in this case, the mesh appears over the model. You'll use the mesh to place pins where you want to control movement (or to ensure there is no movement).

3   Click around the edges of the shirt. Each time you click, Puppet Warp adds a pin. Approximately 10 pins should work.

The pins you've added around the shirt will keep it in place as you tilt the head.

4   Select the pin at the nape of the neck. A white dot appears in the center of the pin to indicate that it's selected.

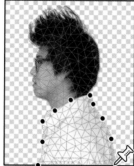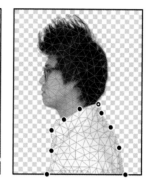

5   Press Alt (Windows) or Option (Mac OS). A larger circle appears around the pin and a curved double arrow appears next to it. Continue pressing Alt or Option as you drag the pointer to rotate the head backwards. You can see the angle of rotation in the options bar; you can enter **135** there to rotate the head back.

Note: Be careful not to Alt-click or Option-click the dot itself, or you'll delete the pin.

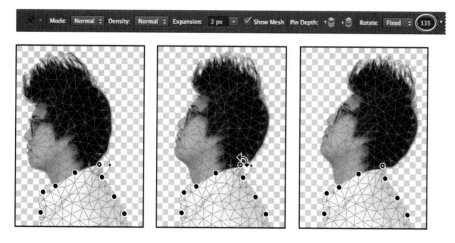

6 When you're satisfied with the rotation, click the Commit Puppet Warp button (✔) in the options bar, or press Enter or Return.

7 Save your work so far.

Working with channels

Just as different information in an image is stored on different layers, channels also let you access specific kinds of information. Alpha channels store selections as gray-scale images. Color information channels store information about each color in an image; for example, an RGB image automatically has red, green, blue, and composite channels.

To avoid confusing channels and layers, think of channels as containing an image's color and selection information; think of layers as containing painting and effects.

You'll use an alpha channel to create a shadow for the model. Then, you'll convert the image to CMYK mode and use the Black channel to add color highlights to the hair.

Using an alpha channel to create a shadow

You've already created a mask of the model. To create a shadow, you want to essentially duplicate that mask and then shift it. You'll use an alpha channel to make that possible.

1 In the Layers panel, Ctrl-click (Windows) or Command-click (Mac OS) the layer icon in the Model layer. The masked area is selected.

2 Choose Select > Save Selection. In the Save Selection dialog box, make sure New is chosen in the Channel menu. Then name the channel **Model Outline,** and click OK.

Nothing changes in the Layers panel or in the image window. However, a new channel named Model Outline has been added to the Channels panel.

3   Click the Create A New Layer icon (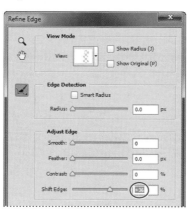) at the bottom of the Layers panel. Drag the new layer below the Model layer, so that the shadow will be below the image of the model. Then double-click the new layer's name, and rename it **Shadow**.

4   With the Shadow layer selected, choose Select > Refine Edge. In the Refine Edge dialog box, move the Shift Edge slider to +**36**%. Then click OK.

5   Choose Edit > Fill. In the Fill dialog box, choose Black from the Use menu, and then click OK.

The Shadow layer displays a filled-in black outline of the model. Shadows aren't usually as dark as the person that casts them. You'll reduce the layer opacity.

6   In the Layers panel, change the layer opacity to **30**%.

The shadow is in exactly the same position as the model, where it can't be seen. You'll shift it.

7   Choose Select > Deselect to remove the selection.

8 Choose Edit > Transform > Rotate. Rotate the shadow by hand, or enter **-15°** in the Rotate field in the options bar. Then drag the shadow to the left, or enter **845** in the X field in the options bar. Click the Commit Transform button (✔) in the options bar, or press Enter or Return, to accept the transformation.

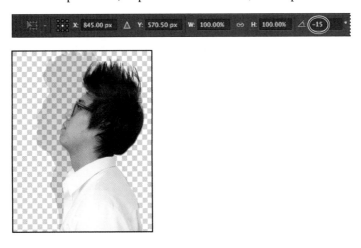

9 Choose File > Save to save your work so far.

Adjusting an individual channel

You're almost done with the magazine cover image. All that remains is to add color highlights to the model's hair. You'll convert the image to CMYK mode so you can take advantage of the Black channel to do just that.

1 Select the Model layer in the Layers panel.

2 Choose Image > Mode > CMYK Color. Click Don't Merge in the dialog box that appears, because you want to keep your layers intact. Click OK if you're prompted about color profiles.

3 Alt-click (Windows) or Option-click (Mac OS) the visibility icon for the Model layer to hide the other layers.

About alpha channels

If you work in Photoshop very long, you're bound to work with alpha channels. It's a good idea to know a few things about them.

- An image can contain up to 56 channels, including all color and alpha channels.

- All channels are 8-bit grayscale images, capable of displaying 256 levels of gray.

- You can specify a name, color, mask option, and opacity for each channel. (The opacity affects the preview of the channel, not the image.)

- All new channels have the same dimensions and number of pixels as the original image.

- You can edit the mask in an alpha channel using the painting tools, editing tools, and filters.

- You can convert alpha channels to spot-color channels.

4 Select the Channels tab. In the Channels panel, select the Black channel. Then choose Duplicate Channel from the Channels panel menu. Name the channel **Hair**, and click OK.

Individual channels appear in grayscale. If more than one channel is visible in the Channels panel, the channels appear in color.

5   Make the Hair channel visible, and hide the Black channel. Then select the Hair channel, and choose Image > Adjustments > Levels.

6   In the Levels dialog box, adjust the levels to move Black to **85**, Midtones to **1**, and White to **165**. Moving the Black and White points create contrast in the hair. Click OK.

 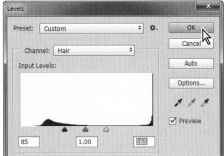

7   With the Hair channel still selected, choose Image > Adjustments > Invert. The channel appears white against a black background.

8   Select the Brush tool, and click the Switch Foreground And Background Colors icon in the Tools panel to make the Foreground color black. Then paint over the glasses, eyes, and anything in the channel that isn't hair.

9 Click the Load Channel As Selection icon at the bottom of the Channels panel.

10 Select the Layers tab. In the Layers panel, select the Model layer.

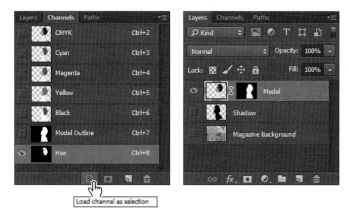

11 Choose Select > Refine Edge. In the Refine Edge dialog box, move the Feather slider to **1.2** px, and then click OK.

12 Choose Image > Adjustments > Hue/Saturation. Select Colorize, and then move the sliders as follows, and click OK:

• Hue: **230**

• Saturation: **56**

• Lightness: **11**

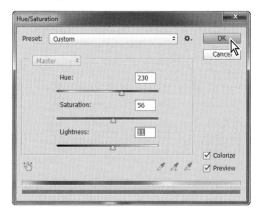 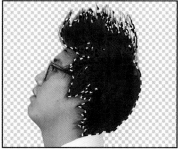

13 Choose Image > Adjustments > Levels. In the Levels dialog box, move the sliders so that the Black slider is positioned where the blacks peak, the White slider where the whites peak, and the Midtones in between. Then click OK.
We used the values 58, 1.65, 255, but your values may vary.

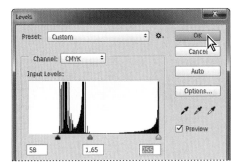 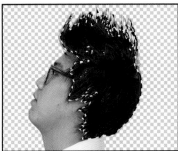

14 In the Layers panel, make the Shadow and Magazine Background layers visible.

15 Choose Select > Deselect.

16 Choose File > Save.

Your magazine cover is ready to go!

Review questions

1 What is the benefit of using a quick mask?

2 What happens to a quick mask when you deselect it?

3 When you save a selection as a mask, where is the mask stored?

4 How can you edit a mask in a channel once you've saved it?

5 How do channels differ from layers?

Review answers

1 Quick masks are helpful for creating quick, one-time selections. In addition, using a quick mask is an easy way to edit a selection using the painting tools.

2 The quick mask disappears when you deselect it.

3 Masks are saved in channels, which can be thought of as storage areas for color and selection information in an image.

4 You can paint on a mask in a channel using black, white, and shades of gray.

5 Channels are used as storage areas for saved selections. Unless you explicitly display a channel, it does not appear in the image or print. Layers can be used to isolate various parts of an image so that they can be edited as discrete objects with the painting or editing tools or other effects.

7 TYPOGRAPHIC DESIGN

Lesson overview

In this lesson, you'll learn how to do the following:

- Use guides to position text in a composition.

- Make a clipping mask from type.

- Merge type with other layers.

- Preview fonts.

- Format text.

- Distribute text along a path.

- Control type and positioning using advanced features.

 This lesson will take less than an hour to complete. Download the Lesson07 project files from the Lesson & Update Files tab on your Account page at www.peachpit.com, if you haven't already done so. As you work on this lesson, you'll preserve the start files. If you need to restore the start files, download them from your Account page.

DIGITAL

VOL 9

THE TREND ISSUE

WHAT'S NEW WITH MUSIC?
WHAT'S NEW WITH GAMES?
WHAT'S NEW WITH PHONES?

What's Hot!
3D MOVIES AT HOME
MUST-HAVE APPS

What's Not!
HARD DRIVES
WIRES, 3G

Coming this Year:
NEXT GEN VIDEO TOOLS
WEARABLE DEVICES

PROJECT: MAGAZINE COVER LAYOUT

Photography © Image Source, www.imagesource.com

Photoshop provides powerful, flexible text tools so
you can add type to your images with great control
and creativity.

About type

Type in Photoshop consists of mathematically defined shapes that describe the letters, numbers, and symbols of a typeface. Many typefaces are available in more than one format, the most common formats being Type 1 or PostScript fonts, TrueType, and OpenType (see "OpenType in Photoshop" later in this lesson).

When you add type to an image in Photoshop, the characters are composed of pixels and have the same resolution as the image file—zooming in on characters shows jagged edges. However, Photoshop preserves the vector-based type outlines and uses them when you scale or resize type, save a PDF or EPS file, or print the image to a PostScript printer. As a result, you can produce type with crisp, resolution-independent edges, apply effects and styles to type, and transform its shape and size.

Getting started

In this lesson, you'll work on the layout for the cover of a technology magazine. You'll start with the artwork you created in Lesson 6: The cover has a model, his shadow, and the orange background. You'll add and stylize type for the cover, including warping the text.

You'll start the lesson by viewing an image of the final composition.

1   Start Photoshop, and then immediately hold down Ctrl+Alt+Shift (Windows) or Command+Option+Shift (Mac OS) to restore the default preferences. (See "Restoring default preferences" on page 4.)

2   When prompted, click Yes to delete the Adobe Photoshop Settings file.

3   Choose File > Browse In Bridge to open Adobe Bridge.

● **Note:** If Bridge is not installed, you'll be prompted to download and install it. See page 3 for more information.

4   In the Favorites panel on the left side of Bridge, click the Lessons folder, and then double-click the Lesson07 folder in the Content panel.

5   Select the 07End.psd file. Increase the thumbnail size to see the image clearly by dragging the thumbnail slider to the right.

You'll apply the type treatment in Photoshop to finish the magazine cover. All of the type controls you need are available in Photoshop, so you don't have to switch to another application to complete the project.

● **Note:** Though this lesson starts where Lesson 6 left off, use the 07Start.psd file. We've included a path and a sticky note in the start file that won't be in the 06Working.psd file you saved.

6   Double-click the 07Start.psd file to open it in Photoshop.

7   Choose File > Save As, rename the file **07Working.psd**, and click Save.

8   Click OK in the Photoshop Format Options dialog box.

9 Choose Typography from the Workspace Switcher in the options bar.

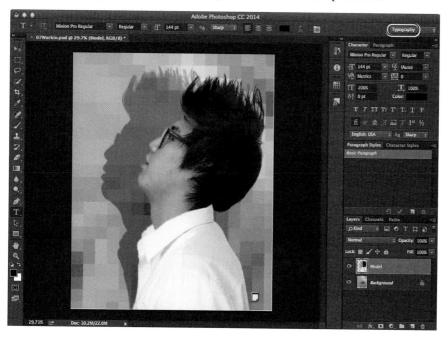

The Typography workspace displays the Character and Paragraph panels that you'll use in this lesson, along with the Paragraph Styles, Character Styles, Layers, Channels, and Paths panels.

Creating a clipping mask from type

A *clipping mask* is an object or a group of objects whose shape masks other artwork so that only areas that lie within the clipping mask are visible. In effect, you are clipping the artwork to conform to the shape of the object (or mask). In Photoshop, you can create a clipping mask from shapes or letters. In this exercise, you'll use letters as a clipping mask to allow an image in another layer to show through the letters.

Adding guides to position type

The 07Working.psd file includes a background layer, which will be the foundation for your typography. You'll start by zooming in on the work area and using ruler guides to help position the type.

1 Choose View > Fit On Screen to see the whole cover clearly.

2 Choose View > Rulers to display rulers along the left and top borders of the image window.

3 Drag a vertical guide from the left ruler to the center of the cover (4.25").

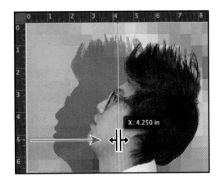

Adding point type

Now you're ready to add type to the composition. You can create horizontal or vertical type anywhere in an image. You can enter *point type* (a single letter, word, or line) or *paragraph type*. You will do both in this lesson. First, you'll create point type.

1 In the Layers panel, select the Background layer.

2 Select the Horizontal Type tool (T), and, in the options bar, do the following:

   • Choose a serif typeface, such as Minion Pro Regular, from the Font Family pop-up menu.

   • Type **144 pt** for the Size, and press Enter or Return.

   • Click the Center Text button.

3 In the Character panel, change the Tracking value to **100**.

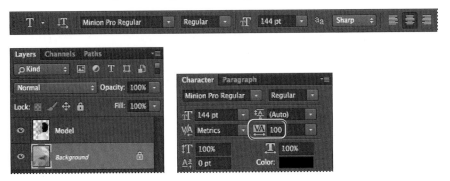

The Tracking value specifies the overall space between letters, which affects the density in a line of text.

4 Click on the center guide you added to set an insertion point, and type **DIGITAL** in all capital letters. Then click the Commit Any Current Edits button (✔) in the options bar.

Note: After you type, you must commit your editing in the layer by clicking the Commit Any Current Edits button or switching to another tool or layer. You cannot commit to current edits by pressing Enter or Return; doing so merely creates a new line of type.

The word "DIGITAL" is added to the cover, and it appears in the Layers panel as a new type layer, DIGITAL. You can edit and manage the type layer as you would any other layer. You can add or change the text, change the orientation of the type, apply anti-aliasing, apply layer styles and transformations, and create masks. You can move, restack, and copy a type layer, or edit its layer options, just as you would for any other layer.

The text is big, but not modern enough for this magazine's style. You'll apply a different font.

5 Select the Horizontal Type tool (T) and select the "Digital" text.

6 Open the Font Family pop-up menu in the options bar. Move the cursor over the fonts, either with the mouse or using arrow keys.

When the cursor is over a font name, Photoshop applies that font to the selected text so you can preview the font in context.

7 Select Myriad Pro Semibold, and then click the Commit Any Current Edits button (✔) in the options bar.

That's much more appropriate.

8 Select the Move tool, and drag the "DIGITAL" text to move it to the top of the cover, if it's not there already.

9 Choose File > Save to save your work so far.

Making a clipping mask and applying a shadow

You added the letters in black, the default text color. However, you want the letters to appear to be filled with an image of a circuit board, so you'll use the letters to make a clipping mask that will allow another image layer to show through.

1　Choose File > Open, and open the circuit_board.tif file, which is in the Lesson07 folder.

2　Choose Window > Arrange > 2-Up Vertical. The circuit_board.tif and 07Working.psd files appear onscreen together. Click the circuit_board.tif file to ensure that it's the active window.

3　With the Move tool selected, hold down the Shift key as you drag the Background layer from the Layers panel in the circuit_board.tif file onto the center of the 07Working.psd file.

Pressing Shift as you drag centers the circuit_board.tif image in the composition.

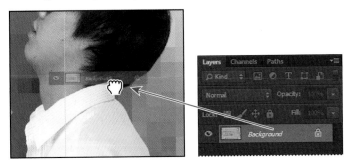

A new layer—Layer 1— appears in the Layers panel for the 07Working.psd file. This new layer contains the image of the circuit board, which will show through the type. But before you make the clipping mask, you'll resize the circuit board image, as it's currently too large for the composition.

4　Close the circuit_board.tif file without saving any changes to it.

5　In the 07Working.psd file, select Layer 1, and then choose Edit > Transform > Scale.

6　Grab a corner handle on the bounding box for the circuit board. Press Alt+Shift (Windows) or Option+Shift (Mac OS) as you resize it to approximately the same width as the area of text.

Pressing Shift retains the proportions; Alt or Option keeps it centered.

7 Reposition the circuit board so that the image covers the text, and press Enter or Return to confirm the transformation.

  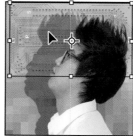

8 Double-click the Layer 1 name, and change it to **Circuit Board**. Then press Enter or Return, or click away from the name in the Layers panel, to apply the change.

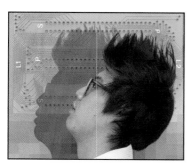 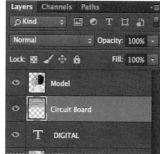

9 Select the Circuit Board layer, if it isn't already selected, and choose Create Clipping Mask from the Layers panel menu (▾☰).

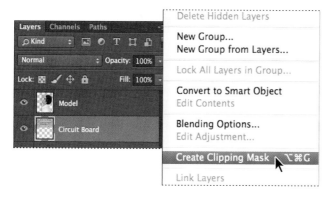

▶ **Tip:** You can also make a clipping mask by holding down the Alt (Windows) or Option (Mac OS) key and clicking between the Circuit Board and DIGITAL type layers.

The circuit board now shows through the DIGITAL letters. A small arrow in the Circuit Board layer and the underlined type layer name indicate the clipping mask is applied. Next, you'll add an inner shadow to give the letters depth.

10 Select the DIGITAL layer to make it active. Then, click the Add A Layer Style button (*fx*) at the bottom of the Layers panel, and choose Inner Shadow from the pop-up menu.

11 In the Layer Style dialog box, change the Blend Mode to Multiply, Opacity to **48**%, Distance to **18**, Choke to **0**, and Size to **16**. Then click OK.

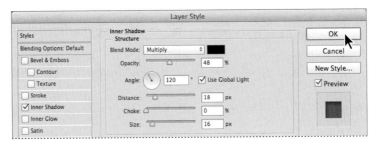

12 Choose File > Save to save your work so far.

Paragraph and Character Styles

If you frequently work with type in Photoshop, or if you need to consistently format a significant amount of type in an image, paragraph and character styles can help you work more efficiently. A paragraph style is a collection of type attributes that you can apply to an entire paragraph with a single click. A character style is a collection of attributes that you can apply to individual characters.

The concept of type styles in Photoshop is similar to that in page layout applications such as Adobe InDesign and word-processing applications such as Microsoft Word. However, styles behave a little differently in Photoshop. For the best results working with styles in Photoshop, keep the following in mind:

- By default, all text you create in Photoshop has the Basic Paragraph style applied. The Basic Paragraph style is defined by your text defaults, but you can change its attributes.

- Deselect all layers before you create a new style.

- If the selected text has been changed from the current paragraph style (usually the Basic Paragraph style), those changes (considered overrides) persist even when you apply a new style. To ensure that all the attributes of a paragraph style are applied to text, apply the style and then click the Clear Overrides button [icon] in the Paragraph Styles panel.

- You can use the same paragraph and character styles across multiple files. To save the current styles as defaults for all new documents, choose Type > Save Default Type Styles. If you want to use your default styles in an existing document, choose Type > Load Default Type Styles.

Creating type on a path

In Photoshop, you can create type that follows along a path you create with a pen or shape tool. The direction the type flows depends on the order in which anchor points were added to the path. When you use the Horizontal Type tool to add text to a path, the letters are perpendicular to the baseline of the path. If you change the location or shape of the path, the type moves with it.

You'll create type on a path to make it look as if questions are coming from the model's mouth. We've already created the path for you.

1   In the Layers panel, select the Background layer.

2   Select the Paths tab in the Layers panel group.

3   In the Paths panel, select the path named Speech Path.

The path appears to be coming out of the model's mouth.

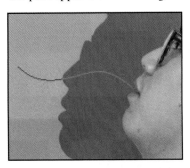

4   Select the Horizontal Type tool.

5   In the options bar, click the Right Align Text button.

Julieanne Kost is an official Adobe Photoshop evangelist.

Tool tips from the Photoshop evangelist

Type tool tricks

- Shift-click in the image window with the Horizontal Type tool to create a new type layer—in case you're close to another block of type and Photoshop tries to autoselect the existing type layer.

- Double-click the thumbnail icon on any type layer in the Layers panel to select all of the type on that layer.

- With any text selected, right-click (Windows) or Control-click (Mac OS) on the text to access the context menu. Choose Check Spelling to run a spell check.

6 In the Character panel, select the following settings:

- Font Family: Myriad Pro Regular
- Font Style: Regular
- Font Size (T): **16** pt
- Tracking (VA): **-10**
- Color: White
- All Caps (TT)

7 Move the Type tool over the path. When a small slanted line appears across the I-bar, click the end of the path closest to the model's mouth, and type **What's new with games?**

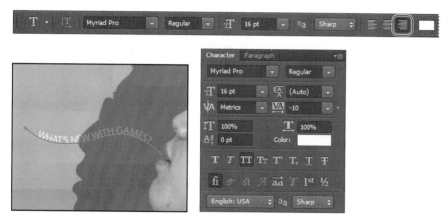

8 Select the word "GAMES," and change its font style to Bold. Click the Commit Any Current Edits button (✔) in the options bar.

9   Click the Layers tab to bring it forward. In the Layers panel, select the What's new with games? layer, and then choose Duplicate Layer from the Layers panel menu. Name the new layer **What's new with music?**, and click OK.

Photoshop creates a duplicate text layer, hiding the text you typed earlier.

10 With the Type tool, select "GAMES," and replace it with **music**. Click the Commit Any Current Edits button in the options bar.

11 Choose Edit > Free Transform Path. Rotate the left side of the path approximately 30 degrees, and then shift the path up above the first path, and a little to the right, as in the image below. Click the Commit Transform button in the options bar.

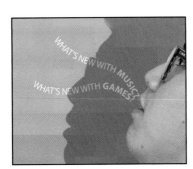

12 Repeat steps 9–11, replacing the word "GAMES" with **phones**. Rotate the left side of the path approximately -30 degrees, and move it below the original path.

13 Choose File > Save to save your work so far.

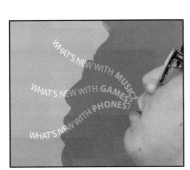

Warping point type

The text on a path is more interesting than straight lines would be, but you'll warp the text to make it more playful. *Warping* lets you distort type to conform to a variety of shapes, such as an arc or a wave. The warp style you select is an attribute of the type layer—you can change a layer's warp style at any time to change the overall shape of the warp. Warping options give you precise control over the orientation and perspective of the warp effect.

1 Scroll or use the Hand tool (🖐) to move the visible area of the image window so that the sentences to the left of the model are in the center of the screen.

2 Right-click (Windows) or Control-click (Mac OS) the What's new with games? layer in the Layers panel, and choose Warp Text from the context menu.

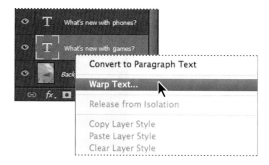

3 In the Warp Text dialog box, choose Wave from the Style menu, and select the Horizontal option. Specify the following values: Bend, +**33**%; Horizontal Distortion, -**23**%; and Vertical Distortion, +**5**%. Then click OK.

The Bend slider specifies how much warp is applied. Horizontal Distortion and Vertical Distortion determine the perspective of the warp.

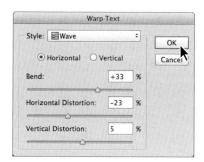 

The words "What's new with games?" appear to float like a wave on the cover.

4 Repeat steps 2 and 3 to warp the other two text layers you typed on a path.

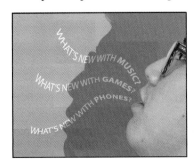 

5 Save your work.

Designing paragraphs of type

All of the text you've written on this cover so far has been a few discrete words or lines—point type. However, many designs call for full paragraphs of text. You can design complete paragraphs of type in Photoshop; you can even apply paragraph styles. You don't have to switch to a dedicated page layout program for sophisticated paragraph type controls.

Using guides for positioning

You will add paragraphs to the cover in Photoshop. First, you'll add some guides to the work area to help you position the paragraph.

1 Drag a guide from the left vertical ruler, placing it approximately ¼" from the right side of the cover.

2 Drag a guide down from the top horizontal ruler, placing it approximately 2" from the top of the cover.

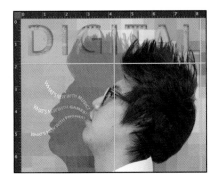

Adding paragraph type from a sticky note

You're ready to add the text. In a real design environment, the text might be provided to you in a word-processing document or the body of an email message, which you could copy and paste into Photoshop. Or you might have to type it in. Another easy way to add a bit of text is for the copywriter to attach it to the image file in a sticky note, as we've done for you here.

1   Select the Move tool, and then double-click the yellow sticky note in the lower right corner of the image window to open the Notes panel. Expand the Notes panel, if necessary, to see all the text.

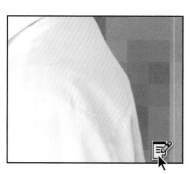 

2   In the Notes panel, select all the text. Press Ctrl+C (Windows) or Command+C (Mac OS) to copy the text to the clipboard. Close the Notes panel.

3   Select the Model layer. Then, select the Horizontal Type tool (T).

4   Press Shift as you click where the guidelines intersect, about ¼" from the right edge and 2" from the top of the cover. Continue to hold the Shift key as you start to drag a text box down and to the left. Then release the Shift key and continue dragging until the box is about 4 inches wide by 8 inches high, the top and right edges aligned with the guides you just added.

5   Press Ctrl+V (Windows) or Command+V (Mac OS) to paste the text. The new text layer is at the top of the Layers panel, so the text appears in front of the model.

The pasted text is 16 pts, and it's right-aligned, because those were the latest text settings you'd used.

▶ **Tip:** Press Shift as you start to drag a text box to ensure that Photoshop creates a new text layer, instead of selecting an existing text layer.

⬤ **Note:** If the text isn't visible, make sure the new type layer is above the Model layer in the Layers panel.

6 Select the first three lines ("The Trend Issue"), and then apply the following settings in the Character panel:

- Font Family: Myriad Pro (or another sans serif font)

- Font Style: Regular

- Font Size (🔠T): **70** pt

● **Note:** *Leading* determines the vertical space between lines.

- Leading (🔠A): **55** pt

- Tracking (🔠A): **50**

- Color: White

7 Select just the word "Trend," and change the Font Style to Bold.

▶ **Tip:** Use the Adobe Illustrator Glyphs panel to preview OpenType options: Copy your text in Photoshop and paste it into an Illustrator document. Then, choose Window > Type > Glyphs. Select the text you want to change, and choose Show > Alternates For Current Selection. Double-click a glyph to apply it, and when you've finished, copy and paste the new type into your Photoshop file.

You've formatted the title. Now you'll format the rest of the text.

8 Select the rest of the text you pasted. In the Character panel, select the following:

- Font Family: Myriad Pro

- Font Style: Regular

- Font Size: **22** pt

- Leading: **28** pt

- Tracking: **0**

- Deselect All Caps (**TT**)

The text looks good, but it's all the same. You'll make the headlines stand out more.

9 Select the "What's Hot!" text, and then change the following in the Character panel:

- Font Style: Bold

- Font Size: **28** pt

10 Repeat step 9 for the "What's Not" and "Coming this year" subheads.

11 Select "Coming this year" and all the text that follows it. Then, in the Character panel, change the text color to Black.

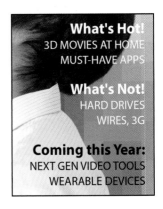

12 Finally, click the Commit Any Current Edits button in the options bar.

13 Save your changes.

OpenType in Photoshop

OpenType is a cross-platform font file format developed jointly by Adobe and Microsoft. The format uses a single font file for both Mac OS and Windows, so you can move files from one platform to another without font substitution or reflowed text. OpenType offers widely expanded character sets and layout features, such as swashes and discretionary ligatures, that aren't available in traditional PostScript and TrueType fonts. This, in turn, provides richer linguistic support and advanced typography control. Here are some highlights of OpenType.

The OpenType menu The Character panel menu includes an OpenType submenu that displays all available features for a selected OpenType font, including ligatures, alternates, and fractions. Dimmed features are unavailable for that typeface; a check mark appears next to features that have been applied.

Discretionary ligatures To add a discretionary ligature to two OpenType letters, such as to "th" in the Bickham Script Standard typeface, select them in the image, and choose OpenType > Discretionary Ligatures from the Character panel menu.

Swashes Adding swashes or alternate characters works the same way. Select the letter, such as a capital "T" in Bickham Script, and choose OpenType > Swash to change the ordinary capital into a dramatically ornate swash T.

True fractions To create true fractions, type the fractions characters—for example, 1/2. Then, select the characters, and from the Character panel menu, choose OpenType > Fractions. Photoshop applies the true fraction (½).

Adding a rounded rectangle

You're almost done with the text for the magazine cover. All that remains is to add the volume number in the upper right corner. First, you'll create a rectangle with rounded corners to serve as a background for the volume number.

1 Select the Rounded Rectangle tool (▣), hidden beneath the Rectangle tool (▭), in the Tools panel.

2 Draw a rectangle in the space above the letter "L" in the upper right corner of the cover, placing its right edge along the guide.

3 In the Properties panel, type **67** px for the width, and then make sure the stroke width is 3 pt.

4 Click the fill color swatch in the Properties panel, and select the Pastel Yellow Orange swatch in the third row.

By default, all the corners in the rectangle have the same radius, but you can adjust the radius for each corner separately. You can even return to edit the corners later if you want to. You'll change the rectangle so that only the lower left corner is rounded, changing the others to right angles.

5 Unlink the corner radius values in the Properties panel. Then change the bottom left corner to **16 px**, and set all the others to **0 px**.

6 With the Move tool, drag the rectangle to the top of the image so it hangs down like a ribbon and its right edge is next to the ruler guide.

7 Select Show Transform Controls in the options bar. Drag the bottom of the rectangle down so that it's close to the letter "L." You want the rectangle to be long enough to contain the text. Then click the Commit Transform button (✔).

Adding vertical text

You're ready to add the volume number on top of the ribbon.

1 Choose Select > Deselect Layers. Then select the Vertical Type tool (↓T), which is hidden under the Horizontal Type tool.

2 Press the Shift key, and click inside the rectangle you just created.

Pressing the Shift key as you click ensures that you create a new text box instead of selecting the title.

3 Type **VOL 9**.

The letters are too large to view. You'll need to change their size to see them.

4 Choose Select > All, and then, in the Character panel, select the following:

- Font Family: a serif typeface, such as Myriad Pro

- Font Style: a light or narrow style, such as Light Condensed

- Font size: **15** pt

- Tracking: **10**

- Color: Black

5 Click the Commit Any Current Edits button (✔) in the options bar. Your vertical text now appears as the layer named VOL 9. Use the Move tool (⊕) to center it in the ribbon, if necessary.

Now, you'll clean up a bit.

6 Click the note to select it. Then right-click (Windows) or Control-click (Mac OS) and choose Delete Note from the context menu; click Yes to confirm that you want to delete the note.

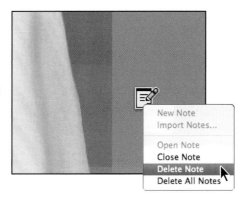

7 Hide the guides: Choose the Hand tool (✋), and then press Ctrl+; (Windows) or Command+; (Mac OS). Then zoom out to get a nice look at your work.

8 Choose File > Save to save your work.

Congratulations! You've added and stylized all of the type on the Digital magazine cover. Now that the magazine cover is ready to go, you'll flatten it and prepare it for printing.

9 Choose File > Save As, rename the file **07Working_flattened**, and click Save. Click OK if you see the Photoshop Format Options dialog box.

Keeping a layered version lets you return to the 07Working.psd file in the future to edit it.

10 Choose Layer > Flatten Image.

11 Choose File > Save, and then close the image window.

Saving as Photoshop PDF

The type you've added consists of vector-based outlines, which remain crisp and clear as you zoom in or resize them. However, if you save the file as a JPEG or TIFF image, Photoshop rasterizes the type, so you lose that flexibility. When you save a Photoshop PDF file, vector type is included.

You can preserve other Photoshop editing capabilities in a Photoshop PDF file, too. For example, you can retain layers, color information, and even notes.

To ensure you can edit the file later, select Preserve Photoshop Editing Capabilities in the Save Adobe PDF dialog box.

To preserve any notes in the file and convert them to Acrobat comments when you save to PDF, select Notes in the Save area of the Save As dialog box.

You can open a Photoshop PDF file in Acrobat or Photoshop, place it in another application, or print it. For more information about saving as Photoshop PDF, see Photoshop Help.

Review questions

1 How does Photoshop treat type?

2 How is a text layer the same as or different from other layers in Photoshop?

3 What is a clipping mask, and how do you make one from type?

Review answers

1 Type in Photoshop consists of mathematically defined shapes that describe the letters, numbers, and symbols of a typeface. When you add type to an image in Photoshop, the characters are composed of pixels and have the same resolution as the image file. However, Photoshop preserves the vector-based type outlines and uses them when you scale or resize type, save a PDF or EPS file, or print the image to a PostScript printer.

2 Type that is added to an image appears in the Layers panel as a text layer that can be edited and managed in the same way as any other kind of layer. You can add and edit the text, change the orientation of the type, and apply anti-aliasing as well as move, restack, copy, and change the options for layers.

3 A clipping mask is an object or group whose shape masks other artwork so that only areas that lie within the shape are visible. To convert the letters on any text layer to a clipping mask, make sure the layer you want to reveal is directly above the text layer, select the layer you want to show through the letters, and choose Create Clipping Mask from the Layers panel menu.

8 VECTOR DRAWING TECHNIQUES

Lesson overview

In this lesson, you'll learn how to do the following:

- Differentiate between bitmap and vector graphics.

- Draw straight and curved paths using the Pen tool.

- Save paths.

- Draw and edit shape layers.

- Draw custom shapes.

- Import and edit a Smart Object from Adobe Illustrator.

- Use Smart Guides.

 This lesson will take about 90 minutes to complete. Download the Lesson08 project files from the Lesson & Update Files tab on your Account page at www.peachpit.com, if you haven't already done so. As you work on this lesson, you'll preserve the start files. If you need to restore the start files, download them from your Account page.

PROJECT: COFFEE SHOP SIGN

Unlike bitmap images, vector images retain their crisp edges when you enlarge them to any size. You can draw vector shapes and paths in your Photoshop images and add vector masks to control what is shown in an image.

About bitmap images and vector graphics

Before working with vector shapes and vector paths, it's important to understand the basic differences between the two main categories of computer graphics: *bitmap images* and *vector graphics*. You can use Photoshop to work with either type of graphic; in fact, you can combine both bitmap and vector data in an individual Photoshop image file.

Bitmap images, technically called *raster images*, are based on a grid of dots known as *pixels*. Each pixel is assigned a specific location and color value. In working with bitmap images, you edit groups of pixels rather than objects or shapes. Because bitmap graphics can represent subtle gradations of shade and color, they are appropriate for continuous-tone images such as photographs or artwork created in painting programs. A disadvantage of bitmap graphics is that they contain a fixed number of pixels. As a result, they can lose detail and appear jagged when scaled up on screen or printed at a lower resolution than they were created for.

Vector graphics are made up of lines and curves defined by mathematical objects called *vectors*. These graphics retain their crispness whether they are moved, resized, or have their color changed. Vector graphics are appropriate for illustrations, type, and graphics such as logos that may be scaled to different sizes.

 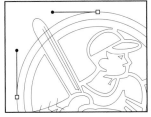

Logo drawn as vector art

Logo rasterized as bitmap art

About paths and the Pen tool

In Photoshop, the outline of a vector shape is a *path*. A path is a curved or straight line segment you draw using the Pen tool, Freeform Pen tool, or a shape tool. The Pen tool draws paths with the greatest precision; shape tools draw rectangles, ellipses, and other shape paths; the Freeform Pen tool draws paths as if you were drawing with a pencil on paper.

Julieanne Kost is an official Adobe Photoshop evangelist.

Tool tips from the Photoshop evangelist

Accessing tools quickly

Each tool in the Tools panel has a single-letter keyboard shortcut. Type the letter, get the tool. Press Shift with the shortcut key to cycle through any nested tools in a group. For example, press P to select the Pen tool, and press Shift+P to toggle between the Pen and Freeform Pen tools.

Paths can be open or closed. An open path (such as a wavy line) has two distinct endpoints. A closed path (such as a circle) is continuous. The type of path you draw affects how it can be selected and adjusted.

Paths that have no fill or stroke do not print when you print your artwork. This is because paths are vector objects that contain no pixels, unlike the bitmap shapes drawn by the Pencil tool and other painting tools.

Getting started

In this lesson, you'll draw a path around a coffee cup in an image, and create another path inside the handle. You'll subtract one selection from the other so that a lightning bolt shape (provided in the Shapes panel) knocks out of the cup shape. Finally, you'll import an Illustrator title treatment as a Smart Object and apply a color and emboss effect.

Before you begin, you'll view the image you'll be creating—a sign for a fictitious coffee shop.

1 Start Photoshop, and then immediately hold down Ctrl+Alt+Shift (Windows) or Command+Option+Shift (Mac OS) to restore the default preferences. (See "Restoring default preferences" on page 4.)

2 When prompted, click Yes to delete the Adobe Photoshop Settings file.

3 Choose File > Browse In Bridge.

4 In the Favorites panel, click the Lessons folder, and then double-click the Lesson08 folder in the Content panel.

5 Select the 08End.psd file, and press the spacebar to see it in full-screen view.

To create this sign, you'll trace the coffee cup in an image, and use that tracing to make a vector logo. You'll resize that logo and combine it with an Illustrator typographic logo imported as a Smart Object. First, you'll practice making paths and selections using the Pen tool.

6 When you've finished looking at the 08End.psd file, press the spacebar again. Then double-click the 08Practice_Start.psd file to open it in Photoshop.

7 Choose File > Save As, rename the file **08Practice_Working.psd**, and click Save. Click OK in the Photoshop Format Options dialog box.

Drawing with the Pen tool

You'll use the Pen tool to select the coffee cup. The cup has long, smooth, curved edges that would be difficult to select using other methods.

The Pen tool works a little differently from most Photoshop tools. We've created a practice file which you can use to get familiar with the Pen tool before making your Kailua Koffee sign.

Paths include anchor points (smooth and corner) and segments (straight and curved). You'll get a feel for the Pen tool by drawing a straight path, a simple curve, and then an S-curve before you practice tracing the coffee cup.

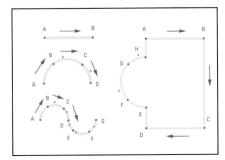

Creating paths with the Pen tool

You can use the Pen tool to create paths that are straight or curved, open or closed. If you're unfamiliar with the Pen tool, it can be confusing to use at first. Understanding the elements of a path and how to create those elements with the Pen tool makes paths much easier to draw.

To create a straight path, click the mouse button. The first time you click, you set the starting point. Each time that you click thereafter, a straight line is drawn between the previous point and the current point. To draw complex straight-segment paths with the Pen tool, simply continue to add points.

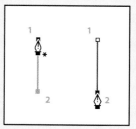

Creating a straight line

To create a curved path, click to place an anchor point, drag to create a direction line for that point, and then click to place the next anchor point. Each direction line ends in two direction points; the positions of direction lines and points determine the size and shape of the curved segment. Moving the direction lines and points reshapes the curves in a path.

Smooth curves are connected by anchor points called *smooth points*. Sharply curved paths are connected by *corner points*. When you move a direction line on a smooth point, the curved segments on both sides of the point adjust simultaneously, but when you move a direction line on a corner point, only the curve on the same side of the point as the direction line is adjusted.

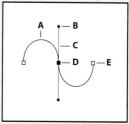

A. Curved line segment
B. Direction point
C. Direction line
D. Selected anchor point
E. Unselected anchor point

Path segments and anchor points can be moved after they're drawn, either individually or as a group. When a path contains more than one segment, you can drag individual anchor points to adjust individual segments of the path, or select all of the anchor points in a path to edit the entire path. Use the Direct Selection tool to select and adjust an anchor point, a path segment, or an entire path.

Creating a closed path differs from creating an open path in the way that you end it. To end an open path, press Enter or Return. To create a closed path, position the Pen tool pointer over the starting point, and click. Closing a path automatically ends the path. After the path closes, the Pen tool pointer appears with a small x, indicating that your next click will start a new path.

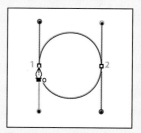

Creating a closed path

As you draw paths, a temporary storage area named Work Path appears in the Paths panel. It's a good idea to save work paths, and it's essential if you use multiple discrete paths in the same image file. If you deselect an existing Work Path in the Paths panel and then start drawing again, a new work path will replace the original one, which will be lost. To save a work path, double-click it in the Paths panel, type a name in the Save Path dialog box, and click OK to rename and save the path. The path remains selected in the Paths panel.

First, you'll configure the Pen tool options and the work area.

1   In the Tools panel, select the Pen tool (✐).

2   In the options bar, select or verify the following settings:

- Choose Shape from the Tool Mode pop-up menu.

- In the Pen Options menu, make sure that Rubber Band is not selected.

- Make sure that Auto Add/Delete is selected.

- Choose No Color from the Fill pop-up menu.

- Choose a green color from the Stroke pop-up menu.

- Enter **4** pt for the stroke width.

- In the Stroke Options window, choose Center (the second option) from the Align menu.

A. *Tool Mode menu* **B.** *Pen Options menu*

Drawing a straight line

You'll start by drawing a straight line. Anchor points mark the ends of path segments; the straight line you'll draw is a single path segment with two anchor points.

1   Click the Paths tab to bring that panel to the front of the Layers panel group.

The Paths panel displays thumbnail previews of the paths you draw. Currently, the panel is empty, because you haven't started drawing.

2   If necessary, zoom in so that you can easily see the lettered points and blue dots on the shape template. Make sure you can see the whole template in the image window, and be sure to reselect the Pen tool after you zoom.

3   Click point A on the first shape, and release the mouse button. You've created an anchor point.

4   Click point B. You've created a straight line with two anchor points.

5 Press Enter or Return to stop drawing.

Create an anchor point.

Click to create a straight line.

Complete the path.

The path you drew appears in the Paths panel and as a new layer in the Layers panel.

Drawing curves

On curved segments, selecting an anchor point displays two direction lines (smooth points) or one direction line (corner point). Direction lines end in direction points, and the positions of the direction lines and direction points determine the size and shape of the curved segment. You'll create curved lines, using smooth points.

1 Click A on the semicircle, and release the mouse to create the first anchor point.

2 Click point B, but don't release the mouse button. Instead, drag the cursor to the blue dot to the right of point B to create a curved path segment and a smooth anchor point. Then release the mouse button.

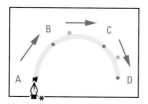
Create an anchor point.

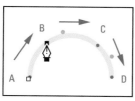
Click and hold.

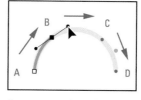
Drag to curve the path segment.

Smooth anchor points have two linked direction lines. When you move one, the curved segments on both sides of the path adjust simultaneously.

3 Click point C, and drag down to the blue dot below. Then release the mouse button. You've created a second curved path segment and another smooth point.

4 Click point D, and release the mouse to create the final anchor point. Press Enter or Return to complete the path.

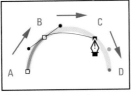 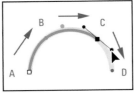 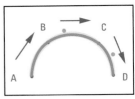

Click C to create a point.　　*Drag to curve the segment.*　　*Click D to finish the semicircle.*

When drawing a freehand path using the Pen tool, use as few points as possible to create the shape you want. The fewer points you use, the smoother the curves are—and the more efficient your file is.

Using the same techniques, you'll draw an S-shaped curve.

5 Click point A, then click point B, and drag the cursor to the first blue dot.

6 Continue with points C, D, E, and F, in each case clicking the point and then dragging to the corresponding green dot.

7 Click point G to create the final anchor point, and then press Enter or Return to complete the path.

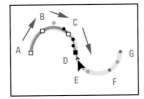 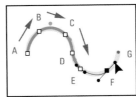 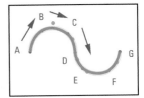

This shape is on its own layer in the Layers panel. Only one path is in the Paths panel because the work path for the second shape overwrote the work path for the first one.

Drawing a more complex shape

Now that you've got the idea, you'll have a chance to draw a more complex object: the outline of a coffee cup.

1 Click point A on the shape on the right side to set the first anchor point.

2 Press the Shift key as you click point B. Pressing the Shift key constrains the line so that it is perfectly straight.

3 Press the Shift key as you click points C, D, and E to create straight path segments.

4 Click point F, and drag to the blue dot to create a curve. Then release the mouse button.

5 Click point G, and drag to the blue dot to create another curve. Then release the mouse button.

6 Click point H. Then press Alt (Windows) or Option (Mac OS) as you click point H again to create a corner point.

When you move a direction line on a corner point, only the curve on the same side of the point as the direction line is adjusted, so you can create a sharp transition between two segments.

7 Click point A to draw the final path segment and close the path. Closing a path automatically ends the drawing; you don't need to press Enter or Return.

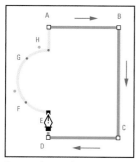
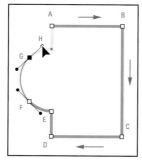
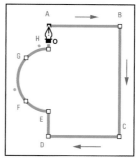

Start with straight segments.   *Drag to create a curve.*   *Close the path.*

Tracing a shape from a photo

Now you're ready to draw a path around the coffee cup in the image. You'll use the techniques you've practiced to draw a path around the outside of the cup and another one inside the handle.

1 Open the 08Start.psd file in Photoshop.

The image includes three layers: the background layer and two template layers to guide you as you draw shapes.

2 Choose File > Save As, rename the file **08Working.psd**, and click Save. Click OK in the Photoshop Format Options dialog box.

▶ Tip: If you'd like to try tracing the cup without using the dots to guide you, hide the Outside Cup layer in the Layers panel.

3   With the Pen tool selected, choose Subtract Front Shape from the Path Operations pop-up menu in the options bar.

Options in the Path Operations menu determine how multiple shapes interact with each other in a path. After you draw the cup outline, you'll subtract the inside of the handle from it.

4   Click point A. Photoshop creates a new layer for the shape.

5   Click point B, and drag the cursor to the red dot on the right to create the initial curve.

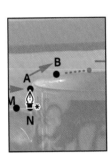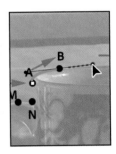

6   Click point C, and drag to the red dot to its right.

7   Continue tracing the cup, clicking each point, and dragging the cursor to corresponding red dots when you need to create a curve.

8   Close the shape by clicking point A again.

9   Evaluate your path. If you want to adjust any segments, use the Direct Selection tool to select a point, and then move its direction lines to edit the segment.

10 Save your work so far.

Adding a second shape to a path

You've drawn a path that outlines the exterior of the cup, but you want the inside of the handle to be transparent. You'll draw a shape to isolate the inside of the cup handle.

1 Hide the Outside Cup layer, and make the Inside Handle layer visible.

2 Make sure the Pen tool is selected.

3 Click point A to begin drawing. Then click point B, drag to the next red dot, and release the mouse button.

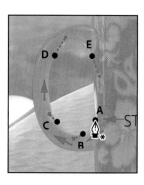 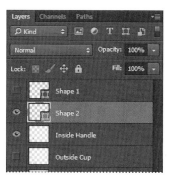

4 Continue drawing, clicking and dragging as indicated at points C and D.

5 Click point E, and drag slightly down to the red dot and release. Then, press Alt (Windows) or Option (Mac OS) as you click point E to convert the point to a corner point.

Converting point E to a corner point enables you to draw a straight path segment between it and point A. If point E remained a smooth point, the path between points E and A would be slightly curved.

6 Click point A to close the shape and stop drawing.

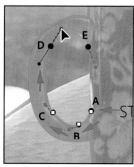 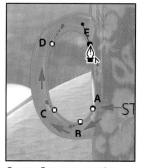 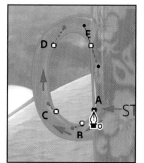

Create the curved path.   *Convert E to a corner point.*   *Create a final straight segment.*

Now you'll save the path to use later.

7 In the Paths panel, double-click Shape 1 Shape Path, type **Cup Outline** in the Save Path dialog box, and click OK to save it.

8 In the Layers panel, delete the Outside Cup and Inside Handle layers because you don't need them anymore.

9 Choose File > Save to save your work.

Working with defined custom shapes

Photoshop includes several predefined custom shapes in the Custom Shape Picker, but you can also create your own. You'll create a custom shape from the cup outline path. Then you'll use that shape and another defined shape to create a logo.

Converting a path to a shape

You'll define the cup outline path as a custom shape that you can use for the logo. The shape will be available in the Custom Shapes Picker.

1 Select the Cup Outline path in the Paths panel.

2 Choose Edit > Define Custom Shape.

3 Name the shape **Coffee Cup**, and click OK.

4 Select the Custom Shape tool ( ), hidden beneath the Rectangle tool ( ) in the Tools panel.

5 Open the Custom Shape Picker in the options menu, and scroll to the bottom of the picker. The shape you added should be the last one displayed.

6 Select the Coffee Cup shape in the Custom Shape Picker. Then press the Shift key as you drag a cup shape in the upper left corner of the image. Make the cup shape about 2 inches tall.

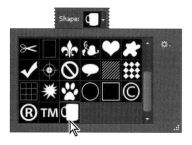 

Pressing the Shift key keeps the shape proportional as you drag.

7 Double-click the Shape 2 layer in the Layers panel, and name it **Coffee Cup**.

Changing the fill color of a shape layer

You've created a custom shape from your path, and you've used the Custom Shape tool to draw the shape on the image. But it's just an outline. You'll add a fill.

1 Make sure the Coffee Cup layer is selected in the Layers panel.

2 Select the Pen tool (✐) in the Tools panel.

3 In the options bar, select black for the Fill color, and None for the stroke.

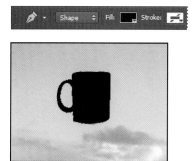

The coffee cup shape is now solid black.

4 Select the Move tool to deselect the coffee cup.

Subtracting shapes from a shape layer

After you create a shape layer, you can subtract new shapes from it. You'll add some interest to the coffee cup shape by subtracting a lightning bolt shape from it, allowing the background to show through.

1 On the options bar, choose Subtract Front Shape from the Path Operations menu. The pointer now appears as cross-hairs with a small minus sign (+).

2 In the Paths panel, select the Coffee Cup shape path.

3 In the Tools panel, select the Custom Shapes tool.

4 Select the lightning bolt from the Custom Shape Picker (it's in the second row). Then press the Shift key as you drag diagonally within the cup silhouette. Start at the upper left corner and drag down to the bottom right.

Working with Photoshop files in Illustrator

In this lesson, you're importing vector artwork that was created in Illustrator to use as the logo in your sign. You can also open, place, or paste Photoshop files in Illustrator.

While you can create and edit vector graphics in Photoshop, its primary purpose is to edit bitmap images. Likewise, you can work with bitmaps in Illustrator, but its strength is to create and edit vector artwork. Depending on the nature of your project, you may want to use both applications to take advantage of features that are available in one but not the other.

Illustrator supports most Photoshop data, including layer comps, layers, editable text, and paths. This means that you can transfer files between Photoshop and Illustrator without losing the ability to edit the artwork. In cases where Illustrator must convert the Photoshop data, it displays a warning message so you'll know what you're losing in the process.

Importing a Smart Object

Smart Objects are layers that you can edit in Photoshop nondestructively; that is, changes you make to the image remain editable and don't affect the actual image pixels, which are preserved. Regardless of how often you scale, rotate, skew, or otherwise transform a Smart Object, it retains its sharp, precise edges.

You can import vector objects from Adobe Illustrator as Smart Objects. If you edit the original object in Illustrator, the changes will be reflected in the placed Smart Object in your Photoshop image file.

When you place a Smart Object, you can link it or embed it. If you link it, Photoshop retains a link to the original file so that you can easily update it later, and it includes a bitmap image of the Smart Object in the Photoshop file. If you embed a Smart Object, Photoshop includes the entire object in the Photoshop file, but does not retain a link. However, you can convert an embedded Smart Object to a linked Smart Object if the original file is still available.

You'll work with a Smart Object now by placing a Kailua Koffee logotype that was created in Illustrator.

1 Select the Move tool (▸✛) in the Tools panel.

2 Select the Coffee Cup layer, and choose File > Place Linked. Select the Logotype.eps file in the Lesson08 folder, and click Place.

The Kailua Koffee logotype is added to the middle of the composition, inside a bounding box with adjustable handles. A new layer, Logotype, appears in the Layers panel.

3 Drag the logotype object to the upper left corner of the sign just to the right of the coffee cup logo, and then press Shift and drag a corner to make the text object proportionally larger—large enough that it fills the top portion of the image, as in the following figure. When you've finished, either press Enter or Return, or click the Commit Transform button (✔) in the options bar.

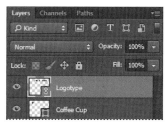

When you commit to the transformation, the layer thumbnail icon changes to reflect that the title layer is a linked Smart Object.

As with any shape layer or Smart Object, you can continue to edit its size and shape if you'd like. Simply select the layer, choose Edit > Free Transform to access the control handles, and drag to adjust them. Or, select the Move tool (⊕), and select Show Transform Controls in the options bar. Then adjust the handles.

Adding color and depth to a shape using layer styles

You created the shape with a black fill. Now you'll make it snazzier by changing the fill color and adding a Bevel & Emboss effect.

1 With the logotype layer selected, choose Color Overlay from the Add A Layer Style button (*fx*) at the bottom of the Layers panel.

2 In the Layer Style dialog box, choose a dark red or burgundy color.

Note: Be sure to click the words Bevel & Emboss. If you click only the check box, Photoshop applies the layer style with its default settings but you won't see the options.

3 Click Bevel & Emboss on the left side of the Layer Style dialog box to add another layer style. Accept the defaults for the Bevel & Emboss layer style, and click OK.

The Color Overlay and Bevel & Emboss layer styles affect the Logotype layer. You'll copy them to the Coffee Cup layer.

4   Press Alt (Windows) or Option (Mac OS) as you drag the layer effects indicator (fx) from the Logotype layer onto the Coffee Cup layer.

5   Clean up the Layers panel: Hide all but the Logotype, Coffee Cup, and Background layers. Then choose Delete Hidden Layers from the Layers panel menu, and click Yes when asked to confirm the deletion.

6   Clean up the Paths panel by deleting the cup outline path.

7   Choose File > Save to save your work. The coffee shop sign is complete.

Extra credit

Smart Guides

Let's take this design to the next level. You can use the coffee cup logo to make a repeated motif at the bottom of the sign. Smart Guides can help you position the images evenly.

1   Choose View > Show, and make sure Smart Guides are enabled. If there's a check mark next to Smart Guides, they're on. If there isn't one, select Smart Guides to enable them.

2   Select the Coffee Cup layer. Then select the Move tool, and press Alt+Shift (Windows) or Option+Shift (Mac OS) as you drag the cup logo to the lower left corner of the sign. The Alt or Option key copies the selected object; the Shift key constrains its movement. The magenta lines that appear as you drag the object are Smart Guides.

3   Choose Edit > Free Transform. Then press Shift to maintain the proportions as you scale the cup to about one-fourth its original size. Press Enter or Return to confirm the transformation.

4   With the Coffee Cup copy layer still selected, press Alt+Shift or Option+Shift and drag to the right until the measurements displayed in pink show you that the images are 3.5 inches apart. As you drag, Smart Guides give you alignment guides and display measurements to help you position objects.

5   Select the second image on the bottom, and repeat step 4. This time, when you drag the image 3.5 inches, Photoshop displays the distance between each of the sets of images.

6   Repeat step 5 so you have a total of 4 equally spaced logos.

Review questions

1 What is the difference between a bitmap image and a vector graphic?

2 How can you create a custom shape?

3 What tool can you use to move and resize paths and shapes?

4 What are Smart Objects, and what is the benefit of using them?

Review answers

1 Bitmap, or raster, images are based on a grid of pixels and are appropriate for continuous-tone images such as photographs or artwork created in painting programs. Vector graphics are made up of shapes based on mathematical expressions and are appropriate for illustrations, type, and drawings that require clear, smooth lines.

2 To create a custom shape, select a path, and then choose Edit > Define Custom Shape. Name the shape; it will appear in the Custom Shape Picker.

3 You use the Direct Selection tool to move, resize, and edit shapes. You can also modify and scale a selected shape or path by choosing Edit > Free Transform.

4 Smart Objects are vector objects that you can place and edit in Photoshop without a loss of quality. Regardless of how often you scale, rotate, skew, or otherwise transform a Smart Object, it retains sharp, precise edges. A great benefit of using Smart Objects is that you can edit the original object in the authoring application, such as Illustrator, and the changes will be reflected in the placed Smart Object in your Photoshop image file.

9 ADVANCED COMPOSITING

Lesson overview

In this lesson, you'll learn how to do the following:

- Apply and edit Smart Filters.

- Use the Liquify filter to distort an image.

- Apply color effects to selected areas of an image.

- Apply filters to create various effects.

- Use the History panel to return to a previous state.

- Upscale a low-resolution image for high-resolution printing.

 This lesson will take about an hour to complete. Download the Lesson09 project files from the Lesson & Update Files tab on your Account page at www.peachpit.com, if you haven't already done so. As you work on this lesson, you'll preserve the start files. If you need to restore the start files, download them from your Account page.

PROJECT: MONSTER MOVIE POSTER DESIGN

Monster makeup imagery courtesy of Russell Brown, with illustration by John Connell

Filters can transform ordinary images into extraordinary digital artwork. Smart Filters let you edit those transformations at any time. The wide variety of features in Photoshop let you be as creative as you want to be.

Getting started

In this lesson, you'll assemble a montage of images for a movie poster as you explore filters in Photoshop. First, look at the final project to see what you'll be creating.

1 Start Photoshop, and then immediately hold down Ctrl+Alt+Shift (Windows) or Command+Option+Shift (Mac OS) to restore the default preferences. (See "Restoring default preferences" on page 4.)

2 When prompted, click Yes to delete the Adobe Photoshop Settings file.

● **Note:** If Bridge isn't installed, you'll be prompted to install it when you choose Browse In Bridge. For more information, see page 3.

3 Choose File > Browse In Bridge.

4 In Bridge, choose Favorites from the menu on the left, and then click the Lessons folder. Double-click the Lesson09 folder.

5 View the 09_End.psd thumbnail. Move the slider on the bottom of the Bridge window if you need to zoom in to see the thumbnail more clearly.

This file is a movie poster that comprises a background, a monster image, and several smaller images. Each image has had one or more filters or effects applied to it.

The monster is composed of an image of a perfectly normal (though slightly threatening) guy with several ghoulish images applied. These monstrous additions are courtesy of Russell Brown, with illustration by John Connell.

6 In Bridge, navigate to the Lesson09/Monster_Makeup folder, and open it.

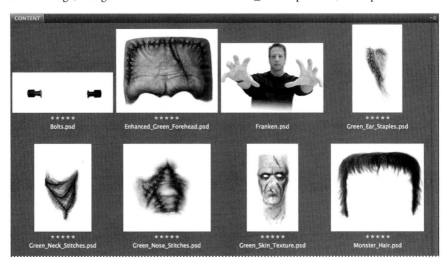

7 Shift-click to select all the files in the Monster_Makeup folder, and then choose Tools > Photoshop > Load Files Into Photoshop Layers.

Photoshop imports all the selected files as individual layers in a new Photoshop file. The visibility icon is labeled red in the layers that create the monster's look.

8 In Photoshop, choose File > Save As. Choose Photoshop for the Format, and name the new file **09Working.psd**. Save it in the Lesson09 folder. Click OK in the Photoshop Format Options dialog box.

Arranging layers

Your image file contains eight layers, imported in alphabetical order. In their current positions, they don't make a very convincing monster. You'll rearrange the layer order and resize their contents as you start to build your monster.

1 Zoom out or scroll so that you can see all the layers on the artboard.

2 In the Layers panel, drag the Monster_Hair layer to the top of the layer stack.

3 Drag the Franken layer to the bottom of the layer stack.

4 Select the Move tool (⊹), and then move the Franken layer (the image of the person) to the bottom of the page.

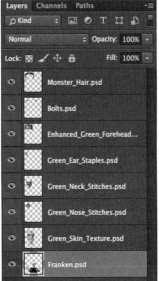

5 In the Layers panel, Shift-select every layer except the Franken layer, and choose Edit > Free Transform.

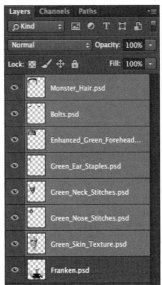

6 Press the Shift key as you drag down from a corner of the selection to resize all the selected layers to about 50% of their original size. (Watch the width and height percentages in the options bar.)

7 With the resized layers still selected, move them over the head of the Franken layer. Then press Enter or Return to commit the transformation.

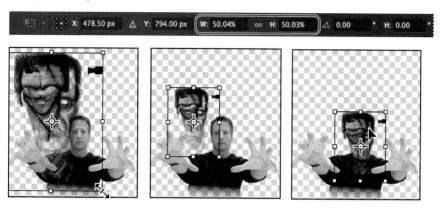

8 Zoom in to see the head area clearly.

9 Hide all layers except the Green_Skin_Texture and Franken layers.

10 Select only the Green_Skin_Texture layer, and use the Move tool to center it over the face.

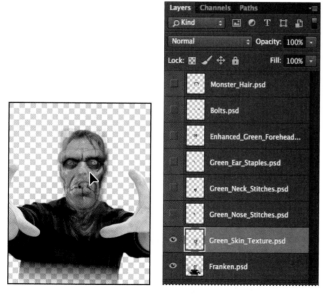

11 Choose Edit > Free Transform again to adjust the fit of the texture to the face. Use the side handles to adjust the width, the bottom and top handles to adjust the height, and arrow keys to nudge the entire layer into position. Use the eyes and mouth as a guide. When you've positioned the skin texture, press Enter or Return to commit the transformation.

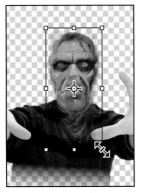  

12 Save your file.

Using Smart Filters

Unlike regular filters, which permanently change an image, Smart Filters are nondestructive: They can be adjusted, turned off and on, and deleted. However, you can apply Smart Filters only to a Smart Object.

Applying the Liquify filter

You'll use the Liquify filter to tighten the eye openings and change the shape of the monster's face. Because you want to be able to adjust the filter settings later, you'll use the Liquify filter as a Smart Filter. So you'll first need to convert the Green_Skin_Texture layer to a Smart Object.

1 Make sure the Green_Skin_Texture layer is selected in the Layers panel, and then choose Convert To Smart Object from the Layers panel menu.

2 Choose Filter > Liquify.

Photoshop displays the layer in the Liquify dialog box.

3 In the Liquify dialog box, select Advanced Mode to see additional options.

4 Select Show Backdrop, and then choose Behind from the Mode menu. Set the Opacity to **75**.

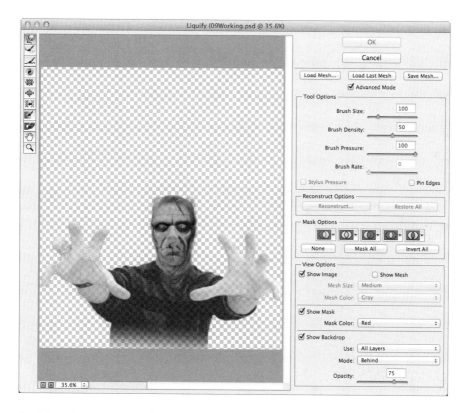

5 Select the Zoom tool (🔍) from the Tools panel on the left side of the dialog box, and zoom in to the eye area.

6 Select the Forward Warp tool (🖌)(the first tool).

The Forward Warp tool pushes pixels forward as you drag.

7 In the Tool Options area, set the Brush Size to **150** and Brush Pressure to **75**.

8 With the Forward Warp tool, pull the right eyebrow down to close the eye opening. Then pull up from under the eye.

9 Repeat step 8 on the left eyebrow and under-eye area.

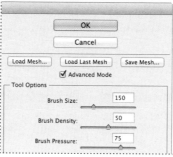

10 When you've closed the gap around the eyes, click OK.

Because you've applied the Liquify filter as a Smart Filter, you can return later to make additional changes to the face.

Positioning other layers

Now that you've got the skin texture in place, you'll move the other layers into position, working up from the lowest layers in the Layers panel.

1 Make the Green_Nose_Stitches layer visible, and select it in the Layers panel.

2 Choose Edit > Free Transform, and then position the layer over the nose, resizing it as necessary. Press Enter or Return to commit the transformation.

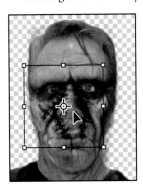 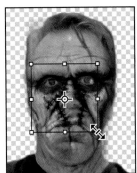 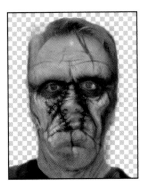

You'll repeat the process to position the rest of the layers.

3 Make the Green_Neck_Stitches layer visible, and select it. Then move it over the neck. If you need to adjust it, choose Edit > Free Transform, resize it, and press Enter or Return.

4   Make the Green_Ear_Staples layer visible, and select it. Move the staples over his right ear. Choose Edit > Free Transform, resize and reposition the staples, and then press Enter or Return.

 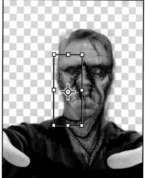

5   Make the Enhanced_Green_Forehead layer visible, and select it. Move it over the forehead; it's probably a bit large. Choose Edit > Free Transform, resize the forehead to fit the space, and press Enter or Return.

 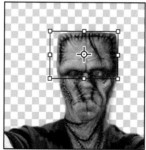

6   Make the Bolts layer visible, and select it. Drag the bolts so they're positioned on either side of the neck. Choose Edit > Free Transform, and resize them so that they fit snugly against the neck. When you have them in position, press Enter or Return to commit the transformation.

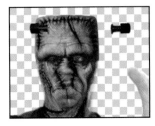 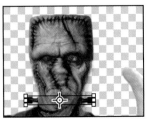

7   Lastly, make the Monster_Hair layer visible, and select it. Move it over the forehead. Choose Edit > Transform, and then resize the hair so it fits properly against the forehead. Press Enter or Return to commit the change.

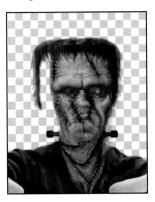 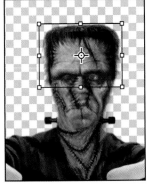

8   Save your work so far.

Editing a Smart Filter

With all the layers in position, you can further refine the eye openings and experiment with the bulges in the eyebrows. You'll return to the Liquify filter to make those adjustments.

1   In the Layers panel, double-click Liquify, listed under Smart Filters in the Green_Skin_Texture layer.

Photoshop opens the Liquify dialog box again. This time, all the layers are visible in Photoshop, so when Show Backdrop is selected, you see them all. Sometimes it's easier to make changes without a backdrop to distract you. Other times, it's useful to see your edits in context.

2   Zoom in to see the eyes more closely.

3   Select the Pucker tool (🐾) in the Tools panel, and click on the outer corner of each eye.

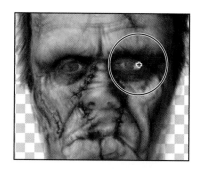

The Pucker tool moves pixels towards the center of the brush as you click or drag, for a puckering effect.

4   Select the Bloat tool (💠), and click the outer edge of an eyebrow to expand it; do the same for the other eyebrow.

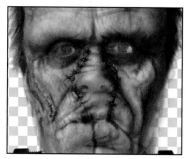

The Bloat tool moves pixels away from the center of the brush as you click or drag.

5   Experiment with the Pucker, Bloat, and other tools in the Liquify filter to customize the monster's face. Remember that you can change the brush size and other settings. You can undo individual steps, but if you want to start over, it's easiest to click Cancel, and then return to the Liquify dialog box.

6   When you're happy with the monster's face, click OK.

Painting a layer

There are many ways to paint objects and layers in Photoshop. One of the simplest is to use the Color blending mode and the Brush tool. You'll use this method to paint the exposed skin green on your monster.

1 Select the Franken layer in the Layers panel.

2 Click the Create A New Layer button at the bottom of the Layers panel.

Photoshop creates a new layer, named Layer 1.

▶ **Tip:** To learn more about blending modes, including a description of each one, see "Blending modes" in Photoshop Help.

3 With Layer 1 selected, choose Color from the Blending Mode menu at the top of the Layers panel.

The Color blending mode combines the luminance of the base color (the color already on the layer) with the hue and saturation of the color you're applying. It's a good blending mode to use when you're coloring monochrome images or tinting color images.

4 Select the Brush tool (✎). In the options bar, select a **60**-pixel brush with a hardness of **0**.

5 Press Alt or Option to temporarily switch to the Eyedropper tool. Sample a green color from the forehead. Then release the Alt or Option key to return to the Brush tool.

6 Ctrl-click or Command-click the thumbnail in the Franken layer to select its contents.

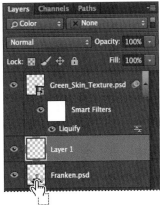

Usually, you select an entire layer in the Layers panel. When you do that, the layer is active, but there isn't actually an active selection. When you Ctrl-click or Command-click the thumbnail of the layer, Photoshop selects the contents of the layer, so you have an active selection. It's a quick way to select all of the contents of a layer—but only the contents of that specific layer.

7   Make sure Layer 1 is still selected in the Layers panel, and then use the Brush tool to paint over the hands and arms. You can paint quickly where the hands are against transparent areas because painting outside the selection has no effect. However, remember that the shirt is part of the selection, so you need to be more careful as you paint the skin where it abuts the shirt colors.

▶ **Tip:** To change the brush size as you paint, press the bracket keys on your keyboard. The Left Bracket key ([) decreases the brush size; the Right Bracket (]) increases it.

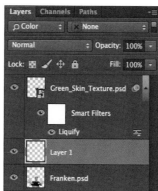

8   Paint any areas of the face or neck where the original flesh color shows through the Green_Skin_Texture layer.

9   When you're happy with the green skin, choose Select > Deselect. Save your work.

Adding a background

You've got a good-looking monster. Now it's time to put him in his spooky environment. To easily move the monster onto a background, you'll first merge the layers.

1   Make sure all the layers are visible. Then choose Merge Visible from the Layers panel menu.

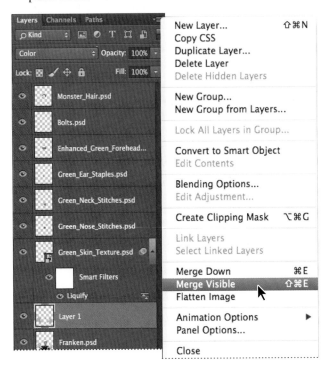

Photoshop merges all the layers into one, named Layer 1.

2   Rename Layer 1 **Monster**.

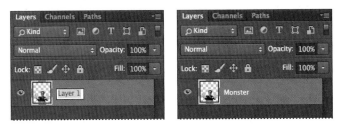

3   Choose File > Open. Navigate to and open the Backdrop.psd file in the Lesson09 folder.

4   Choose Window > Arrange > 2-Up Vertical to display both the monster and backdrop files.

5   Click the 09Working.psd file to make it active.

6   Select the Move tool (✛), and then drag the Monster layer onto the Backdrop.psd file. Position the monster so his hands are just above the movie title.

7   Close the 09Working.psd file, saving the changes when prompted.

From now on, you'll work on the movie poster file itself.

8   Choose File > Save As, and save the file with the name **Movie-Poster.psd**. Click OK in the Photoshop Format Options dialog box.

Using the History Panel to undo tasks

You've used the Undo command to move backward one step. That's as far back as Undo can take you. This is a practicality, because Photoshop files can be very large, and maintaining multiple Undo steps can tie up a lot of memory, which tends to degrade performance. If you press Ctrl+Z or Command+Z to undo, and then press the shortcut again, Photoshop restores the step you removed initially.

When you want to go back more than one step, you could use the Step Backward command to undo steps one at a time, but it's faster and easier to reverse multiple actions using the History panel.

Photoshop stores a record of the steps you perform in the History panel. Knowing this, you can try a creative approach, easily return to your starting point if you don't get the results you want, and try going a different direction.

Applying filters and effects

You'll add a tombstone to the poster, and you'll experiment with filters and effects to see what works, using the History panel to reverse course if necessary.

1   In Photoshop, choose File > Open.

2   Navigate to the Lesson09 folder, and double-click the T1.psd file to open it.

The tombstone image is plain, but you'll add texture and color to it.

3   In the Tools panel, click the Default Foreground And Background Colors button (◧) to return the foreground color to black.

You'll start by adding a little atmosphere to the tombstone.

4   Choose Filter > Render > Difference Clouds.

The original is dull.

Clouds add drama.

You'll leave the top of the tombstone in focus, but blur the rest using an iris blur. The default blur settings will work fine.

5   Choose Filter > Blur Gallery > Iris Blur.

6   In the image window, drag the Iris Blur ellipse up so that the top of the tombstone is in focus. Then click OK.

By default, it's centered.

Shift the focus higher.

You'll use adjustment layers to make the image darker and change its color.

7   Click the Brightness/Contrast icon in the Adjustments panel. Then, in the Properties panel, move the Contrast slider to **70**.

8   Click the Channel Mixer icon in the Adjustments panel.

9   In the Properties panel, choose Green from the Output Channel menu, and then change the Red value to **+37** and the Blue value to **+108**.

The tombstone takes on a green cast. You can use the Channel Mixer adjustment to create high-quality grayscale, sepia tone, or other tinted images. You can also make creative color adjustments to an image.

10 Click the Exposure icon in the Adjustments panel. In the Properties panel, move the Exposure slider to **+.90** to increase the contrast in the image.

Undoing multiple steps

The tombstone certainly looks different than it did when you started, but it doesn't quite match the tombstones that are already in the poster. You'll use the History panel to revisit the steps you've taken.

1 Choose Window > History to open the History panel. Drag the bottom of the panel down so that you can see everything in it.

The History panel records the recent actions you've performed on the image. The current state is selected.

2 Click the Blur Gallery state in the History panel.

The states below the selected state are dimmed, and the image has changed. The color is gone, as are the Brightness/Contrast settings. At this point, the Difference Clouds filter has been run and the iris blur has been applied. Everything else has been removed. There are no adjustment layers listed in the Layers panel.

3 Click the Modify Channel Mixer Layer state in the History panel.

Many of the states are restored. The color has returned, along with the brightness and contrast settings. There are two adjustment layers in the Layers panel. However, the states below the one you selected remain dimmed, and the Exposure adjustment layer is not listed in the Layers panel.

You'll return almost to the beginning to apply different effects to the tombstone.

4 Click Difference Clouds in the History panel.

Everything following that state is dimmed.

5 Choose Filter > Noise > Add Noise.

Adding noise will give the tombstone a grainier look.

6 In the Add Noise dialog box, set the Amount to **3**%, select Gaussian, and select Monochromatic. Then click OK.

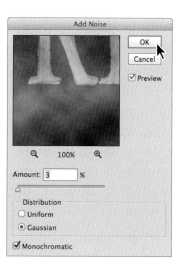 

The states that were dimmed are no longer in the History panel. Instead, the History panel has added a state for the task you just performed (Add Noise), following the state you had selected (Difference Clouds). You can click any state to return to that point in the process, but as soon as you perform a new task, Photoshop deletes all dimmed states.

Note: The Lighting Effects filter is unavailable if Use Graphics Processor is not selected in the Performance Preferences dialog box. If your video card does not support the Use Graphics Processor option, skip steps 16-20.

7 Choose Filter > Render > Lighting Effects.

8 In the options bar, choose Flashlight from the Presets menu.

9 In the Properties panel, click the Color swatch, and select a light blue color.

10 In the image window, drag the light source to the upper third of the tombstone, centered over the letters "RIP."

11 In the Properties panel, change the Ambience to **46**.

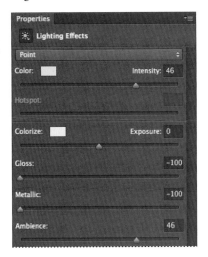

12 Click OK in the options bar to accept the Lighting Effects settings.

The tombstone is ready to join the others in your movie poster.

13 Save the file.

14 Choose Window > Arrange > Tile All Vertically.

15 Drag the tombstone you just created to the Movie-Poster.psd file. Click OK if you see a color management warning.

16 Drag the tombstone to the bottom left corner, with the top third of it showing.

17 Choose File > Save to save the Movie-Poster.psd file. Then close the T1.psd file without saving it.

You've had a chance to try out some new filters and effects, and to use the History panel to backtrack. By default, the History panel retains only the last 20 states. You can change the number of levels in the History panel by choosing Edit > Preferences > Performance (Windows) or Photoshop > Preferences > Performance (Mac OS), and entering a different value for History States.

Upscaling a low-resolution image

Low-resolution images are fine—even desirable—for web pages and social media. If you need to enlarge them, though, they may not contain enough information for high-quality printing. To scale an image up in size, Photoshop needs to resample it. That is, it needs to create new pixels where none existed, approximating their values. The Preserve Details (Enlargement) algorithm in Photoshop gives the best results when you upscale low-resolution images.

In your movie poster, you want to use a low-resolution image that was posted on a social media site. You'll need to resize it without compromising quality for your printed poster.

1   Choose File > Open, navigate to the Lesson09 folder, and open the Faces.jpg file.

2   Zoom in to 300%, so you can see the pixels.

3   Choose Image > Image Size.

4   Change the width and height measurements to Percent, and then change their values to **400**%.

The width and height are linked by default, so that images resize proportionally. If you need to change the width and height separately for a project, click the link icon to unlink the values.

5   Pan in the preview window so that you can see the glasses.

6   Make sure Resample is selected, and choose Preserve Details (Enlargement) from the Resample menu.

The image is much sharper, but the sharpening has introduced some noise.

7 Move the Reduce Noise slider to **50**% to smooth the image.

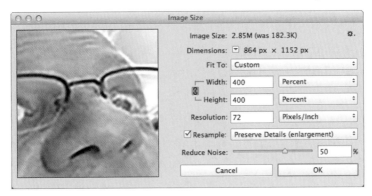

8 Click and hold on the preview window to see the original image, so you can compare it to the altered image.

9 Click OK.

The final image quality is softer, but it holds up well, considering you've quadrupled the image size and made a low-resolution image usable for print. You'll paste the image into a feathered selection on the poster.

10 Choose Select > All, and then choose Edit > Copy.

11 Select the Movie-Poster.psd tab to bring it to the front, and then select the Elliptical Marquee tool (○), hidden beneath the Rectangular Marquee tool (▭).

12 In the options bar, enter **50 px** for Feather to soften the edge of the pasted image.

13 Draw an oval in the upper right corner of the poster, above the monster's head. The oval should overlap the window and fire escape.

14 Choose Edit > Paste Special > Paste Into. Click OK if you see the Paste Profile Mismatch dialog box.

15 Select the Move tool (▸✛), and center the pasted image in the feathered area.

16 In the Layers panel, choose Luminosity from the Blending Mode menu, and move the Opacity slider to **50**%.

17 Choose File > Save. Then close the Faces.jpg file without saving it.

Review questions

1 What are the differences between using a Smart Filter and a regular filter to apply effects to an image?

2 What do the Bloat and Pucker tools in the Liquify filter do?

3 What does the History panel do?

Review answers

1 Smart Filters are nondestructive: They can be adjusted, turned off and on, and deleted at any time. In contrast, regular filters permanently change an image; once applied, they cannot be removed. A Smart Filter can be applied only to a Smart Object layer.

2 The Bloat tool moves pixels away from the center of the brush; the Pucker tool moves pixels toward the center of the brush.

3 The History panel records recent steps you've performed in Photoshop. You can return to an earlier step by selecting it in the History panel.

10 PAINTING WITH THE MIXER BRUSH

Lesson overview

In this lesson, you'll learn how to do the following:

- Customize brush settings.

- Clean the brush.

- Mix colors.

- Use an erodible tip.

- Create a custom brush preset.

- Use wet and dry brushes to blend color.

 This lesson will take about an hour to complete. Download the Lesson10 project files from the Lesson & Update Files tab on your Account page at www.peachpit.com, if you haven't already done so. As you work on this lesson, you'll preserve the start files. If you need to restore the start files, download them from your Account page.

PROJECT: DIGITAL PAINTING

The Mixer Brush tool gives you flexibility, color-mixing abilities, and brush strokes as if you were painting on a physical canvas.

About the Mixer Brush

In previous lessons, you've used brushes in Photoshop to perform various tasks. The Mixer Brush is unlike other brushes in that it lets you mix colors with each other. You can change the wetness of the brush and how it mixes the brush color with the color already on the canvas.

Photoshop brushes have realistic bristles, so you can add textures that resemble those in paintings you might create in the physical world. While this is a great feature in general, it's particularly useful when you're using the Mixer Brush. You can also use an erodible tip to achieve the effects you might get with charcoal pencils and pastels in the physical world. Combining different bristle settings and brush tips with different wetness, paint-load, and paint-mixing settings gives you opportunities to create exactly the look you want.

Getting started

In this lesson, you'll get acquainted with the Mixer Brush as well as the brush tip and bristle options available in Photoshop. Start by taking a look at the final projects you'll create.

1 Start Photoshop, and then immediately hold down Ctrl+Alt+Shift (Windows) or Command+Option+Shift (Mac OS) to restore the default preferences. (See "Restoring default preferences" on page 4.)

Note: If Bridge isn't installed, you'll be prompted to install it when you choose Browse In Bridge. For more information, see page 3.

2 When prompted, click Yes to delete the Adobe Photoshop Settings file.

3 Choose File > Browse In Bridge to open Adobe Bridge.

4 In Bridge, click Lessons in the Favorites panel. Double-click the Lesson10 folder in the Content panel.

5 Preview the Lesson10 end files.

You'll use the palette image to explore brush options and learn to mix colors. You'll then apply what you've learned to transform the landscape image into a watercolor.

Note: If you plan to do a lot of painting in Photoshop, consider using a tablet, such as a Wacom tablet, instead of a mouse. Photoshop can sense the way you hold and use the pen to change the brush width, strength, and angle on the fly.

6 Double-click 10Palette_start.psd to open the file in Photoshop.

7 Choose File > Save As, and name the file **10Palette_working.psd**. Click OK if the Photoshop Format Options dialog box appears.

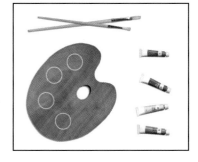

Selecting brush settings

The image includes a palette and four tubes of color, which you'll use to sample the colors you're working with. You'll change settings as you paint different colors, exploring brush tip settings and wetness options.

1 Select the Zoom tool (🔍), and zoom in to see the tubes of paint.

2 Select the Eyedropper tool (🖋), and click the red tube to sample its color.

The foreground color changes to red.

3 Select the Mixer Brush tool (✏), hidden under the Brush tool (✏).

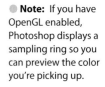

Note: If you have OpenGL enabled, Photoshop displays a sampling ring so you can preview the color you're picking up.

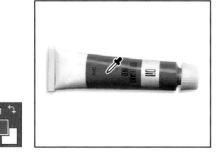

4 Choose Window > Brush to open the Brush panel. Select the first brush.

The Brush panel contains brush presets and several options for customizing brushes.

Experimenting with wetness options and brushes

The effect of the brush is determined by the Wet, Load, and Mix fields in the options bar. *Wet* controls how much paint the brush picks up from the canvas. *Load* controls how much paint the brush holds when you begin painting (as with a physical brush, it runs out of paint as you paint with it). *Mix* controls the ratio of paint from the canvas and paint from the brush.

You can change these settings separately. However, it's faster to select a standard combination from the pop-up menu.

1   In the options bar, choose Dry from the pop-up menu of blending brush combinations.

When you select Dry, Wet is set to 0%, Load to 50%, and Mix is not applicable. With the Dry preset, you paint opaque color; you cannot mix colors on a dry canvas.

2   Paint in the area above the red tube. Solid red appears. As you continue painting without releasing the mouse, the paint eventually fades and runs out.

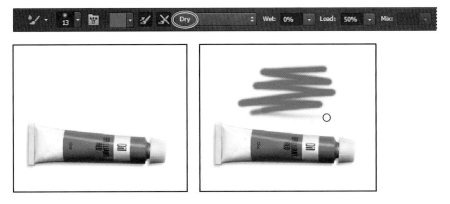

● **Note:** When you Alt-click or Option-click to load paint, the brush picks up color variations in the sample area. To sample only solid colors, select Load Solid Colors Only in the Current Brush Load menu in the options bar.

3   Sample the blue color from the blue tube of paint. You can use the Eyedropper tool or Alt-click (Windows) or Option-click (Mac OS) to sample the color. If you use the Eyedropper tool, return to the Mixer Brush tool after you sample the color.

4   In the Brush panel, select the round fan-shaped brush. Choose Wet from the pop-up menu in the options bar.

5 Paint above the blue tube. The paint mixes with the white background.

6 Choose Dry from the menu in the options bar, and then paint again above the blue tube. A much darker, more opaque blue appears, and doesn't mix with the white background.

The bristles from the fan brush you selected are much more apparent than the bristles you used originally. Changing bristle qualities makes a big difference in the texture you paint.

7 In the Brush panel, decrease the number of bristles to **40**%. Paint a little more with the blue brush to see the change in texture. The bristles are much more obvious in the stroke.

▶ **Tip:** The Live Tip Brush Preview shows you the direction of the bristles as you paint. To show or hide the Live Tip Brush Preview, click the Toggle The Live Tip Brush Preview button at the bottom of the Brush or Brush Presets panel. The Live Tip Brush Preview is available only with OpenGL enabled.

8 Sample the yellow color from the yellow paint tube. In the Brush panel, select the flat-point brush with fewer bristles (the one to the right of the fan brush). Choose Dry from the menu in the options bar, and then paint in the area over the yellow paint tube.

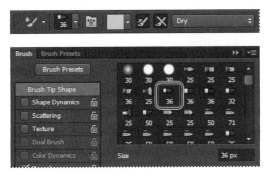

9 Choose Very Wet from the menu in the options bar, and then paint some more. Now the yellow mixes with the white background.

Using an erodible tip

When you use an erodible tip, the width of the brush changes as you paint. Erodible tips are represented in the Brush panel by pencil icons, because in the physical world, pencils and pastels have erodible tips. You'll experiment with erodible point and triangle tips.

1 Sample the green color from the green paint tube, and choose Dry, Heavy Load in the options bar.

2 Select one of the erodible tips (any tip with a pencil icon), and then choose Erodible Point from the Shape menu. Change the brush's Size to **30 px**, and Softness to **100%**.

The Softness value determines how quickly the tip erodes. A higher value results in faster erosion.

3 Draw a zig-zag line above the green paint tube.

The line gets thicker as the tip erodes.

4 Click Sharpen Tip in the Brush panel, and then draw a line next to the one you just drew.

The sharper tip draws a much narrower line.

5 Choose Erodible Triangle from the Shape menu in the Brush panel, and draw a zig-zag line with it.

You can choose from several erodible tips, depending on the effect you want.

Mixing colors

You've used wet and dry brushes, changed brush settings, and mixed the paint with the background color. Now, you'll focus more on mixing colors with each other as you add paint to the painter's palette.

1 Zoom out just enough to see the full palette and the paint tubes.

2 Select the Paint mix layer in the Layers panel, so the color you paint won't blend with the brown palette on the Background layer.

The Mixer Brush tool mixes colors only on the active layer unless you select Sample All Layers in the options bar.

3 Use the Eyedropper tool to sample the red color from the red paint tube. Then, with the Mixer Brush tool selected, select the round blunt brush in the Brush panel (the fifth brush). Then choose Wet from the pop-up menu in the options bar, and paint in the top circle on the palette.

Note: Depending on the complexity of your project, you may need to be patient. Mixing colors can be a memory-intensive process.

4 Click the Clean The Brush After Each Stroke icon (✖) in the options bar to deselect it.

5 Use the Eyedropper tool to sample the blue color from the blue paint tube, and then use the Mixer Brush tool to paint in the same circle, mixing the red with the blue until the color becomes purple.

Use the Eyedropper tool to sample a color when the layer that contains the color (in this case, the Background layer) isn't selected.

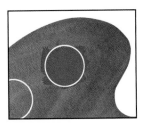

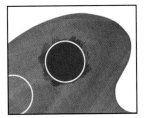

6 Paint in the next circle. You're painting in purple because the paint stays on the brush until you clean it.

7 In the options bar, choose Clean Brush from the Current Brush Load pop-up menu. The preview changes to indicate transparency, meaning the brush has no paint loaded.

To remove the paint load from a brush, you can choose Clean Brush in the options bar. To replace the paint load in a brush, sample a different color.

If you want Photoshop to clean the brush after each stroke, select the Clean Brush icon in the options bar. To load the brush with the foreground color after each stroke, select the Load Brush icon in the options bar. By default, both of these options are selected.

8   Choose Load Brush from the Current Brush Load pop-up menu in the options bar to load the brush with blue, the current foreground color. Paint blue in half of the next circle.

9   Sample the yellow color from the yellow paint tube, and paint over the blue with a wet brush to mix the two colors.

10 Fill the last circle with yellow and red paint, mixing the two with a wet brush to create an orange color.

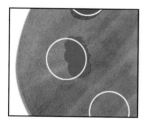 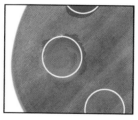 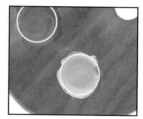

11 Hide the Circles layer in the Layers panel to remove the outlines on the palette.

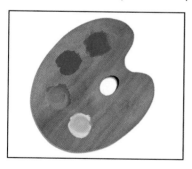 

12 Choose File > Save.

▶ **Tip:** Use the Eyedropper tool to sample the color, since it's on a different layer. You can press I to temporarily select the Eyedropper tool. When you release the I key, Photoshop returns to the Mixer Brush tool..

Julieanne Kost is an official Adobe Photoshop evangelist.

Tool tips from the Photoshop evangelist

Mixer Brush shortcuts

There are no default keyboard shortcuts for the Mixer Brush tool, but you can create your own.

To create custom keyboard shortcuts:

1   Choose Edit > Keyboard Shortcuts.

2   Choose Tools from the Shortcuts For menu.

3   Scroll down to the bottom of the list.

4   Select a command, and then enter a custom shortcut. You can create shortcuts for the following commands:

- Load Mixer Brush
- Clean Mixer Brush
- Toggle Mixer Brush Auto-Load
- Toggle Mixer Brush Auto-Clean
- Toggle Mixer Brush Sample All Layers
- Sharpen Erodible Tips

Creating a custom brush preset

Photoshop includes numerous brush presets, which are very handy. But if you need to tweak a brush for your project, you might find it easier to create your own preset. You'll create a brush preset to use in the following exercise.

Note: Due to an anomaly, numbers you enter in the Size, Bristles, Thickness, and Stiffness fields may not appear in the correct order. To avoid the issue, select only the digits (not the percentage sign) in the field before entering a new value.

1   In the Brush panel, select the following settings:

- Size: **36** px
- Shape: Round Fan
- Bristles: **35%**
- Length: **32%**
- Thickness: **2%**
- Stiffness: **75%**
- Angle: **0°**
- Spacing: **2%**

2 Choose New Brush Preset from the Brush panel menu.

3 Name the brush **Landscape**, and click OK.

4 Click Brush Presets in the Brush panel to open the Brush Presets panel.

The Brush Presets panel displays samples of the strokes created by different brushes. If you know which brush you want to use, it can be easier to find by name. You'll list them by name now, so you can find your preset for the next exercise.

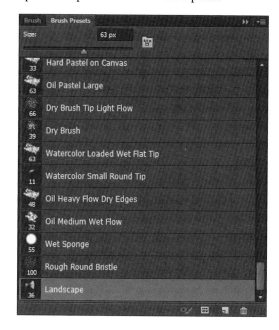

5 Choose Large List from the Brush Presets panel menu.

6 Scroll to the bottom of the list. The preset you created, named Landscape, is the last preset in the list.

7 Close the 10Palette_working.psd file.

Mixing colors with a photograph

Earlier, you mixed colors with a white background and with each other. Now, you'll use a photograph as your canvas. You'll add colors and mix them with each other and with the background colors to transform a photograph of a landscape into a watercolor.

1 Choose File > Open. Double-click the 10Landscape_Start.jpg file in the Lesson10 folder to open it.

2 Choose File > Save As. Rename the file **10Landscape_working.jpg**, and click Save. Click OK in the JPEG Options dialog box.

You'll paint the sky first. Start by setting up the color and selecting the brush.

3 Click the Foreground color swatch in the Tools panel. Select a medium-light blue color (we chose R=185, G=204, B=228), and then click OK.

4 Select the Mixer Brush tool (✔), if it isn't already selected. Choose Dry from the pop-up menu in the options bar. Then select the Landscape brush from the Brush Presets panel.

Presets are saved on your system, so they're available when you work with any image.

5 Paint over the sky, moving in close to the trees. Because you're using a dry brush, the paint isn't mixing with the colors beneath it.

6 Select a darker blue color (we used R=103, G=151, B=212), and add darker color at the top of the sky, still using the dry brush.

7 Select a light blue color again, and choose Very Wet, Heavy Mix from the pop-up menu in the options bar. Use this brush to scrub diagonally across the sky, blending the two colors in with the background color. Paint in close to the trees, and smooth out the entire sky.

Adding a darker color with a dry brush   Blending colors with a wet brush

When you're satisfied with the sky, move on to the grass and trees.

8 Select a light green (we used R=92, G=157, B=13). Choose Dry from the pop-up menu in the options bar. Then paint along the top section of the grass to highlight it.

9 Sample a darker green from the grass itself. Choose Very Wet, Heavy Mix in the options bar. Then paint using diagonal strokes to blend the colors in the grass.

▶ **Tip:** Remember that you can Alt-click (Windows) or Option-click (Mac OS) to sample a color instead of using the Eyedropper tool. To sample only solid colors using the keyboard shortcut, choose Load Solid Colors Only from the Current Brush Load pop-up menu in the options bar.

Adding light green with a dry brush   Blending colors with a wet brush

10 Sample a light green, and then use a dry brush to highlight the lighter areas of the trees and the small tree in the middle of the landscape. Then select a dark green (we used R=26, G=79, B=34), and choose Very Wet, Heavy Mix in the options bar. Paint with the wet brush to mix together the colors in the trees.

Highlighting the trees

Mixing the colors

▶ **Tip:** For different effects, paint in different directions. With the Mixer Brush tool, you can go wherever your artistic instincts lead you.

So far, so good. The background trees and the brown grasses are all that remain to be painted.

11 Select a bluer color for the background trees (we used R=65, G=91, B=116). Paint with a dry brush to add the blue at the top. Then choose Wet in the options bar, and paint to mix the blue into the trees.

12 Sample a brown color from the tall grasses, and then select Very Wet, Heavy Mix in the options bar. Paint along the top of the tall grass with up-and-down strokes for the look of a field. Across the back area, behind the small center tree, paint back and forth to create smooth strokes.

Voilà! You've created a masterpiece with your paints and brushes, and there's no mess to clean up.

Brush variations

You can go beyond the settings in these projects to explore numerous variations in brush tips and settings. In particular, you may want to play with Brush Pose and Shape Dynamics options.

Brush Pose settings change the tilt, rotation, and pressure of the brush. In the Brush panel, select Brush Pose from the list on the left. Move the Tilt X slider to tilt the brush from left to right. Move the Tilt Y slider to tilt the brush forward and backward. Change the Rotation value to rotate the bristles. (Rotation is more obvious when using a flat fan-shaped brush, for example.) Change the Pressure setting to determine how much effect the brush has on the artwork.

Shape Dynamics settings affect the steadiness of the stroke. Move the sliders up to increase the variability in the stroke.

If you're using a supported stylus or Wacom tablet, Photoshop recognizes the angle and pressure of the pen you're using and applies them to the brush. You can use the pen to control such things as Size Jitter. Choose Pen Pressure or Pen Tilt from the Control menu in the Shape Dynamics settings to determine how the value changes.

There are many more options—some subtle, some not so subtle—to create variety in brush effects. Which options are available depend on the brush tip shape you've selected. For more information about all the options, see Photoshop Help.

Painting gallery

The painting tools and brush tips in Photoshop let you create all kinds of painting effects.

Erodible brush tips give an added realism to your art. The following pages show examples of art created with the brush tips and tools in Photoshop.

Image © Janet Stoppee for m2media.com

Image © John Derry, www.pixelart.com

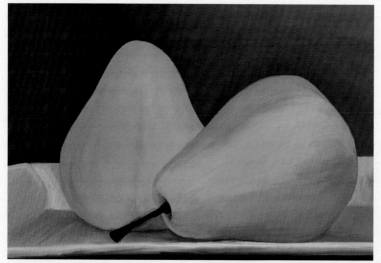

Image © Victoria Pavlov, www.pavlovphotography.com

Image © sholby, www.sholby.net

Image © sholby, www.sholby.net

Image © sholby, www.sholby.net

Continues on next page

Painting gallery (continued)

Image © John Derry, www.pixelart.com

Image © Lynette Kent, www.LynetteKent.com

Review questions

1   What does the Mixer Brush do that other brushes don't?

2   How do you load a mixer brush?

3   How do you clean a brush?

4   How can you display the names of brush presets?

5   What is the Live Tip Brush Preview, and how can you hide it?

6   What is an erodible tip?

Review answers

1   The Mixer Brush mixes the color of the paintbrush with colors on the canvas.

2   You can load a mixer brush by sampling a color, either by using the Eyedropper tool or keyboard shortcuts (Alt-click or Option-click). Or, you can choose Load Brush from the pop-up menu in the options bar to load the brush with the foreground color.

3   To clean a brush, choose Clean Brush from the pop-up menu in the options bar.

4   To display brush presets by name, open the Brush Presets panel, and then choose Large List (or Small List) from the Brush Presets panel menu.

5   The Live Tip Brush Preview shows you the direction the brush strokes are moving. It's available if OpenGL is enabled. To hide or show the Live Tip Brush Preview, click the Toggle The Live Tip Brush Preview icon at the bottom of the Brush panel or the Brush Presets panel.

6   An erodible tip erodes, changing thickness, as you paint or draw. It's similar to the way a pencil or pastel tip changes shape as it erodes.

11 EDITING VIDEO

Lesson overview

In this lesson, you'll learn how to do the following:

- Create a video timeline in Photoshop.
- Add media to a video group in the Timeline panel.
- Add motion to still images.
- Animate type and effects using keyframes.
- Add transitions between video clips.
- Include audio in a video file.
- Render a video.

 This lesson will take about 90 minutes to complete. Download the Lesson11 project files from the Lesson & Update Files tab on your Account page at www.peachpit.com, if you haven't already done so. As you work on this lesson, you'll preserve the start files. If you need to restore the start files, download them from your Account page.

PROJECT: FAMILY VIDEO FROM MOBILE PHONE

You can edit video files in Photoshop using many
of the same effects you use to edit image files. You
can create a movie from video files, still images, Smart
Objects, audio files, and type layers; apply transitions;
and animate effects using keyframes.

Getting started

In this lesson, you'll edit a video that was shot using a camera phone. You'll create a video timeline, import clips, add transitions and other video effects, and render the final video. First, look at the final project to see what you'll be creating.

1 Start Photoshop, and then immediately hold down Ctrl+Alt+Shift (Windows) or Command+Option+Shift (Mac OS) to restore the default preferences. (See "Restoring default preferences" on page 4.)

2 When prompted, click Yes to delete the Adobe Photoshop Settings file.

● **Note:** If Bridge isn't installed, you'll be prompted to install it when you choose Browse In Bridge. For more information, see page 3.

3 Choose File > Browse In Bridge.

4 In Bridge, select the Lessons folder in the Favorites panel. Then, double-click the Lesson11 folder in the Content panel.

5 Double-click the 11End.mp4 file to open it in QuickTime or Windows Media Player.

6 Click the Play button to view the final video.

The short video is a compilation of clips from a day at the beach. It includes transitions, layer effects, animated text, and a musical track.

7 Close QuickTime or Windows Media Player, and return to Bridge.

8 Double-click the 11End.psd file to open it in Photoshop.

About the Timeline panel

If you've used a video-editing application such as Adobe Premiere® Pro or Adobe After Effects®, the Timeline panel is probably familiar. You use the Timeline panel to assemble and arrange video clips, images, and audio files for a movie file. You can edit the duration of each clip, apply filters and effects, animate attributes such as position and opacity, mute sound, add transitions, and perform other standard video-editing tasks without ever leaving Photoshop.

1 Choose Window > Timeline to open the Timeline panel.

Each video clip or image included in the project is represented in a box in the Timeline panel and as a layer in the Layers panel. Video clips have a blue background in the Timeline panel; image files have a purple background. At the bottom of the Timeline panel is the audio track.

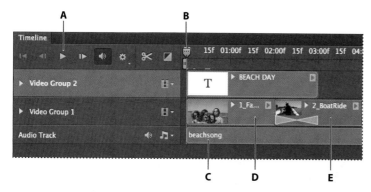

A. *Play button* **B.** *Playhead* **C.** *Audio track* **D.** *Image file* **E.** *Video clip*

2 Click Play in the Timeline panel to view the movie.

The playhead moves across the time ruler, displaying each frame of the movie.

3 Press the spacebar to pause playback.

4 Drag the playhead to another point in the time ruler.

The playhead's location determines what appears in the document window.

On the left side of the Timeline panel are animation keyframe controls. You'll use these to animate the position and other attributes of image and video files across time.

When you work with video, Photoshop displays guidelines across the document window. The guidelines identify the area that would be visible if you broadcast the video.

5   When you've finished exploring the end file, close it, but leave Photoshop open. Don't save any changes you might have made.

Creating a new video project

Working with video is a little different from working with still images in Photoshop. You may find it easiest to create the project first, and then import the assets you'll be using. You'll choose the video preset for this project, and then add nine video and image files to include in your movie.

Creating a new file

● **Note:** The video in this lesson was shot using an Apple iPhone, so one of the HDV presets is appropriate. The 720p preset provides good quality without providing too much data for easy streaming online.

Photoshop includes several film and video presets for you to choose from. You'll create a new file and select an appropriate preset.

1   Choose File > New.

2   Name the file **11Start.psd**.

3   Choose Film & Video from the Preset menu.

4   Choose HDV/HDTV 720p/29.97 from the Size menu.

5   Accept the default settings for the other options, and click OK.

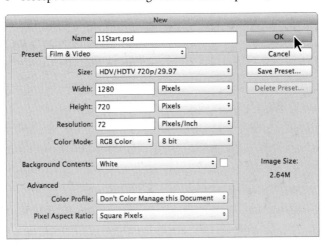

6   Choose File > Save As, and save the file in the Lesson11 folder.

Importing assets

Photoshop provides tools specifically for working with video, such as the Timeline panel, which may already be open because you previewed the end file. To ensure you have access to the resources you need, you'll select the Motion workspace and organize your panels. Then you'll import the video clips, images, and audio file you need to create the movie.

1   Choose Window > Workspace > Motion.

2   Pull the top edge of the Timeline panel up so that the panel occupies the bottom half of the workspace.

3   Select the Zoom tool (🔍), and then click Fit Screen in the options bar so that you can see the entire canvas within the top half of the screen.

4   In the Timeline panel, click Create Video Timeline. Photoshop creates a new video timeline, including two default tracks: Layer 0 and Audio Track.

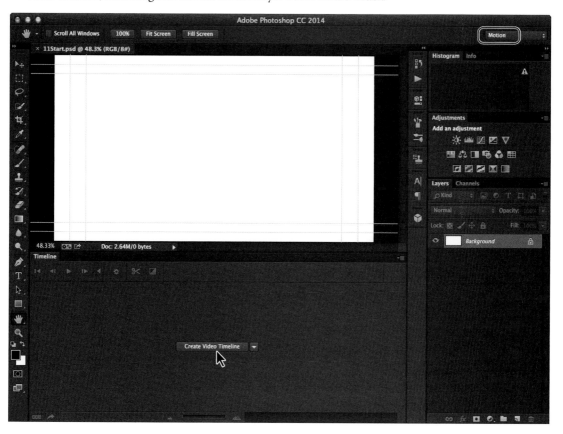

5 Click the Video menu in the Layer 0 track, and choose Add Media.

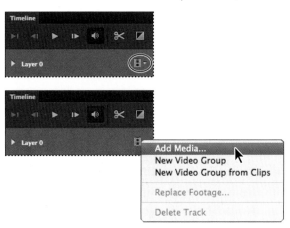

6 Navigate to the Lesson11 folder.

7 Shift-select the video and photo assets numbered 1–6, and click Open.

● **Note:** When you use the Add Media button with an unspecified canvas, Photoshop determines the project size based on the size of the first video file it finds—or, if you're importing only images, based on the image size.

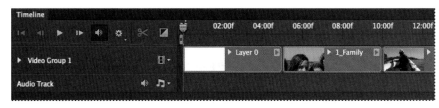

Photoshop imports all six of the assets you selected onto the same track, now named Video Group 1, in the Timeline panel. It displays still images with a purple background and video clips with a blue background. In the Layers panel, the assets appear as individual layers within the layer group named Video Group 1. You don't need the Layer 0 layer, so you'll delete it.

8 Select Layer 0 in the Layers panel, and click the Delete Layer button at the bottom of the panel. Click Yes to confirm the deletion.

Changing the duration and size of clips in the timeline

The clips are of very different lengths, meaning they'd play for different amounts of time. For this video, you want all the clips to be the same length, so you'll shorten them all to 3 seconds. The length of a clip (its *duration*) is measured in seconds and frames: 03:00 is 3 seconds; 02:25 is 2 seconds and 25 frames.

1 Drag the Control Timeline Magnification slider to the right at the bottom of the Timeline panel to zoom in on the timeline. You want to be able to see a thumbnail of each clip and enough detail in the time ruler that you can accurately change the duration of each clip.

2 Drag the right edge of the first clip (1_Family) to 03:00 on the time ruler. Photoshop displays the end point and the duration as you drag so that you can find the right stopping point.

● **Note:** You're shortening each clip to the same length here, but you can have clips of varying lengths, depending on what's appropriate for the project.

3 Drag the right edge of the second clip (2_BoatRide) to a duration of 03:00.

Shortening a video clip doesn't compress it; it removes part of the clip from the video. In this case, you want to use the first three seconds of each clip. If you wanted to use a different portion of a video clip, you would shorten the clip from each end. As you drag the end point of a video clip, Photoshop displays a preview so you can see which part of the clip is included.

4 Repeat step 3 for each of the remaining clips so that each has a duration of 3 seconds.

▶ **Tip:** To quickly change the duration of a video clip, click the arrow in the upper right corner, and then type a new Duration value. This option isn't available for still images.

The clips are now the right duration, but some of the images are the wrong size for the canvas. You'll resize the first image before continuing.

5 Select the 1_Family layer in the Layers panel. The clip is also selected in the Timeline panel.

6 Click the triangle in the upper right corner of the 1_Family clip in the Timeline panel to open the Motion panel.

▶ **Tip:** The arrow on the left side of a clip (next to the clip's thumbnail) reveals the attributes you can animate using keyframes. The arrow on the right side of a clip opens the Motion panel.

7 Choose Pan & Zoom from the menu, and make sure Resize To Fill Canvas is selected. Then click an empty area of the Timeline panel to close the Motion panel.

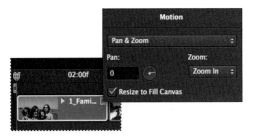 

The image resizes to fit the canvas, which is what you wanted. However, you don't actually want to pan and zoom. You'll remove the effect.

8 Open the Motion panel from the 1_Family clip again, and choose No Motion from the menu. Click an empty area of the Timeline panel to close the Motion panel.

9 Choose File > Save. Click OK in the Photoshop Format Options dialog box.

Animating text with keyframes

Keyframes let you control animation, effects, and other changes that occur over time. A keyframe marks the point in time where you specify a value, such as a position, size, or style. To create a change over time, you must have at least two keyframes: one for the state at the beginning of the change and one for the state at the end. Photoshop interpolates the values for the positions in between so that the change takes effect smoothly over the specified time. You'll use keyframes to animate a movie title (Beach Day) from left to right over the opening image.

1 Click the Video pop-up menu in the Video Group 1 track, and choose New Video Group. Photoshop adds Video Group 2 to the Timeline panel.

2 Select the Horizontal Type tool (T), and then click on the left edge of the image, about halfway down from the top.

Photoshop creates a new type layer, named Layer 1, in the Video Group 2 track.

3 In the options bar, select a sans serif font such as Myriad Pro, set the type size to **600 pt**, and select white for the type color.

4 Type **BEACH DAY**.

The text is large enough that it doesn't all fit on the image. That's okay; you'll animate it to move across the image.

5 In the Layers panel, change the opacity for the BEACH DAY layer to **25%**.

6 In the Timeline panel, drag the end point of the type layer to 03:00 so that it has the same duration as the 1_Family layer.

7 Click the arrow next to the thumbnail in the BEACH DAY clip to display the clip's attributes.

8 Make sure the playhead is at the beginning of the time ruler.

9 Click the stopwatch icon (⏱) next to the Transform property to set an initial keyframe for the layer.

The keyframe appears as a yellow diamond in the timeline.

10 Select the Move tool (➕), and use it to drag the type layer over the canvas so that the top of the letters align with the lower of the two top guidelines. Drag it to the right so that only the left edge of the letter "B" in the word "BEACH" is visible on the canvas. The keyframe you set ensures that the text will be in this position at the beginning of the movie.

▶ **Tip:** Photoshop displays the playhead's location in the lower left corner of the Timeline panel.

11 Move the playhead to the last frame of the first clip (02:29).

12 Press the Shift key as you drag the type layer to the left over the canvas so that only the right edge of the "Y" in the word "DAY" is visible. Pressing the Shift key ensures the type remains level as you move it across.

Because you've changed the position, Photoshop creates a new keyframe.

13 Move the playhead across the first three seconds of the time ruler to preview the animation. The title moves across the image.

14 Click the triangle next to the thumbnail of the text clip to close the clip's attributes, and then choose File > Save to save your work so far.

Creating effects

One of the benefits of working with video files in Photoshop is that you can create effects using adjustment layers, styles, and simple transformations.

Adding adjustment layers to video clips

You've used adjustment layers with still images throughout this book. They work just as well on video clips. When you apply an adjustment layer in a video group, Photoshop applies it only to the layer immediately below it in the Layers panel.

1. Select the 3_DogAtBeach layer in the Layers panel.

2. In the Timeline panel, move the playhead to the beginning of the 3_DogAtBeach layer so you can see the effect as you apply it.

3. In the Adjustments panel, click the Black & White button.

4. In the Properties panel, leave the default preset, and select Tint. The default tint color creates a sepia effect that works well for this clip. You can experiment with the sliders and the tint color to modify the black-and-white effect to your taste.

Note: If you had imported the video file using the Place command, so that it was not in a video group, you would need to create a clipping layer to limit the adjustment layer to a single layer.

5. Move the playhead across the 3_DogAtBeach clip in the Timeline panel to preview the effect.

Animating a zoom effect

Even simple transformations become interesting effects when you animate them. You'll use animation to zoom in on the 4_Dogs clip.

1. Move the playhead to the beginning of the 4_Dogs clip in the Timeline panel (09:00).

2. Click the arrow in the 4_Dogs clip to display the Motion panel.

3. Choose Zoom from the pop-up menu, and choose Zoom In from the Zoom menu. On the Zoom From grid, select the upper left corner to zoom in from that point. Make sure Resize To Fill Canvas is selected, and then click an empty area of the Timeline panel to close the Motion panel.

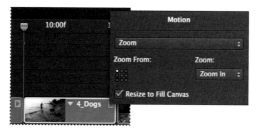

4 Drag the playhead across the clip to preview the effect.

You'll enlarge the image in the last keyframe to make the zoom more dramatic.

5 Click the arrow on the left side of the 4_Dogs clip to reveal the attributes for the clip.

There are two keyframes, one for the beginning of the Zoom In effect, and one for the end.

Tip: You can move to the next keyframe by clicking the right arrow next to the attribute in the Timeline panel. Click the left arrow to move to the previous keyframe.

6 Click the right arrow next to the Transform attribute (under Video Group 1 on the left side of the Timeline panel) to move the playhead to the last keyframe if it's not already there, and choose Edit > Free Transform. Then enter **120%** for Width and Height in the options bar. Press Enter or Return to confirm the transformation.

7 Drag the playhead across the 4_Dogs clip in the time ruler to preview the animation again.

8 Choose File > Save.

Animating an image to create a motion effect

You'll animate another transformation to create the appearance of motion. You want the image to begin with the diver's legs and end with his hands.

1 Move the playhead to the end of the 5_Jumping clip (14:29), and select the clip. Press Shift while you move the image down in the document window so that the hands are near the top of the canvas, putting the diver in the final position.

2 Display the attributes for the clip, and click the stopwatch icon for the Position attribute to add a keyframe.

3 Move the playhead to the beginning of the clip (12:00). Press Shift while you move the image up so that the feet are near the bottom of the canvas.

Photoshop adds a keyframe.

4 Move the playhead across the time ruler to preview the animation.

5 Close the clip's attributes. Then choose File > Save to save your work so far.

Adding pan & zoom effects

You can easily add features similar to the pan and zoom effects used in documentaries. You'll add them to the sunset to bring the video to a dramatic close.

1 Move the playhead to the beginning of the 6_Sunset clip.

2 Open the Motion panel for the clip. Choose Pan & Zoom from the pop-up menu, choose Zoom Out from the Zoom menu, and make sure Resize To Fill Canvas is selected. Then click an empty area of the Timeline panel to close the Motion panel.

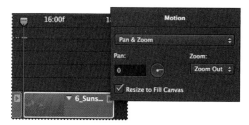

3 Move the playhead across the last clip to preview the effects.

Adding transitions

A transition moves a scene from one shot to the next. Simply drag and drop to add transitions to clips in Photoshop.

1   Click the Go To First Frame button (◄) in the upper left corner of the Timeline panel to return the playhead to the beginning of the time ruler.

2   Click the Transitions button (◢) in the upper left corner of the Timeline panel. Select Cross Fade, and change the Duration value to **.25 s** (for a quarter of a second).

3   Drag the Cross Fade transition between the 1_Family and 2_BoatRide clips.

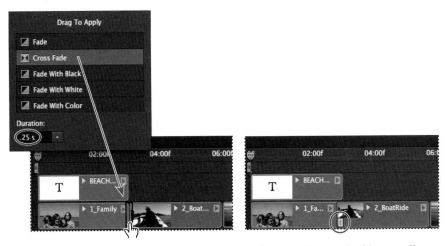

Photoshop adjusts the ends of the clips to apply the transition, and adds a small white icon in the lower corner of the second clip.

4   Drag Cross Fade transitions between each of the other clips.

5   Drag a Fade With Black transition onto the end of the final clip.

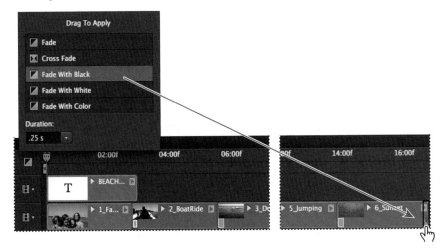

6 To make the transition smoother, extend the Fade With Black transition by stretching its left side to about one-third the total length of the clip.

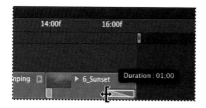

7 Choose File > Save.

Adding audio

You can add a separate audio track to a video file in Photoshop. In fact, the Timeline panel includes an audio track by default. You'll add an MP3 file to play as the soundtrack for this short video.

1 Click the note icon in the Audio Track at the bottom of the Timeline panel, and choose Add Audio from the pop-up menu.

▶ Tip: You can also add an audio track by clicking the + sign at the far right end of the track in the Timeline panel.

2 Select the beachsong.mp3 file from the Lesson11 folder, and click Open.

The audio file is added to the timeline, but it's much longer than the video. You'll use the Split At Playhead tool to shorten it.

3 Move the playhead to the end of the 6_Sunset clip. With the audio file still selected, click the Split At Playhead tool.

The audio file is clipped at that point, becoming two audio clips.

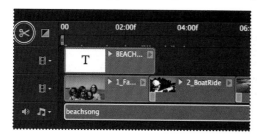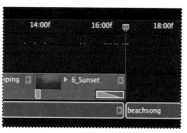

4 Select the second audio file segment, the one that begins after the end of the 6_Sunset clip. Press the Delete key on your keyboard to delete the selected clip.

Now the audio file is the same length as the video. You'll add a fade so that it ends smoothly.

5 Click the small arrow at the right edge of the audio clip to open the Audio panel. Then enter **3** seconds for Fade In and **5** seconds for Fade Out.

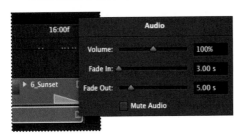

6 Save your work so far.

Muting unwanted audio

So far, you've previewed portions of the video by moving the playhead across the time ruler. Now you'll preview the entire video using the Play button in the Timeline panel, and then mute any extraneous audio from the video clips.

▶ **Tip:** To create a smoother preview, disable the audio playback button in the Timeline panel the first time you play the video. With audio playback disabled, Photoshop can create a more complete cache, resulting in a more accurate preview.

1 Click the Play button (▶) in the upper left corner of the Timeline panel to preview the video so far.

It's looking good, but there is some unwanted background noise from the video clips. You'll mute that extra sound.

2 Click the small triangle at the right end of the 2_BoatRide clip.

3 Click the Audio tab to see audio options, and then select Mute Audio. Click an empty area of the Timeline panel to close the panel.

256 LESSON 11 Editing Video

4 Click the small triangle at the right end of the 3_DogAtBeach clip.

5 Click the Audio tab to see audio options, and then select Mute Audio. Click an empty area of the Timeline panel to close the panel.

Rendering video

You're ready to render your project to video. Photoshop provides several rendering options. You'll select options appropriate for streaming video to share on the Vimeo website. For information about other rendering options, see Photoshop Help.

1 Choose File > Export > Render Video, or click the Render Video button (↪) in the lower left corner of the Timeline panel.

2 Name the file **11Final.mp4**.

3 Click Select Folder, and then navigate to the Lesson11 folder, and click OK or Choose.

4 From the Preset menu, choose Vimeo HD 720p 25.

5 Click Render.

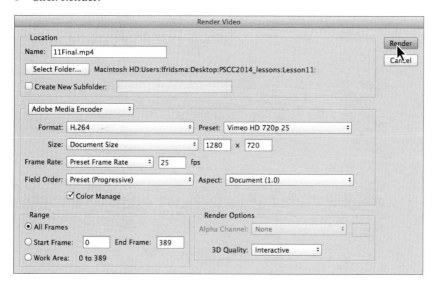

Photoshop displays a progress bar as it exports the video. Depending on your system, the rendering process may take several minutes.

 Depending on your system, this may take a while.

6 Locate the 11Final.mp4 file in the Lesson11 folder in Bridge. Double-click it to view the video you made.

Review questions

1 What is a keyframe, and how do you create one?

2 How do you add a transition between clips?

3 How do you render a video?

Review answers

1 A keyframe marks the point in time where you specify a value, such as a position, size, or style. To create a change over time, you must have at least two keyframes: one for the state at the beginning of the change and one for the state at the end. To create an initial keyframe, click the stopwatch icon next to the attribute you want to animate for the layer. Photoshop creates additional keyframes each time you change the values of that attribute.

2 To add a transition, click the Transition icon in the upper left corner of the Timeline panel, and then drag a transition onto a clip.

3 To render a video, choose File > Export > Render Video, or click the Render Video button in the lower left corner of the Timeline panel. Then select the video settings that are appropriate for your intended output.

12 WORKING WITH CAMERA RAW

Lesson overview

In this lesson, you'll learn how to do the following:

- Open a proprietary camera raw image in Adobe Camera Raw.

- Adjust tone and color in a raw image.

- Sharpen an image in Camera Raw.

- Synchronize settings for multiple images.

- Open a Camera Raw image as a Smart Object in Photoshop.

- Apply Camera Raw as a filter in Photoshop.

 This lesson will take about an hour to complete. Download the Lesson12 project files from the Lesson & Update Files tab on your Account page at www.peachpit.com, if you haven't already done so. As you work on this lesson, you'll preserve the start files. If you need to restore the start files, download them from your Account page.

PROJECT: ADVANCED PHOTO RETOUCHING

Raw images give you greater flexibility, especially in setting color and tone. Camera Raw lets you tap into that potential. It can be a useful tool even when you're starting with a JPEG or TIFF image, or when you apply it as a filter in Photoshop.

Getting started

● **Note:** We used Adobe Camera Raw 8.5, which was the current version at the time of publication. Adobe updates Camera Raw frequently; if you're using a later version, some of the steps in this lesson may not match what you see.

● **Note:** If you haven't installed Bridge, you'll be prompted to do so when you choose Browse In Bridge. For more information, see page 3.

In this lesson, you'll edit several digital images using Photoshop and Adobe Camera Raw, which comes with Photoshop. You'll use a variety of techniques to touch up and improve the appearance of digital photographs. You'll start by viewing the before and after images in Adobe Bridge.

1 Start Photoshop, and then immediately hold down Ctrl+Alt+Shift (Windows) or Command+Option+Shift (Mac OS) to restore the default preferences. (See "Restoring default preferences" on page 4.)

2 When prompted, click Yes to delete the Adobe Photoshop Settings file.

3 Choose File > Browse In Bridge to open Adobe Bridge.

4 In the Favorites panel in Bridge, click the Lessons folder. Then, in the Content panel, double-click the Lesson12 folder to open it.

5 Adjust the thumbnail slider, if necessary, so that you can see the thumbnail previews clearly. Then look at the 12A_Start.crw and 12A_End.psd files.

12A_Start.crw *12A_End.psd*

The original photograph of a Spanish-style church is a camera raw file, so it doesn't have the usual .psd or .jpg file extension you've worked with so far in this book. It was shot with a Canon Digital Rebel camera and has the Canon proprietary .crw file extension. You'll process this proprietary camera raw image to make it brighter, sharper, and clearer, and then save it as a JPEG file for the web and as a PSD file so that you could work on it further in Photoshop.

6 Compare the 12B_Start.nef and 12B_End.psd thumbnail previews.

12B_Start.nef   *12B_End.psd*

This time, the start file was taken with a Nikon camera, and the raw image has an .nef extension. You'll perform color corrections and image enhancements in Camera Raw and Photoshop to achieve the end result.

About camera raw files

A *camera raw* file contains unprocessed picture data from a digital camera's image sensor. Many digital cameras can save images in camera raw format. The advantage of camera raw files is that they let the photographer—rather than the camera—interpret the image data and make adjustments and conversions. (In contrast, shooting JPEG images with your camera locks the camera's processing into the image.) Because the camera doesn't do any image processing when you shoot a camera raw photo, you can use Adobe Camera Raw to set the white balance, tonal range, contrast, color saturation, and sharpening. Think of camera raw files as photo negatives: You can go back and reprocess the file any time you like to achieve the results you want.

To create camera raw files, set your digital camera to save files in its own, possibly proprietary, raw file format. When you download the file from your camera, it has a file extension such as .nef (from Nikon) or .crw (from Canon). In Bridge or Photoshop, you can process camera raw files from a myriad of supported digital cameras from Canon, Kodak, Leica, Nikon, and other makers—and even process multiple images simultaneously. You can then export the proprietary camera raw files to DNG, JPEG, TIFF, or PSD file format.

Note: The Photoshop Raw format (.raw extension) is a file format for transferring images between applications and computer platforms. Don't confuse Photoshop Raw with camera raw file formats.

You can process camera raw files obtained from supported cameras, but you can also open TIFF and JPEG images in Camera Raw, which includes some editing features that aren't in Photoshop. However, you won't have the same flexibility with white balance and other settings if you're using a TIFF or JPEG image. Although Camera Raw can open and edit a camera raw image file, it cannot save an image in camera raw format.

Processing files in Camera Raw

When you make adjustments to an image in Camera Raw, such as straightening or cropping the image, Photoshop and Bridge preserve the original file data. This way, you can edit the image as you desire, export the edited image, and keep the original intact for future use or other adjustments.

Opening images in Camera Raw

You can open Camera Raw from either Bridge or Photoshop, and you can apply the same edits to multiple files simultaneously. This is especially useful if you're working with images that were all shot in the same environment, and which therefore need the same lighting and other adjustments.

Camera Raw provides extensive controls for adjusting white balance, exposure, contrast, sharpness, tone curves, and much more. In this exercise, you'll edit one image and then apply the settings to similar images.

1 In Bridge, open the Lessons/Lesson12/Mission folder, which contains three shots of the Spanish church you previewed earlier.

2 Shift-click to select all of the images—Mission01.crw, Mission02.crw, and Mission03.crw—and then choose File > Open In Camera Raw.

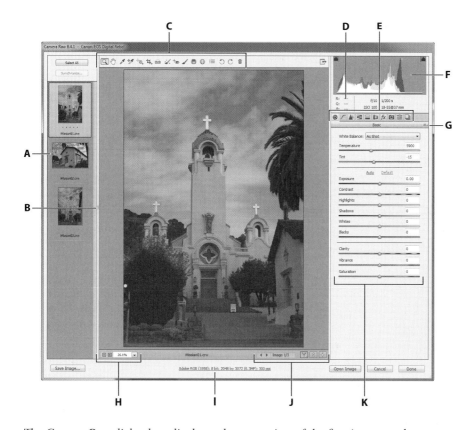

A. *Filmstrip*

B. *Toggle Filmstrip*

C. *Toolbar*

D. *RGB values*

E. *Image adjustment tabs*

F. *Histogram*

G. *Camera Raw Settings menu*

H. *Zoom levels*

I. *Click to display workflow options*

J. *Multi-image navigation controls*

K. *Adjustment sliders*

The Camera Raw dialog box displays a large preview of the first image, and a filmstrip down the left side displays all open images. The histogram in the upper right corner shows the tonal range of the selected image; the workflow options link below the preview window displays the selected image's color space, bit depth, size, and resolution. Tools along the top of the dialog box let you zoom, pan, straighten, and make other adjustments to the image. Tabbed panels on the right side of the dialog box give you more nuanced options for adjusting the image: You can correct the white balance, adjust the tone, sharpen the image, remove noise, adjust color, and make other changes. You can also save settings as a preset, and then apply them later.

For the best results using Camera Raw, plan your workflow to move from left to right and top to bottom. That is, you'll often want to use the tools across the top first, and then move through the panels in order, making changes as necessary.

You will explore these controls now as you edit the first image file.

3   Click each thumbnail in the filmstrip to preview all the images before you begin. Or, you can click the Forward button under the main preview window to cycle through them. When you've seen all three, select the Mission01.crw image again.

Adjusting white balance

An image's white balance reflects the lighting conditions under which it was captured. A digital camera records the white balance at the time of exposure; this is the value that initially appears in the Camera Raw dialog box image preview.

White balance comprises two components. The first is *temperature*, which is measured in kelvins and determines the level of "coolness" or "warmness" of the image—that is, its cool blue-green tones or warm yellow-red tones. The second component is *tint*, which compensates for magenta or green color casts in the image.

Depending on the settings you're using on your camera and the environment in which you're shooting (for example, if there's glare or uneven lighting), you may want to adjust the white balance for the image. If you plan to modify the white balance, make that the first thing you do, as it will affect all other changes in the image.

1   If the Basic panel isn't already displayed on the right side of the dialog box, click the Basic button (⊙) to open it.

By default, As Shot is selected in the White Balance menu. Camera Raw applies the white balance settings that were in your camera at the time of exposure. Camera Raw includes several White Balance presets, which you can use as a starting point to see different lighting effects.

2   Choose Cloudy from the White Balance menu.

Camera Raw adjusts the temperature and tint for a cloudy day. Sometimes a preset does the trick. In this case, though, there's still a blue cast to the image. You'll adjust the white balance manually.

3   Select the White Balance tool (✎) at the top of the Camera Raw dialog box.

To set an accurate white balance, select an object that should be white or gray. Camera Raw uses that information to determine the color of the light in which the scene was shot, and then adjusts for scene lighting automatically.

4 Click the white clouds in the image. The lighting of the image changes.

5 Click a different area of the clouds. The lighting shifts.

You can use the White Balance tool to find the best lighting for the scene quickly and easily. Clicking different areas changes the lighting without making any permanent changes to the file, so you can experiment freely.

6 Click the clouds directly to the left of the steeple. This selection removes most of the color casts and results in realistic lighting.

▶ **Tip:** To undo the settings, press Ctrl+Z (Windows) or Command+Z (Mac OS).

7 Move the Tint slider to **-22** to intensify the greens.

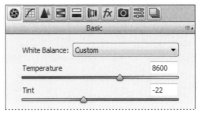

8 To see the changes you've made, click the Preview mode button () at the bottom of the window, and choose Before/After Left/Right from the pop-up menu.

▶ **Tip:** To expand Camera Raw to fill the screen, click the Toggle Full-Screen Mode button (⊡) on the far right side of the toolbar, or press F.

Camera Raw displays the Before image on the left and the After image on the right so you can see the changes you've made.

9 To see only the After image again, choose Single View from the Preview mode pop-up menu. If you prefer, you can leave both views visible so you can see how the image has changed as you continue to alter it.

Making tonal adjustments in Camera Raw

Other sliders in the Basic panel affect exposure, brightness, contrast, and saturation in the image. Except for Contrast, moving a slider to the right lightens the affected areas of the image, and moving it to the left darkens those areas. Exposure essentially defines the *white point*, or the lightest point of the image, so that Camera Raw adjusts everything else accordingly. Conversely, the Blacks slider sets the *black point*, or the darkest point in the image. The Highlights and Shadows sliders increase detail in the highlights and the shadows, respectively.

> **Tip:** For the best effect, increase the Clarity slider until you see halos near the edge details, and then reduce the setting slightly.

The Contrast slider adjusts the contrast. For more nuanced contrast adjustments, you can use the Clarity slider, which adds depth to an image by increasing local contrast, especially on the midtones.

The Saturation slider adjusts the saturation of all colors in the image equally. The Vibrance slider, on the other hand, has a greater effect on undersaturated colors. You can use it to bring life to a background without oversaturating any skin tones in the image, for example.

You can use the Auto option to let Camera Raw attempt to correct the image tone, or you can select your own settings.

1   Click Auto in the Basic panel.

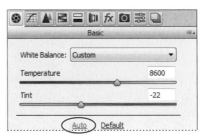

Camera Raw increases the exposure and changes several other settings. You could use this as a starting point. However, in this exercise, you'll return to the default settings and adjust them yourself.

2 Click Default in the Basic panel.

3 Change the sliders as follows:

- Exposure: **+0.20**
- Contrast: **+18**
- Highlights: **+8**
- Shadows: **+63**
- Whites: **+12**
- Blacks: **-14**
- Clarity: **+3**
- Vibrance: **+4**
- Saturation: **+1**

These settings help pump up the midtones of the image so that it looks bolder and more dimensional without being oversaturated.

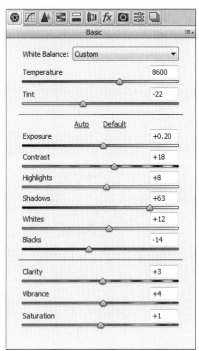

About the Camera Raw histogram

The histogram in the upper right corner of the Camera Raw dialog box simultaneously shows the red, green, and blue channels of the selected image, and updates interactively as you adjust any settings. Also, as you move any tool over the preview image, the RGB values for the area under the cursor appear below the histogram.

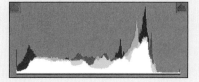

Applying sharpening

Photoshop offers several sharpening filters, but when you need to sharpen an entire image, Camera Raw provides the best control. The sharpening controls are in the Detail panel. To see the effect of sharpening in the preview panel, you must view the image at 100% or greater.

1   Double-click the Zoom tool (Q) on the left side of the toolbar to zoom in to 100%. Then select the Hand tool (✋), and pan the image to see the cross at the top of the mission tower.

2   Click the Detail button (▲) to open the Detail panel.

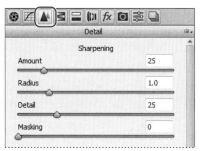

The Amount slider determines how much sharpening Camera Raw applies. Typically, you'll want to exaggerate the amount of sharpening at first, and then adjust it after you've set the other sliders.

3 Move the Amount slider to **100**.

The Radius slider determines the pixel area Camera Raw analyzes as it sharpens the image. For most images, you'll get the best results if you keep the radius low, even below one pixel. A larger radius can begin to cause an unnatural look, almost like a watercolor.

4 Move the Radius slider to **0.9**.

The Detail slider determines how much detail you'll see. Even when this slider is set to 0, Camera Raw performs some sharpening. Typically, you'll want to keep the Detail setting relatively low.

5 Move the Detail slider to **25**, if it isn't already there.

The Masking slider determines which parts of the image Camera Raw sharpens. When the Masking value is high, Camera Raw sharpens only those parts of the image that have strong edges.

6 Move the Masking slider to **61**.

▶ **Tip:** Press Alt (Windows) or Option (Mac OS) as you move the Masking slider to see what Camera Raw will sharpen.

After you've adjusted the Radius, Detail, and Masking sliders, you can lower the Amount slider to finalize the sharpening.

7 Decrease the Amount slider to **70**.

 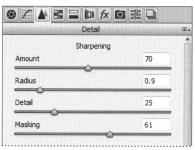

Sharpening the image gives stronger definition to the details and edges. The Masking slider lets you target the sharpening effect to the lines in the image, so that artifacts don't appear in unfocused or background areas.

● **Note:** If you zoom out, the image won't appear to be sharpened. You can preview sharpening effects only at zoom levels of 100% or greater.

When you make adjustments in Camera Raw, the original file data is preserved. Your adjustment settings for the image are stored either in the Camera Raw database file or in "sidecar" XMP files that accompany the original image file in the same folder. These XMP files retain the adjustments you made in Camera Raw when you move the image file to a storage medium or another computer.

Synchronizing settings across images

All three of the mission images were shot at the same time under the same lighting conditions. Now that you've made the first one look stunning, you can automatically apply the same settings to the other two images. You do this using the Synchronize command.

1 In the upper left corner of the Camera Raw dialog box, click Select All to select all of the images in the filmstrip.

2 Click the Synchronize button.

The Synchronize dialog box appears, listing all the settings you can apply to the images. By default, all options except Crop, Spot Removal, and Local Adjustments are selected. You can accept the default for this project, even though you didn't change all the settings.

3 Click OK in the Synchronize dialog box.

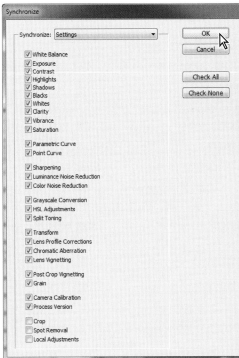

When you synchronize the settings across all of the selected images, the thumbnails update to reflect the changes you made. To preview the images, click each thumbnail in the filmstrip.

Saving Camera Raw changes

You can save your changes in different ways for different purposes. First, you'll save the images with adjustments as low-resolution JPEG files that you can share on the web. Then, you'll save one image, Mission01, as a Photoshop file that you can open as a Smart Object in Photoshop. When you open an image as a Smart Object in Photoshop, you can return to Camera Raw at any time to make further adjustments.

1 Click Select All in the Camera Raw dialog box to select all three images.

2 Click Save Images in the lower left corner.

3 In the Save Options dialog box, do the following:

- Choose Save In Same Location from the Destination menu.
- In the File Naming area, leave "Document Name" in the first box.
- Choose JPEG from the Format menu.
- In the Image Sizing area, select Resize To Fit, and then choose Long Side from the Resize To Fit menu.
- Enter **640** pixels to designate the dimension of the long side, whether it's a portrait or landscape image. (The dimension of the short side will automatically be adjusted proportionally.)
- Type **72** pixels/inch for the Resolution value.

These settings will save your corrected images as smaller, downsampled JPEG files, which you can share with colleagues on the web. They'll be resized so that most viewers won't need to scroll to see the entire image when it opens. Your files will be named Mission01.jpg, Mission02.jpg, and Mission03.jpg.

4 Click Save.

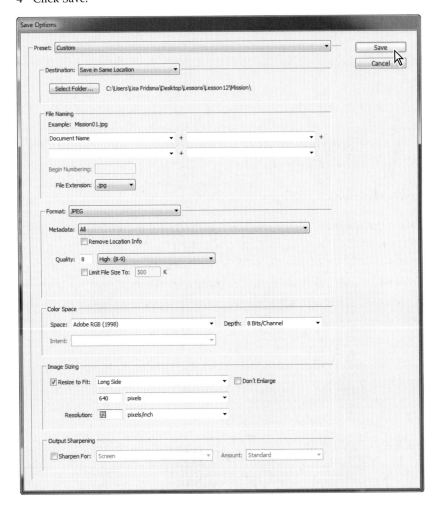

Bridge returns you to the Camera Raw dialog box, and indicates how many images have been processed until all the images have been saved. The CRW thumbnails still appear in the Camera Raw dialog box. In Bridge, however, you now also have JPEG versions as well as the original CRW image files, which you can continue to edit or leave for another time.

Now, you'll open a copy of the Mission01 image in Photoshop.

5 Select the Mission01.crw image thumbnail in the filmstrip in the Camera Raw dialog box. Then press the Shift key, and click Open Object at the bottom of the dialog box.

The Open Object button opens the image as a Smart Object in Photoshop; you can double-click the Smart Object thumbnail in the Layers panel to return to Camera Raw to continue making adjustments at any time.

If, instead, you had clicked Open Image, the image would open as a standard Photoshop image. Pressing the Shift key changes the Open Image button to the Open Object button.

▶ **Tip:** To make the Open Object button the default, click the workflow options link (in blue) below the preview window, select Open In Photoshop As Smart Objects, and click OK.

6 In Photoshop, choose File > Save As. In the Save As dialog box, choose Photoshop for the format, rename the file **Mission_Final.psd**, navigate to the Lesson12 folder, and click Save. Click OK if the Photoshop Format Options dialog box appears. Then close the file.

About saving files in Camera Raw

Every camera model saves raw images in a unique format, but Adobe Camera Raw can process many raw file formats. Camera Raw processes the raw files with default image settings based on built-in camera profiles for supported cameras and the EXIF data.

You can save the proprietary files in DNG format (the format saved by Adobe Camera Raw), JPEG, TIFF, and PSD. All of these formats can be used to save RGB and CMYK continuous-tone, bitmapped images, and all of them except DNG are also available in the Photoshop Save and Save As dialog boxes.

- The **DNG (Adobe Digital Negative)** format contains raw image data from a digital camera and metadata that defines what the image data means. DNG is meant to be an industry-wide standard format for raw image data, helping photographers manage the variety of proprietary raw formats and providing a compatible archival format. (You can save this format only from the Camera Raw dialog box.)

- The **JPEG (Joint Photographic Experts Group)** file format is commonly used to display photographs and other continuous-tone RGB images on the web. Higher-resolution JPEG files may be used for other purposes, including high-quality printing. JPEG format retains all color information in an image, but compresses file size by selectively discarding data. The greater the compression, the lower the image quality.

- **TIFF (Tagged Image File Format)** is used to exchange files between applications and computer platforms. TIFF is a flexible format supported by virtually all paint, image-editing, and page layout applications. Also, virtually all desktop scanners can produce TIFF images.

- **PSD format** is the Photoshop native file format. Because of the tight integration between Adobe products, other Adobe applications such as Adobe Illustrator and Adobe InDesign can directly import PSD files and preserve many Photoshop features.

Once you open a file in Photoshop, you can save it in many different formats, including Large Document Format (PSB), Cineon, Photoshop Raw, or PNG. Not to be confused with camera raw file formats, the Photoshop Raw format (RAW) is a file format for transferring images between applications and computer platforms.

For more information about file formats in Camera Raw and Photoshop, see Photoshop Help.

Applying advanced color correction

You'll use Levels, the Healing Brush tool, and other Photoshop features to enhance the image of this model.

Tip: In addition to opening files in Camera Raw when you start the editing process, you can apply Camera Raw settings as a filter to any file in Photoshop. Choose Filter > Camera Raw Filter, adjust the settings, and click OK.

Adjust the white balance in Camera Raw

The original image of the bride has a slight color cast. You'll start your color corrections in Camera Raw, setting the white balance and adjusting the overall tone of the image.

1 In Bridge, navigate to the Lesson12 folder. Select the 12B_Start.nef file, and choose File > Open In Camera Raw.

2 In Camera Raw, select the White Balance tool (🖋), and then click a white area in the model's dress to adjust the temperature and remove a green color cast.

3 Adjust other sliders in the Basic panel to brighten and intensify the image:

- Increase Exposure to **0.30**.
- Increase Contrast to **15**.
- Increase Clarity to **+8**.

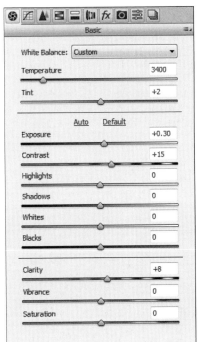

4 Press the Shift key, and click Open Object.

The image opens in Photoshop as a Smart Object.

Adjusting levels

The tonal range of an image represents the amount of contrast, or detail, in the image and is determined by the image's distribution of pixels, ranging from the darkest pixels (black) to the lightest pixels (white). You'll use a Levels adjustment layer to fine-tune the tonal range in this image.

1 In Photoshop, choose File > Save As. Name the file **Model_final.psd**, and click Save. Click OK if you see the Photoshop Format Options dialog box.

2 Click the Levels button in the Adjustments panel.

Photoshop adds a Levels adjustment layer to the Layers panel. The Levels controls and a histogram appear in the Properties panel. The histogram displays the range of dark and light values in the image. The left (black) triangle represents the shadows; the right (white) triangle represents the highlights; and the middle (gray) triangle represents the midtones, or gamma. Unless you're aiming for a special effect, the ideal histogram has its black point at the beginning of the data and its white point at the end of the data, and the middle portion has fairly uniform peaks and valleys, representing adequate pixel data in the midtones.

3 Click the Calculate A More Accurate Histogram button () on the left side of the histogram. Photoshop replaces the histogram.

There is a small bump on the far right side of the histogram, representing the current white point, but the bulk of the data ends further to the left. You want to set the white point to match the end of that data.

4 Drag the right (white) triangle toward the left to the point where the histogram indicates the lightest colors begin.

A photographer for more than 25 years, Jay Graham began his career designing and building custom homes. Today, Graham has clients in the advertising, architectural, editorial, and travel industries.

See Jay Graham's portfolio on the web at jaygraham.com.

Pro photo workflow

Good habits make all the difference

A sensible workflow and good work habits will keep you enthused about digital photography, help your images shine—and save you from the night terrors of losing work you never backed up. Here's an outline of the basic workflow for digital images from a professional photographer with more than 25 years' experience. To help you get the most from the images you shoot, Jay Graham offers guidelines for setting up your camera, creating a basic color workflow, selecting file formats, organizing images, and showing off your work.

Graham uses Adobe Photoshop Lightroom® to organize thousands of images.

"The biggest complaint from people is they've lost their image. Where is it? What does it look like?" says Graham. "So naming is important."

Start out right by setting up your camera preferences

If your camera has the option, it's generally best to shoot in its camera raw file format, which captures all the image information you need. With one camera raw photo, says Graham, "you can go from daylight to an indoor tungsten image without degradation" when it's reproduced. If it makes more sense to shoot in JPEG for your project, use fine compression and high resolution.

Start with the best material

Get all the data when you capture—at fine compression and high resolution. You can't go back later.

Organize your files

Name and catalogue your images as soon after downloading them as possible. "If the camera names files, eventually it resets and produces multiple files with the same name," says Graham. Use Adobe Photoshop Lightroom to rename, rank, and add metadata to the photos you plan to keep; cull those you don't.

Graham names his files by date (and possibly subject). He would store a series of photos taken Dec. 12, 2013 at Stinson Beach in a folder named "20131212_Stinson_01"; within the folder, he names each image incrementally, and each image has a unique filename. "That way, it lines up on the hard drive real easily," he says. Follow Windows naming conventions to keep filenames usable on non-Macintosh platforms (32 characters maximum; only numbers, letters, underscores, and hyphens).

Convert raw images to Adobe Camera Raw

It may be best to convert all your camera raw images to the DNG format. Unlike many cameras' proprietary raw formats, this open-source format can be read by any device.

Keep a master image

Save your master in PSD, TIFF, or DNG format, not JPEG. Each time a JPEG is re-edited and saved, compression is reapplied, and the image quality degrades.

Show off to clients and friends

When you prepare your work for delivery, choose the appropriate color file for the destination. Convert the image to that profile, rather than assigning the profile. sRGB is generally best for viewing electronically or for printing from most online printing services. Adobe 1998 or Colormatch are the best profiles to use for RGB images destined for traditionally printed material such as brochures. Adobe 1998 or ProPhoto RGB are best for printing with inkjet printers. Use 72 dpi for electronic viewing and 180 dpi or higher for printing.

Back up your images

You've devoted a lot of time and effort to your images: don't lose them. Because the lifespan of CDs and DVDs is uncertain, it's best to back up to an external hard drive (or drives!), ideally set to back up automatically. "The question is not if your [internal] hard drive is going to crash," says Graham, reciting a common adage. "It's when."

As you drag, the third Input Levels value (beneath the histogram graph) changes, and so does the image itself.

5   Pull the middle (gray) triangle a little bit to the right to slightly darken the midtones. We moved it to a value of .90.

Editing the saturation in Camera Raw

The Levels adjustments helped significantly, but our bride looks a little sunburned. You'll adjust the saturation in Camera Raw to even out her skin tone.

1   Double-click the 12B_Start layer thumbnail to open the Smart Object in Camera Raw.

2   Click the HSL/Grayscale button (▦) to display that panel.

3   Click the Saturation tab.

4   Move the following sliders to reduce the amount of red in the skin:

- Reduce Reds to -**2**.

- Reduce Oranges to -**10**.

- Reduce Magentas to -**3**.

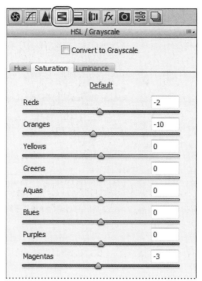

5   Click OK to return to Photoshop.

Using the healing brush tools to remove blemishes

Now you're ready to give the model's face some focused attention. You'll use the Healing Brush and Spot Healing Brush tools to heal blemishes, smooth the skin, remove red veins from the eyes, and even hide the nose jewelry.

1   In the Layers panel, select the 12B_Start layer. Then, choose Duplicate Layer from the Layers panel menu.

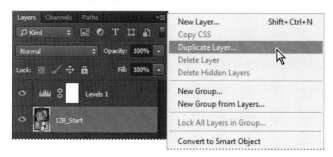

2 Name the new layer **Corrections**, and click OK.

Working on a duplicate layer preserves the original pixels so you can make changes later. You can't make changes using the healing brush tools on a Smart Object, so first you'll rasterize the layer.

3 Choose Layer > Smart Objects > Rasterize.

4 Zoom in on the model's face so that you can see it clearly.

5 Select the Spot Healing Brush tool (✐).

6 In the options bar, select the following settings:

- Brush size: **35** px

- Mode: Normal

- Type: Content-Aware

7 With the Spot Healing Brush tool, brush out the nose jewelry. A single click may be enough.

Because you've selected Content-Aware in the options bar, the Spot Healing Brush tool replaces the nose stud with skin that is similar to that around it.

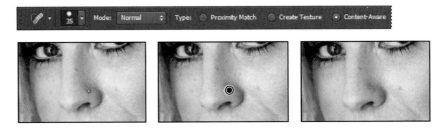

8 Paint over fine lines around the eyes and mouth. You can also brush away freckles and moles on her face, neck, arms, and chest. Experiment with simply clicking, using very short strokes, and creating longer brush strokes. You can also experiment with different settings. For example, to soften the lines around the mouth, we selected Proximity Match in the options bar and the Lighten blending mode. Remove obtrusive or distracting lines and blemishes, but leave enough that the face retains its character.

The Healing Brush tool may be a better option for larger blemishes. With the Healing Brush tool, you have more control over the pixels Photoshop samples.

9 Select the Healing Brush tool (✐), hidden under the Spot Healing Brush tool (✐). Select a brush with a size of **45** pixels and a hardness of **100%**.

10 Alt-click (Windows) or Option-click (Mac OS) an area on her cheek to create the sampling source.

11 Brush over the large mole on her cheek to replace it with the color you sampled. You'll smooth out the texture later.

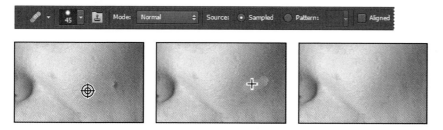

12 Use the Healing Brush tool to heal any larger blemishes that remain.

13 Choose File > Save to save your work so far.

Enhancing an image using the Dodge and Sponge tools

You'll use the Sponge and Dodge tools to brighten the eyes and lips.

1 Select the Sponge tool (⬤), hidden under the Dodge tool (🔍). In the options bar, make sure Vibrance is selected, and then select the following settings:

- Brush size: **35** px
- Brush hardness: **0%**
- Mode: Saturate
- Flow: **50%**

2 Move the Sponge tool over the irises in the eyes to increase their saturation.

3 Change the brush size to **70** px and the flow to **10%**. Then brush the Sponge tool over the lips to saturate them.

You can use the Sponge tool to desaturate color, too. You'll reduce the red in the corner of the eye.

4 Change the brush size to **45** px, and the flow to **50%**. Then choose Desaturate from the Mode menu in the options bar.

5 Brush over the corner of the eye to reduce the red.

6 Select the Dodge tool (🔍), hidden beneath the Sponge tool.

7 In the options bar, change the brush size to **60** px and the Exposure to **10%**. Choose Highlights from the Range menu.

8 Brush the Dodge tool over the eyes—the whites and the irises—to brighten them.

9 With the Dodge tool still selected, select Shadows from the Range menu in the options bar.

10 Use the Dodge tool to lighten the shadow area above the eyes and the areas around the irises to bring out the color.

Adjusting skin tones

In Photoshop, you can select a color range that targets skin tones so that it's easier to adjust the levels and color tone of skin without affecting the entire image. The skin tone color range selects other areas of the image with a similar color, but if you're making slight adjustments, this is usually acceptable.

1 Choose Select > Color Range.

2 In the Color Range dialog box, choose Skin Tones from the Select menu.

The preview shows that much of the image has been selected.

3 Select Detect Faces.

The preview in the selection changes. Now the face, hair highlights, and lighter areas of the dress are selected.

4 Decrease the Fuzziness slider to **10** to refine the selection. Then click OK.

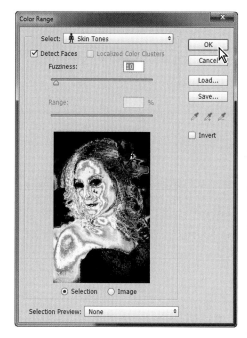 

The selection appears on the image itself as animated dotted lines (sometimes called *marching ants*). You'll apply a Curves adjustment layer to the selection to reduce the overall red in the skin tone of the image.

5 Click the Curves icon in the Adjustments panel.

Photoshop adds a Curves adjustment layer above the Corrections layer.

6　Choose Red from the color channel menu in the Properties panel. Then click in the middle of the graph, and pull the curve down very slightly. The selected areas become less red. Be careful not to pull the curve down too far, or a green cast will appear. You can see the difference you've made by clicking the Toggle Layer Visibility button.

Because you selected the skin tones before applying the Curves adjustment layer, the skin color shifts but the background is unchanged. The adjustment affects slightly more of the image than the skin itself, but the effect blends well and is subtle.

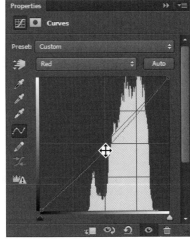

Applying surface blur

You're almost done with the model. As a finishing touch, you'll apply the Surface Blur filter to give her a smooth appearance.

1　Select the Corrections layer, and choose Layer > Duplicate Layer. Name the layer **Surface Blur**, and click OK in the Duplicate Layer dialog box.

2　With the Surface Blur layer selected, choose Filter > Blur > Surface Blur.

3　In the Surface Blur dialog box, leave the Radius at 5 pixels, and move the Threshold to **10** levels. Then click OK.

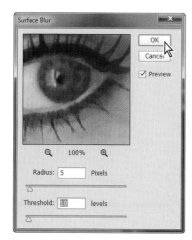

The Surface Blur filter has left the model looking a little glassy. You'll reduce its effect by reducing the opacity of the blur.

4   With the Surface Blur layer selected, change the Opacity to **40%** in the Layers panel.

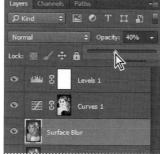

She looks more realistic now, but you can target the surface blur more precisely using the Eraser tool.

5   Select the Eraser tool (🖎). In the options bar, select a brush between **10** and **50** pixels, with **10**% hardness. Set the opacity to **90**%.

6   Brush over the eyes, eyebrows, the defining lines of the nose, and the detail in the dress. You're erasing part of the blurred layer to let the sharper layer below show through in these areas.

7   Zoom out so you can see the entire image.

8   Save your work.

9   Choose Layer > Flatten Image to flatten the layers and reduce the image size.

10 Save the image again, and then close it.

You've taken advantage of features in both Camera Raw and Photoshop to help this bride look her best. As you've seen, you can move between Photoshop and Camera Raw to perform different tasks as you enhance and improve an image.

Extra credit

Painting with Light : Using Camera Raw as a Filter

In addition to opening files in Camera Raw to start the editing process, you can apply Camera Raw settings as a filter to any file in Photoshop. You'll use Camera Raw as a filter to make adjustments to this still-life image. First, you'll convert the image to a Smart Object so you can use Camera Raw as a Smart Filter, applying changes without affecting the original file.

1   In Photoshop, choose File > Open. Navigate to the Lessons/Lesson12 folder, and double-click the Fruit.jpg file to open it.

2   Choose Filter > Convert for Smart Filters. Click OK in the informational dialog box.

3   Select Filter > Camera Raw Filter. The image opens in Camera Raw.

You converted the image to a Smart Object so you can apply Camera Raw as a Smart Filter. You can also apply Camera Raw as a standard filter, but then you can't return to adjust your settings or hide the adjustments in your image file.

4   Select the Adjustment Brush in the toolbar.

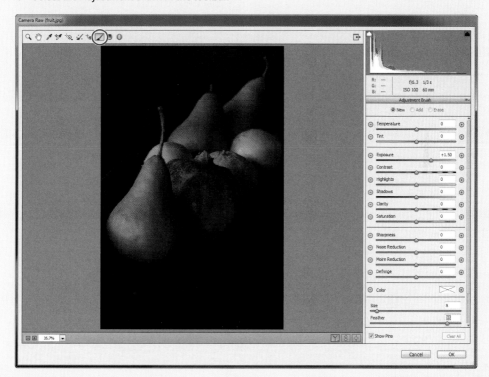

Continues on next page

Extra credit (continued)

With the Adjustment Brush tool in Camera Raw, you can apply Exposure, Brightness, Clarity, and other adjustments to specific areas of a photo by painting them directly onto those areas. The Graduated Filter tool is similar, but it applies the same types of adjustments gradually across a region of the photo that you define.

5　In the Adjustment Brush panel, change Exposure to **+1.50**. Then, at the bottom of the panel, change Size to **8** and Feather to **85**.

6　Brush the fruit where you want to increase the exposure, which reveals more of the color. Continue brushing until the fruit is too bright.

 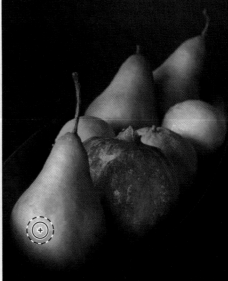

7　Once you've brushed all the fruit, reduce the Exposure setting in the Adjustment Brush panel so the image looks more realistic.

8　To see how your changes have affected the image in Camera Raw, click the Before/After Views button at the bottom of the image window, and choose Before/After Left/Right from the pop-up menu.

9　When you're satisfied with the changes, click OK.

Photoshop displays the image. In the Layers panel, the Camera Raw filter is listed beneath the layer name. You can toggle the visibility icon for the Camera Raw filter to see the image before and after the adjustment.

Review questions

1 What happens to camera raw images when you edit them in Camera Raw?

2 What is the advantage of the Adobe Digital Negative (DNG) file format?

3 How can you apply the same settings to multiple images in Camera Raw?

4 How can you apply Camera Raw as a filter?

Review answers

1 A camera raw file contains unprocessed picture data from a digital camera's image sensor. Camera raw files give photographers control over interpreting the image data, rather than letting the camera make the adjustments and conversions. When you edit the image in Camera Raw, it preserves the original raw file data. This way, you can edit the image as you desire, export it, and keep the original intact for future use or other adjustments.

2 The Adobe Digital Negative (DNG) file format contains the raw image data from a digital camera as well as metadata that defines what the image data means. DNG is an industry-wide standard for camera raw image data that helps photographers manage proprietary camera raw file formats and provides a compatible archival format.

3 To apply the same settings to multiple images in Camera Raw, select the images in the filmstrip, and click Synchronize. Then select the settings you want to apply, and click OK.

4 To apply Camera Raw as a filter, choose Filter > Camera Raw Filter in Photoshop. Make the changes you want to make in Camera Raw, and then click OK. If you want to be able to edit the changes later, apply Camera Raw as a Smart Filter.

13 PREPARING FILES FOR THE WEB

Lesson overview

In this lesson, you'll learn how to do the following:

- Create & stylize a button for a website.

- Use layer groups.

- Optimize images for the web and make good compression choices.

- Record an action to automate a series of steps.

- Play an action to affect multiple images.

- Save assets using Adobe Generator.

- Evaluate assets and revise them with Generator.

 This lesson will take about an hour to complete. Download the Lesson13 project files from the Lesson & Update Files tab on your Account page at www.peachpit.com, if you haven't already done so. As you work on this lesson, you'll preserve the start files. If you need to restore the start files, download them from your Account page.

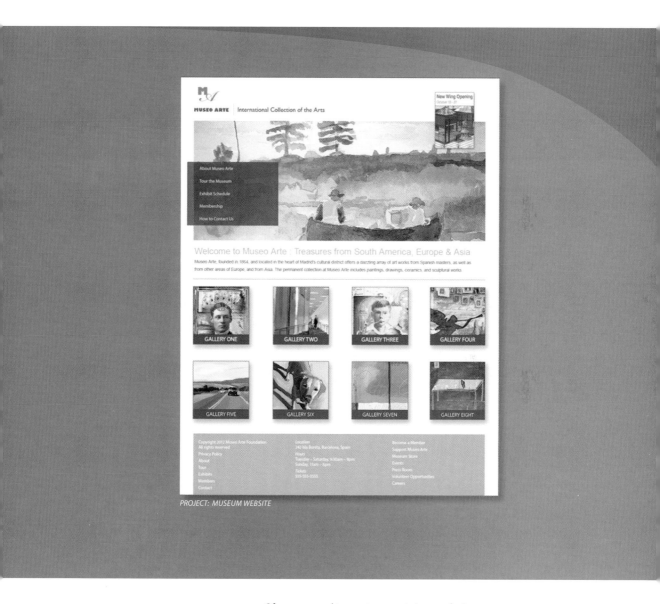

PROJECT: MUSEUM WEBSITE

Often, you need to create separate images for buttons or other objects in a website. Adobe Generator, built into Photoshop, makes it easy to save layers and layer groups as separate image files.

Getting started

In this lesson, you will build buttons for the home page of a Spanish art museum's website, and then generate appropriate graphics files for each button. You'll use layer groups to assemble the buttons, and actions to prepare a set of images for use as a second group of buttons. First, you'll view the final web design.

1   Start Photoshop, and then immediately hold down Ctrl+Alt+Shift (Windows) or Command+Option+Shift (Mac OS) to restore the default preferences. (See "Restoring default preferences" on page 4.)

2   When prompted, click Yes to delete the Adobe Photoshop Settings file.

3   Choose File > Browse In Bridge.

● **Note:** If Bridge isn't installed, you'll be prompted to install it when you choose Browse In Bridge. For more information, see page 3.

4   In Bridge, click Lessons in the Favorites panel. Double-click the Lesson13 folder in the Content panel.

5   View the 13End.psd file in Bridge.

There are eight buttons at the bottom of the page, arranged in two rows. You'll transform images into buttons for the top row, and use an action to prepare the buttons for the second row.

6   Double-click the 13Start.psd thumbnail to open the file in Photoshop. Click OK if you see the Missing Profile dialog box.

7   Choose File > Save As, and rename the file **13Working.psd**. Click OK in the Photoshop Format Options dialog box.

Using layer groups to create button graphics

Layer groups make it easier to organize and work with layers in complex images, especially when there are sets of layers that work together. You'll use layer groups to assemble the layers that make up each button, and they'll come in handy when you save assets using Adobe Generator later.

Four images have been arranged in the start file to serve as the basis for buttons. You'll add a label to each, identifying the gallery it represents, and then add a drop shadow and a stroke.

Creating the first button

You'll design the first button, and then duplicate layers and edit them to quickly apply the same treatment to the other three. First, you'll change the units of measurement to pixels.

1 Choose Edit > Preferences > Units & Rulers (Windows) or Photoshop > Preferences > Units & Rulers (Mac OS). In the Units area of the dialog box, choose Pixels from the Rulers menu, and then click OK.

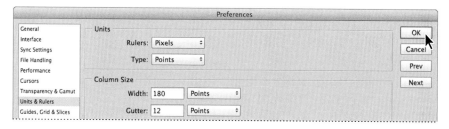

2 Choose View > Snap to turn off snapping. (A check mark appears next to Snap when it's enabled.)

3 Choose Window > Info to open the Info panel.

The Info panel displays information dynamically as you move the pointer or make selections. Which information it displays depends on the tool that is selected. You'll use it to determine the position of the ruler guide (based on the Y coordinate) and the size of an area you select (based on the width and height). It's also very handy for seeing the RGB and CMYK values of colors in an image.

4 Choose View > Rulers. Then drag a ruler guide down until the Y value reported in the Info panel is 795 pixels.

You'll use this guide to draw a band across the bottom of the image for the label.

5 Zoom in on the first image, the image of the man. Then select Image 1 in the Layers panel.

You'll use this image to design the first button.

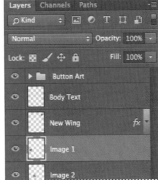

6 Click the New Layer button (◻) at the bottom of the Layers panel. The new layer is named Layer 13 and appears directly above the Image 1 layer. Rename it **band**.

7 Select the Rectangular Marquee tool (▢) in the Tools panel. Then, drag a selection across the bottom of the image, as indicated by the guides. The selection should be 180 pixels wide and 32 pixels high.

8 Choose Edit > Fill. In the Fill dialog box, choose Color from the Use menu, and then, in the Color Picker, select a dark blue (R=**25**, G=**72**, B=**121**). Click OK to apply the fill.

A dark blue band appears at the bottom of the image, where you made your selection. You'll add text to it next.

9 Choose Select > Deselect.

10 Select the Horizontal Type tool, and select the following settings in the options bar:

- Font Family: Myriad Pro
- Font Style: Regular
- Font Size: **18** pt
- Anti-aliasing: Strong
- Alignment: Center
- Color: White

11 Click in the center of the blue band, and type **GALLERY ONE**. Use the Move tool to adjust the position of the type layer if necessary.

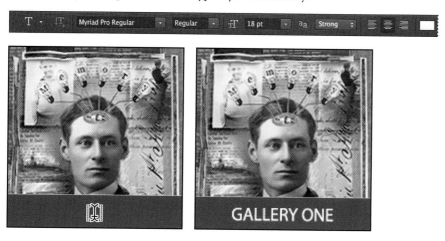

The label is in place. Now you'll add a drop shadow and stroke to improve the appearance of the button.

12 Select the Image 1 layer in the Layers panel. Then, click the Add Layer Style button (*fx*) at the bottom of the Layers panel, and choose Drop Shadow.

13 In the Layer Style dialog box, change the following settings in the Structure area:

- Opacity: **27**%

- Distance: **9** px

- Spread: **19**%

- Size: **18** px

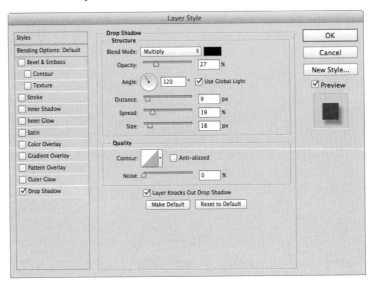

● **Note:** Be sure to click the word Stroke. If you click only the check box, Photoshop applies the layer style with its default settings but you won't see the options.

14 With the Layer Style dialog box still open, select Stroke on the left, and apply the following settings:

- Size: **1** px

- Position: Inside

- Color: Click the color swatch to open the Color Picker. Then click the blue band to sample its color, and click OK to select it.

15 Click OK to apply both layer styles.

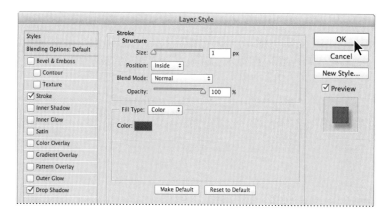

The button looks good. Now you'll assemble all of its layers into a single group.

16 Select the GALLERY ONE, band, and Image 1 layers in the Layers panel, and choose Layer > Group Layers.

Photoshop creates a group named Group 1.

17 Double-click the Group 1 layer group, and rename it **Gallery 1**. Then expand the group. The layers you selected are indented, indicating they're part of that group.

18 Choose File > Save.

Duplicating buttons

You've designed the initial button. You could go through all those steps again to create each of the other buttons, but it will be faster to duplicate layers or even layer groups, and then edit them as necessary.

1   Click the Create A New Group button at the bottom of the Layers panel. Name the group Gallery 2.

2   Drag Image 2 into the Gallery 2 layer group, and then press Alt or Option as you drag the Effects line or the fx symbol from Image 1 to Image 2.

The drop shadow and stroke you applied to Image 1 are applied to both images now.

3   Select the band layer, and choose Duplicate Layer from the Layers panel menu. Name it **band 2**, and drag it into the Gallery 2 layer group above the Image 2 layer.

▶ **Tip:** You can also duplicate layers by dragging a layer down to the New Layer icon in the Layers panel.

4   Select the Move tool, and then, in the image window, drag the duplicate band layer from the first image to the second one.

5   Select the GALLERY ONE layer, and choose Duplicate Layer from the Layers panel menu. Name the duplicate layer **GALLERY TWO**, and drag it into the Gallery 2 layer group above the band 2 layer.

▶ **Tip:** Press the Shift key as you move the type to drag it in a straight line.

6   Use the Move tool to drag the duplicate type from the first image to the band on the second image. Then select the Horizontal Type tool, and change the type to **GALLERY TWO**.

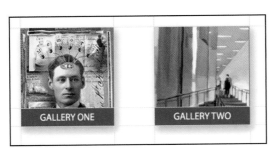 

The second button is done. You'll create the third button by duplicating the entire layer group and making the necessary changes.

7   Select the Gallery 2 layer group, and choose Duplicate Group from the Layers panel menu. Rename the group **Gallery 3**.

8   Delete the Image 2 layer in the Gallery 3 layer group, and then drag Image 3 into the group, below the band 2 layer.

9   Press Alt or Option as you drag the layer effects from the Image 2 layer (in the Gallery 2 group) onto the Image 3 layer to copy them.

10 In the Gallery 3 group, rename the band 2 layer **band 3**, and select it. Then, in the image window, drag the blue band from the second image to the third image.

11 Rename the type layer in the Gallery 3 group **GALLERY THREE**. Then select the layer, and drag the duplicate type from the second image to the blue band on the third image. Finally, select the Horizontal Type tool, and change the type to **GALLERY THREE**.

12 Repeat steps 1-6 or steps 7-11 to copy the design elements for the fourth button.

13 Save the file, and then close it.

Automating a multistep task

An *action* is a set of one or more commands that you record and then play back to apply to a single file or a batch of files. In this exercise, you'll create an action to prepare a set of images to serve as buttons for additional galleries on the web page you're designing.

▶ **Tip:** You can create conditional actions that change their behavior based on criteria you define.

Recording an action

You'll start by recording an action that resizes an image, changes its canvas size, and adds layer styles, so that the additional buttons match the ones you've already created. You use the Actions panel to record, play, edit, and delete individual actions. You also use the Actions panel to save and load action files.

There are four images in the Buttons folder that will serve as the basis for new gallery buttons on your website. The images are large, so the first thing you'll need to do is resize them to match the existing buttons. You'll perform each of the steps on the Gallery5.jpg file as you record the action. You'll then play the action to make the same changes on the other images in the folder automatically.

1   Choose File > Open, and navigate to the Lesson13/Buttons folder. Double-click the Gallery5.jpg file to open it in Photoshop.

2   Choose Window > Actions to open the Actions panel. Close the Default actions folder to keep the Actions panel tidy.

3   Click the Create New Set button (📁) at the bottom of the Actions panel. In the New Set dialog box, name the set **Buttons**.

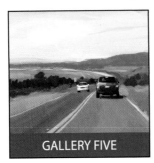

Photoshop comes with several pre-recorded actions, all in the Default Actions set. You can use actions sets to organize your actions so that it's easier to find the one you want.

4   Click the Create New Action button (🔖) at the bottom of the Layers panel. Name the action **Resizing and Styling Images**, and click Record.

It's a good idea to name actions in a way that makes it clear what the actions do so you can find them easily later.

Don't let the fact that you're recording rush you. Take all the time you need to do the procedure accurately. The speed at which you work has no effect on the amount of time required to play a recorded action.

You'll start by resizing and sharpening the image.

5 Choose Image > Image Size. Choose Pixels from the Units menu for the Width, and then change the Width to **180**. By default, the Width and Height values are linked. Confirm that the Height changes to **180** pixels, too. Then click OK.

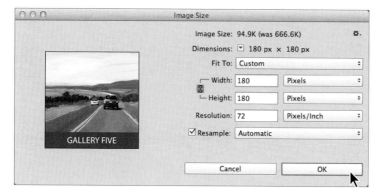

6 Choose Filter > Sharpen > Smart Sharpen, apply the following settings, and click OK:

- Amount: **100**%

- Radius: **1** px

You need to make some additional changes to the image that you can't make as long as the Background layer is locked. You'll convert it to a regular layer.

7 Double-click the Background layer name in the Layers panel. In the New Layer dialog box, name the layer **Button**, and click OK.

When you rename a Background layer, you're converting it to a regular layer, so Photoshop displays the New Layer dialog box. But the new layer replaces the Background layer; Photoshop doesn't add a layer to the image.

Now that you've converted the Background layer, you can change the canvas size and add layer styles.

8 Choose Image > Canvas Size, and do the following:

- Make sure the canvas is measured in pixels.

- Change the Width to **220** pixels and the Height to **220** pixels.

- Click the center square in the anchor area to ensure the canvas is extended evenly on all sides.

- Click OK.

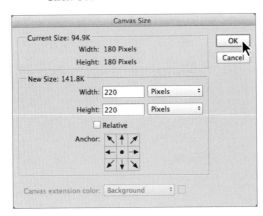 

9 Choose Layer > Layer Style > Drop Shadow.

10 In the Layer Style dialog box, change the following settings:

- Opacity: **27**%

- Angle: **120**°

- Distance: **9** px

- Spread: **19**%

- Size: **18** px

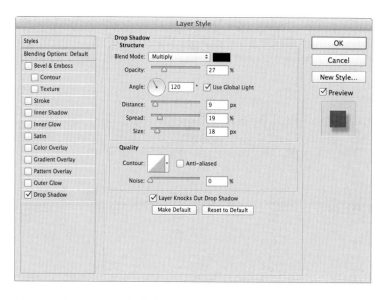

11 With the Layer Style dialog box still open, select Stroke on the left, and apply the following settings:

- Size: **1** px

- Position: Inside

- Color: Click the color swatch to open the Color Picker. Then click the blue band to sample its color, and click OK to select it.

12 Click OK to apply both layer styles.

13 Choose File > Save As, choose Photoshop for the Format, and click Save. Then close the file.

14 Click the Stop Recording button at the bottom of the Actions panel.

● **Note:** Be sure to click the word Stroke. If you click only the check box, Photoshop applies the layer style with its default settings but you won't see the options.

The action you just recorded (Resizing and Styling Images) is now saved in the Buttons set in the Actions panel. Click the arrows to expand different sets of steps. You can examine each recorded step and the specific selections you made.

Batch-playing an action

Applying actions is a timesaving process for performing routine tasks on files, but you can streamline your work even further by applying actions to multiple files at once. You'll apply the action you've created to the three remaining images.

1   Choose File > Open, and navigate to the Lesson13/Buttons folder. Shift-select the Gallery6.jpg, Gallery7.jpg, and Gallery8.jpg files, and click Open.

2   Choose File > Automate > Batch.

3   In the Batch dialog box, do the following:

   •   Confirm that Buttons is chosen in the Set menu and Resizing and Styling Images—the action you just created—is chosen in the Action menu.

   •   Choose Opened Files from the Source menu.

   •   Make sure None is chosen for the Destination.

   •   Click OK.

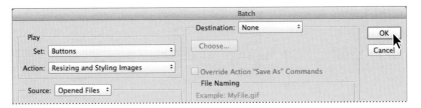

Photoshop plays the action, applying its steps to all the files that are open. You can also apply an action to an entire folder of images without opening them.

Because you saved the file and closed it while you were recording the action, Photoshop saves each of the images as a PSD file in its original folder, and then closes the file.

Placing Files in Photoshop

The four additional button images are ready to be placed into the design. You probably noticed that each already has a blue band with its gallery name included in the image, so you don't need to perform those steps. They're ready to go.

1   Choose File > Open, navigate to the Lesson13 folder, and double-click the 13Working.psd file to open it in Photoshop.

2   in the Layers panel, select a layer group name or the logo layer. New layers are added above the selected layer; don't add them to the Gallery 4 layer group.

3 Choose File > Place Embedded.

You'll place these files as embedded Smart Objects. Because they're embedded, the entire image is included in the Photoshop file.

4 In the Place Embedded dialog box, navigate to the Lesson13/Buttons folder, and double-click the Gallery5.psd file.

Photoshop places the Gallery5.psd file in the center of the 13Working.psd file. But that's not where you want it to go. You'll move it.

5 Drag the image into position below the Gallery One button. Use the guides to place the image. When it's in position, press Enter or Return to commit the change.

6 Repeat steps 2–4 to place the Gallery6.psd, Gallery7.psd, and Gallery8.psd files so that they line up below the Gallery Two, Gallery Three, and Gallery Four buttons.

7 Choose File > Save to save your work so far.

Saving assets with Adobe Generator

When you're preparing files for a website, often you need to create separate image files for buttons and other content. With Adobe Generator, you can easily generate a JPEG, PNG, or GIF image from the contents of a layer or layer group in a Photoshop file—simply by renaming the layer or layer group. You can append the appropriate file extension to save an image with default settings, but you can also specify quality and size parameters for the image, all determined by how you name it.

Renaming layers and layer groups

You'll generate assets from the 13Working.psd file for a website. Initially, you'll save only one of the buttons, so you can preview the generated image and see if it meets your needs.

1   Choose File > Generate > Image Assets.

Once you've enabled Generator, it continues to be enabled for the current document until you disable it again. It's a document-specific setting, which means it can be enabled for one PSD file you're working in but not for another.

● **Note:** Your layers may be in a different order, depending on how you copied the gallery folders and placed the gallery files. Any layer order is fine.

2   In the Layers panel, double-click the Gallery 1 layer group name, and rename it **gallery1.jpg5**.

The JPG extension specifies that the resulting asset should be a JPEG file. The 5 specifies a quality of 50%. (See the sidebar "Specifying quality and size parameters in generated assets" for more information.)

3   Rename the New Wing layer so that its new name is **new-wing.gif**.

When you're naming layers and layer groups to generate assets, it's a good idea to use names that don't include spaces or special characters.

4   Rename the Logo layer **logo.jpg5**.

You won't see any changes in the Photoshop file itself when you generate assets. But Adobe Generator has saved the renamed layer or layer group in the specified format to a subfolder alongside the source PSD file. In this case, the assets you've generated have been saved to the Lesson13/13Working-assets folder.

If you generate an asset from a layer group, the group is flattened to produce the resulting image.

Evaluating and revising generated assets

Look at the assets that were generated to ensure they meet your needs. You can quickly evaluate them using Bridge.

1   Choose File > Browse In Bridge to open Adobe Bridge.

2   Navigate to the Lesson13/13Working-assets folder.

There are three images in the folder: gallery1.jpg, logo.jpg, and new-wing.gif. Each of the images is surrounded by a white border. That's fine for the buttons and the logo, because they're on a white background on the site. But the New Wing artwork overlaps another image, so the white border won't work. Additionally, the images all appear pixelated. The file sizes are currently very small, so there's room to increase the file resolutions. You'll return to Photoshop and generate the assets again, using different settings.

First, you'll increase the quality of the gallery button and logo files from 50% to 100%.

3   In Photoshop, rename the gallery1.jpg5 layer group **gallery1.jpg10**. Then rename the logo.jpg5 layer **logo.jpg10**.

Next, you'll try a different format for the New Wing image. GIF images are saved with a white border, but PNG files have a semitransparent background and shadows.

4   Rename the new-wing.gif layer **new-wing.png**.

5   Return to Bridge.

The images look better. Their files sizes are much larger, but they're still reasonable for use on the web. These settings should work.

6 Return to Photoshop, and rename each of
   the gallery layer groups and the layers for
   galleries 5-8, appending **.jpg10** to each one
   to generate the rest of the buttons.

Generating assets is as simple as renaming layers and layer groups, but the renaming
process can still be tedious if you have a large number of layers to rename. To reduce
possible frustration, test your settings on a single layer or layer group first, before
renaming them all.

Generating multiple image sizes and formats from the same layer

If you're preparing images for print, you know how people will view them, and you
can be sure that one size and format will work well. However, the web is a very different environment. People view websites on a variety of devices, from cellphones
to desktop computers, and webmasters construct their sites in different ways. You
often need to provide the same image in multiple sizes and formats, so that the
appropriate one is available for any particular viewing environment.

You can use Adobe Generator to create multiple versions of a single asset by adding
image filenames to the layer or layer group name. You need only separate them with
a comma for Generator to recognize that you want to generate multiple assets.

For this project, you'll generate multiple versions of the logo so that it can be used
on various sites that promote the museum.

1 Expand the Layers panel to make it wider so that you can see a long layer name.

2 Rename the logo.jpg10 layer with the following name: **300% logo.jpg8, 100%
   logo.gif, 50% logo.png24**.

Photoshop generates a logo.jpg file that is an 80% quality JPEG image scaled to
300%, a logo.gif file that is a GIF image scaled to 100%, and a logo.png file that is a
24-bit PNG image scaled to 50%.

The first image is a larger version of the logo that will work for a full-page web
banner. Because the original logo layer is a Smart Object, it can be resized to 300%
without losing resolution.

Previewing images in a browser

A web browser displays all image files at 72 dpi. You can compare the logo assets you generated to see how they have been scaled.

1 Open a web browser.

2 Choose File > Open File, and then navigate to the Lesson13/13Working-assets folder.

3 Double-click the logo.jpg file to open it.

The logo is three times its original size, but kept the same resolution.

4 Open the logo.png file.

It's half the size it was in the Photoshop file.

You've successfully generated the images you need to build the website.

5 Return to Photoshop. Choose File > Generate > Image Assets.

The assets you generated are unaffected, but Generator is disabled.

6 Save the file, and then close it.

Specifying quality and size parameters in generated assets

When you rename a layer or layer group with just the appended file extension (.jpg, .png, or .gif), Generator uses default settings to create the assets. JPEG files are generated at 90% quality, PNG assets are generated as 32-bit images, and GIF assets include basic alpha transparency.

To generate assets with different parameters, add more information to the name.

Specifying the quality of an asset

- To specify the quality of a JPEG asset, add a number from 1 to 10 or a percentage from 1 to 100% as a suffix. (For example, .jpg6 and .jpg60% both create JPEG files at 60% quality.)

- To specify whether a PNG file is an 8-bit, 24-bit, or 32-bit file, add the number as a suffix. (Gallery1.png32 generates a 32-bit PNG file.)

- Quality parameters are not available for GIF images.

Specifying the image size

To specify the output image size, add a prefix, followed by a space, before the asset name. You can specify a percentage or an absolute size. The default unit is pixels; specify other units—in, cm, or mm—in the name. You can mix units as well. The same naming method applies for JPEG, PNG, and GIF images.

If your asset is named Gallery1, for example, you could use the following prefixes:

- 200% Gallery1.jpg scales the image to 200%.

- 300 x 200 Gallery1.png scales the image to 300 x 200 pixels.

- 10in x 200mm Gallery1.gif scales the image to 10 inches by 200 millimeters.

Extra credit

Copying layer properties for CSS

In Photoshop, you can generate cascading style sheet (CSS) properties from shape and text layers without writing code. For shape layers, the Copy CSS feature captures size, location, fill color (including gradients), stroke color, and drop shadows created with layer styles. For text layers, it also captures font family, font size, font weight, line height, underline, strikethrough, superscript, subscript, and text alignment. You'll generate CSS properties from the Flyer.psd file and paste them into the site's HTML file in Adobe Dreamweaver®.

1 In Photoshop, navigate to the Lesson13/Extra_Credit folder, and open the Flyer.psd file.

2 Select the new_wing layer, and choose Layer > Copy CSS.

Photoshop copies the CSS properties for the new_wing layer to the clipboard.

3 Open Dreamweaver, and open the New-Wing_Start.html file (in the Lesson13/Extra_Credit folder).

4 Choose File > Save As, and save the file as **New-Wing_Finished.html** in the Lesson13/Extra_ Credit folder.

5 In Dreamweaver, choose View > Code to see the source code, if it's not visible. Then select the entire comment between the <style> and </style> tags ("<! -- Paste your CSS code here -- >"), and choose Edit > Paste.

```
<style type="text/css">
<!-- Paste your CSS code here -->
</style>
```

```
<style type="text/css">

.new_wing {
    font-size: 0.436in;
    font-family: "Trajan Pro";
    color: rgb( 254, 242, 147 );
    text-align: center;
    -moz-transform: matrix( 1.43355542890517, 0, 0, 1.43355542890517, 0, 0);
    -webkit-transform: matrix( 1.43355542890517, 0, 0, 1.43355542890517, 0, 0);
    text-shadow: 0.021in 0.036in 0.069444444444444in rgb( 0, 0, 0 );
    position: absolute;
    left: 1.051in;
    top: 3.88in;
    height: 0.625in;
    z-index: 3;
}

</style>
```

Continues on next page

Extra credit (continued)

The CSS code Photoshop copied is pasted into your Dreamweaver file. Not all of the boilerplate code may be necessary for a website. In this case, you'll delete some lines you don't need.

6 Delete the lines that specify position, left, top, and height.

7 In Photoshop, select the info layer, and choose Layer > Copy CSS.

8 In Dreamweaver, click beneath the close brace (}) that follows the CSS code you pasted from the new_wing layer, and then choose Edit > Paste to add the CSS code from the info layer.

```
info {
  font-size: 0.222in;
  font-family: "Myriad Pro";
  color: rgb( 254, 242, 146 );
  line-height: 1.752;
  text-align: center;
  position: absolute;
  left: 1.848in;
  top: 4.589in;
  height: 0.611in;
  z-index: 2;
}
```

9 Delete the lines that specify position, left, top, and height. Then, choose File > Save to save the changes to the HTML file.

10 Click the Preview/Debug In Browser button, and then choose a browser.

11 Preview the website. Notice that the text, font size, color, and even the drop shadow were copied from Photoshop.

It's a good idea to preview a website in multiple browsers, as results may vary. You may want to edit the CSS code to specify type size and position, for example.

Review questions

1   What is a layer group?

2   What is an action? How do you create one?

3   How can you generate assets from layers and layer groups in Photoshop?

Review answers

1   A layer group is a group of layers. Layer groups make it easier to organize and work with layers in complex images, especially when there are sets of layers that work together.

2   An action is a set of one or more commands that you record and then play back to apply to a single file or a batch of files. To create one, click the Create New Action button in the Actions panel, name the action, and click Record. Then perform the tasks you want to include in your action. When you've finished, click the Stop Recording button at the bottom of the Actions panel.

3   Use Adobe Generator to generate assets from layers and layer groups in Photoshop. First, enable Generator for your document by choosing File > Generate > Image Assets. Then rename layers or layer groups to append format file extensions (.jpg, .png, or .gif), as well as size and quality parameters.

14 PRODUCING AND PRINTING CONSISTENT COLOR

Lesson overview

In this lesson, you'll learn how to do the following:

- Define RGB, grayscale, and CMYK color spaces for displaying, editing, and printing images.

- Prepare an image for printing on a PostScript CMYK printer.

- Proof an image for printing.

- Save an image as a CMYK EPS file.

- Create and print a four-color separation.

- Understand how images are prepared for printing on presses.

 This lesson will take less than an hour to complete. Download the Lesson14 project files from the Lesson & Update Files tab on your Account page at www.peachpit.com, if you haven't already done so. As you work on this lesson, you'll preserve the start files. If you need to restore the start files, download them from your Account page.

PROJECT: TRAVEL POSTER

To produce consistent color, you define the color space in which to edit and display RGB images, and the color space in which to edit, display, and print CMYK images. This helps ensure a close match between onscreen and printed colors.

Preparing files for printing

● **Note:** One exercise in this lesson requires that your computer be connected to a PostScript color printer. If it isn't, you can do most, but not all, of the exercises.

After you've edited an image to get the effect you want, you probably want to share or publish it in some way. Ideally, you've been editing with the final output in mind and you've managed file resolution, colors, file size, and other aspects of the image accordingly. But as you prepare to output the file, you have another opportunity to make sure your image will look its best.

If you plan to print the image—whether you'll print it to your own inkjet printer or send it to a service provider for professional printing—you should perform the following tasks for the best results. (Many of these tasks are described in greater detail later in this lesson.)

- Determine the final destination. Whether you're printing the file yourself or sending it away, identify whether it will be printed to a PostScript printer, an inkjet printer, an offset press, or some other device. If you're working with a service provider, ask what format they prefer; often, they request a PDF file.

- Verify that the image resolution is appropriate. For professional printing, the resolution should be 300 dpi when the image size matches the intended output size. For an inkjet printer, you may get the best results with a 300-dpi image, but you might also get good results with a lower resolution; if you own the printer, you can experiment with settings to find what works best. Generally, 300 dpi is a safe resolution for most printed output.

- Do a "zoom test": Take a close look at the image. Zoom in to check and correct sharpness, color correction, noise, and other issues that can affect the final printed image quality.

- Allow for bleeds if you're sending an image for professional printing: If any color runs to the edge of the image, extend the canvas by ¼ inch on all sides to ensure that the color is properly printed even if the trim line is not exact. Your service provider can help you determine whether you have bleeds and how to prepare your file to ensure it prints correctly.

- Unless you're printing to an inkjet printer, convert the file to CMYK. Note: Some high-quality printers are inkjets; ask your service provider what color space your image should be saved in.

- Flatten the file to reduce its size for faster transfer and printing speeds. Make sure you keep an unflattened copy of the original so you can make changes or reuse the content later, if necessary. Photoshop prompts you to merge layers when you convert to CMYK.

- Soft-proof the image to ensure the colors will print as you expect them to.

Getting started

You'll prepare an 11"x17" travel poster for professional printing. The Photoshop file is quite large, because it contains several layers and has a resolution of 300 dpi, which is necessary for quality printing.

First, start Photoshop and restore its default preferences.

1   Start Photoshop, and then immediately hold down Ctrl+Alt+Shift (Windows) or Command+Option+Shift (Mac OS) to restore the default preferences. (See "Restoring default preferences" on page 4.)

2   When prompted, click Yes to delete the Adobe Photoshop Settings file.

3   Choose File > Open, navigate to the Lesson14 folder, and double-click the 14Start.psd file. Because the file is large, it may open slowly, depending on your system.

4   Choose File > Save As, navigate to the Lesson14 folder, and save the file as **14Working.psd**.

Performing a "zoom test"

When you've finished editing your image, take a few minutes to make sure everything is appropriate for your output device and that you haven't overlooked any potentially problematic details. Start with the image resolution.

1 Choose Image > Image Size.

2 Verify that the width and height are the final output size, and that the resolution is appropriate. For most printing, 300 dpi produces good results.

This image has a width of 11" and a height of 17", which is the final size of the poster. Its resolution is 300 dpi. The size and resolution are appropriate.

3 Click OK to close the dialog box.

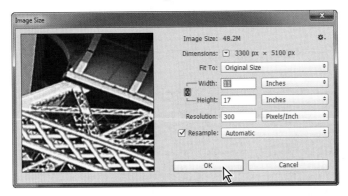

Next, you'll look closely at the image and correct any problems. When you prepare your own images for printing, zoom in and scroll to view the entire image closely.

4 Select the Zoom tool in the Tools panel, and zoom in on the photos in the lower third of the poster.

The photo of tourists is flat and a little muddy-looking.

5 Select the Tourists layer in the Layers panel, and then click the Curves icon in the Adjustments panel to add a Curves adjustment layer.

6 Click the Clip To Layer button () at the bottom of the Properties panel to create a clipping mask.

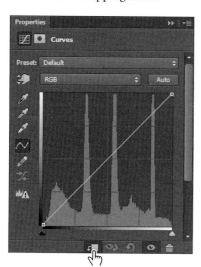

The clipping mask ensures that the adjustment layer affects only the layer directly below it in the Layers panel.

7 In the Properties panel, select the White Point eyedropper tool, and then click the light area of the building behind the tourists to brighten and correct the color in the image.

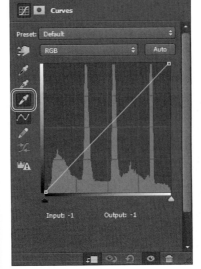

The image of tourists looks better. But the image of the statue appears flat and lacks contrast. You'll fix that with a Levels adjustment layer.

8 Select the Statue layer in the Layers panel, and then click the Levels icon in the Adjustments panel to add a Levels adjustment layer.

9 Click the Clip To Layer button at the bottom of the Properties panel to create a clipping mask, so that the adjustment layer affects only the Statue layer.

10 In the Properties panel, click the Calculate A More Accurate Histogram icon to refresh the histogram display.

 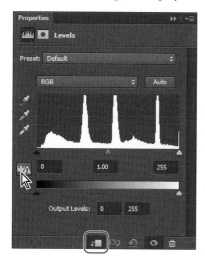

Cached histogram data displays more quickly, but is often less accurate. It's a good idea to refresh the histogram before you make edits based on information in it.

11 Move the sliders to punch up the image. We used the values 31, 1.60, 235.

 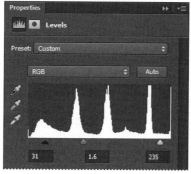

12 Save the file.

RGB model

A large percentage of the visible spectrum can be represented by mixing red, green, and blue (RGB) colored light in various proportions and intensities. Where the colors overlap, they create cyan, magenta, yellow, and white.

Because the RGB colors combine to create white, they are also called *additive* colors. Adding all colors together creates white—that is, all light is transmitted back to the eye. Additive colors are used for lighting, video, and monitors. Your monitor, for example, creates color by emitting light through red, green, and blue phosphors.

CMYK model

The CMYK model is based on the light-absorbing quality of ink printed on paper. As white light strikes translucent inks, part of the spectrum is absorbed, while other parts are reflected back to your eyes.

In theory, pure cyan (C), magenta (M), and yellow (Y) pigments should combine to absorb all color and produce black. For this reason, these colors are called *subtractive* colors. But because all printing inks contain some impurities, these three inks actually produce a muddy brown, and must be combined with black (K) ink to produce a true black. (K is used instead of B to avoid confusion with blue.) Combining these inks to reproduce color is called four-color process printing.

Identifying out-of-gamut colors

Colors on a monitor are displayed using combinations of red, green, and blue light (called RGB), while printed colors are typically created using a combination of four ink colors—cyan, magenta, yellow, and black (called CMYK). These four inks are called process colors because they are the standard inks used in the four-color printing process.

Most scanned photographs contain RGB colors within the CMYK gamut, so changing them to CMYK mode converts all the colors with relatively little substitution. Images that are created or altered digitally, however, often contain RGB colors that are outside the CMYK gamut—for example, neon-colored logos and lights.

Before you convert an image from RGB to CMYK, you can preview the CMYK color values while still in RGB mode.

1　Choose View > Gamut Warning to see out-of-gamut colors. Photoshop builds a color-conversion table, and displays a neutral gray in the image window where the colors are out of gamut.

Because the gray can be hard to spot in the image, you'll convert it to a more visible color.

2　Choose Edit > Preferences > Transparency & Gamut (Windows) or Photoshop > Preferences > Transparency & Gamut (Mac OS).

3　Click the color sample in the Gamut Warning area at the bottom of the dialog box. Select a vivid color, such as purple or bright green, and click OK.

4　Click OK to close the Preferences dialog box.

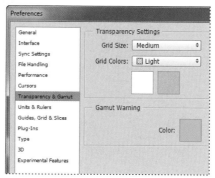

The bright new color you chose appears instead of the neutral gray as the gamut warning color.

5　Choose View > Gamut Warning to turn off the preview of out-of-gamut colors.

Photoshop will automatically correct these out-of-gamut colors when you save the file in Photoshop EPS format later in this lesson. Photoshop EPS format changes the RGB image to CMYK, adjusting the RGB colors as needed to bring them into the CMYK color gamut.

Adjusting an image

The next step in preparing an image for output is to make any necessary color and tonal adjustments. In this exercise, you'll add some tonal and color adjustments to correct an off-color scan of the original poster.

So that you can compare the image before and after making corrections, you'll start by making a copy.

1 Choose Image > Duplicate, and click OK to duplicate the image.

2 Choose Window > Arrange > 2 Up Vertical so you can compare the images as you work.

You'll adjust the hue and saturation of the image to move all colors into gamut.

3 Select 14Working.psd (the original image) to make it active, and then select the Visit Paris layer in the Layers panel.

4 Choose Select > Color Range.

5 In the Color Range dialog box, choose Out Of Gamut from the Select menu, and then click OK.

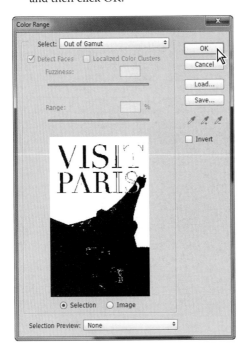

The areas that were marked as out of gamut earlier are now selected, so you can make changes that affect only those areas.

6 Choose View > Extras to hide the selection while you work with it.

The selection border can be distracting. When you hide extras, you no longer see the selection, but it's still in effect.

7   Click the Hue/Saturation button in the Adjustments panel to create a Hue/Saturation adjustment layer. (Choose Window > Adjustments if the panel isn't open.) The Hue/Saturation adjustment layer includes a layer mask, created from your selection.

8   In the Properties panel, do the following:

- Leave Hue setting at the default value.

- Drag the Saturation slider until the intensity of the colors looks more realistic (we used -14).

- Drag the Lightness to darken (we used -2).

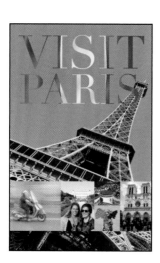

9   Choose View > Gamut Warning. You have removed most of the out-of-gamut colors from the image. Choose View > Gamut Warning again to deselect it.

10 Close the duplicate image file without saving it.

Converting an image to CMYK

It's generally a good idea to work in RGB mode as long as possible. Converting between modes causes color values to be rounded—and therefore less accurate if you convert multiple times. Once you've made any last-minute corrections, you're ready to convert the image to CMYK. If you think you may want to output the image to an inkjet printer or distribute it digitally later, save a copy in RGB mode before converting to CMYK mode.

1 Click the Channels tab to bring the Channels panel to the front.

The image is currently in RGB mode, so there are three channels listed: red, green, and blue. The RGB channel is not actually a channel, but a composite of all three.

2 Choose Image > Mode > CMYK Color.

3 Click Merge in the message that warns you that you might lose some adjustment layers.

Adjustment layers are lost when you convert the color mode from RGB to CMYK. Merging the layers ensures the adjustments you made are preserved.

4 Click OK in the message about the color profile used in the conversion.

You'll learn more about color profiles when you work with color management.

The Channels panel now displays four channels: cyan, magenta, yellow, and black. Additionally, it lists the CMYK composite. The layers were merged during conversion, so there is only one layer in the Layers panel.

About color management

Because the RGB and CMYK color models use different methods to display colors, each reproduces a different *gamut*, or range, of colors. For example, RGB uses light to produce color, so its gamut includes neon colors, such as those you'd see in a neon sign. In contrast, printing inks excel at reproducing certain colors that can lie outside the RGB gamut, such as some pastels and pure black.

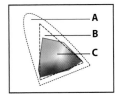 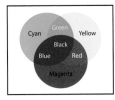

A. *Natural color gamut*
B. *RGB color gamut*
C. *CMYK color gamut*

RGB color model

CMYK color model

But not all RGB and CMYK gamuts are alike. Each monitor and printer model differs, and so each displays a slightly different gamut. For example, one brand of monitor may produce slightly brighter blues than another. The *color space* for a device is defined by the gamut it can reproduce.

The color management system in Photoshop uses International Color Consortium (ICC)-compliant color profiles to convert colors from one color space into another. A color profile is a description of a device's color space, such as the CMYK color space of a particular printer. You specify which profiles to use to accurately proof and print your images. Once you've selected the profiles, Photoshop can embed them into your image files, so that Photoshop and other applications can accurately manage color for the image.

For information on embedding color profiles, see Photoshop Help.

Before you begin working with color management, you should calibrate your monitor. If your monitor doesn't display colors accurately, color adjustments you make based on the image you see on your monitor may not be accurate. For information about calibrating your monitor, see Photoshop Help.

Specifying color-management settings

In order to accurately preview your colors onscreen, you need to set up color management in Photoshop. Most of the color-management controls you need are in the Color Settings dialog box.

By default, Photoshop is set up for RGB as part of a digital workflow. If you are preparing artwork for print production, however, you'll want to change the settings to be more appropriate for images that will be printed on paper rather than displayed on a screen.

You'll create customized color settings.

1   Choose Edit > Color Settings to open the Color Settings dialog box.

The bottom of the dialog box interactively describes each option.

2   Move the pointer over each part of the dialog box, including the names of areas (such as Working Spaces), the menu names, and the menu options. As you move the pointer, Photoshop displays information about each item. When you've finished, return the options to their defaults.

Now, you'll choose a set of options designed for a print workflow, rather than an online workflow.

3   Choose North America Prepress 2 from the Settings menu. The working spaces and color-management policy options change for a prepress workflow. Then click OK.

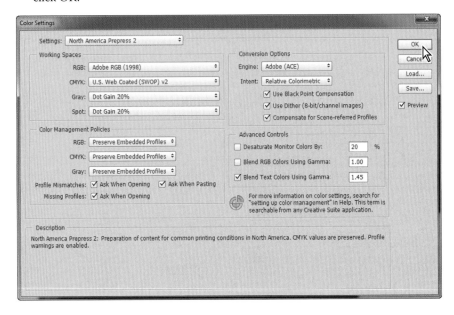

Proofing an image

You'll select a proof profile so that you can view a close onscreen representation of what an image will look like when printed. An accurate proof profile lets you proof on the screen (*soft-proof*) for printed output.

A proof profile (also called a *proof setup*) defines how the document is going to be printed, and adjusts the onscreen appearance accordingly. Photoshop provides a variety of settings that can help you proof images for different uses, including print and display on the web. For this lesson, you'll create a custom proof setup. You can then save the settings for use on other images that will be output the same way.

1   Choose View > Proof Setup > Custom. The Customize Proof Condition dialog box opens. Make sure Preview is selected.

2   From the Device To Simulate menu, choose a profile that represents the final output device, such as that for the printer you'll use to print the image. If you don't have a specific printer, the profile Working CMYK–U.S. Web Coated (SWOP) v2, the current default, is generally a good choice.

3   If you've chosen a different profile, make sure Preserve CMYK Numbers is *not* selected.

The Preserve CMYK Numbers option simulates how colors will appear if they're not converted to the output device color space.

4 Make sure Relative Colorimetric is selected for the Rendering Intent.

A rendering intent determines how the color is converted from one color space to another. Relative Colorimetric, which preserves color relationships without sacrificing color accuracy, is the standard rendering intent for printing in North America and Europe.

5 If it's available for the profile you chose, select Simulate Black Ink. Then deselect it, and select Simulate Paper Color; notice that selecting this option automatically selects Simulate Black Ink.

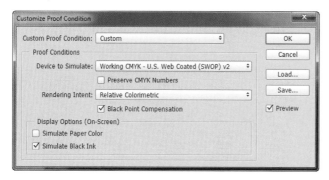

Notice that the image appears to lose contrast. Paper Color simulates the dingy white of real paper, according to the proof profile. Black Ink simulates the dark gray that actually prints to most printers, instead of solid black. Not all profiles support these options.

> **Tip:** To display the document with and without the proof settings, toggle View > Proof Colors.

6 Toggle the Preview option to see the difference between the image as it is displayed on screen and as it will print, based on the profile you selected. Then click OK.

Normal image

Image with Paper Color and Black Ink options selected

Saving the image as a CMYK EPS file

Many professional printers request that Photoshop images be submitted in EPS format. You'll save this image as an EPS file in CMYK mode.

1   Choose File > Save As.

2   In the Save As dialog box, do the following, and then click Save:

   • Choose Photoshop EPS from the Format menu.

   • Under Color, select Use Proof Setup. Don't worry about the warning icon; you'll save a copy.

   • Accept the filename 14Working.eps.

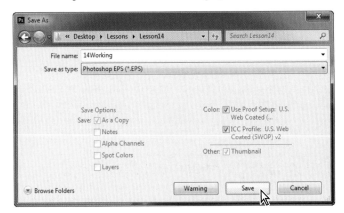

3   Click OK in the EPS Options dialog box that appears.

4   Save and then close the 14Working.psd file.

5   Choose File > Open, navigate to the Lessons/Lesson14 folder, and double-click the 14Working.eps file.

Printing to a desktop inkjet printer

Many consumer-level inkjet printers do a good job printing photographs and other image files. The precise settings available vary from printer to printer, but when you're printing images from Photoshop to a desktop inkjet printer, you'll get the best results if you do the following:

- Make sure the appropriate printer driver is installed, and that you've selected it.

- Use the appropriate paper for your intended use. Special photographic and coated papers are a good choice when you're printing photos for framing.

- Select the correct paper source in the printer settings. The printer lays ink differently on different types of paper. If you're using photographic paper, make sure you've selected it in the printer settings.

- Select the image quality in the printer settings. For framed prints, you probably want to print the highest quality. If you're printing a proof to get a sense of the color, you may want to select a lower quality for speedier printing and to use less ink.

Printing a CMYK image from Photoshop

If you're printing an image directly from Photoshop, use the following guidelines for best results:

- Print a *color composite*, often called a *color comp,* to proof your image. A color composite is a single print that combines the red, green, and blue channels of an RGB image (or the cyan, magenta, yellow, and black channels of a CMYK image). This indicates what the final printed image will look like.

- Set the parameters for the halftone screen.

- Print separations to make sure the image separates correctly.

- Print to film or plate.

When you print color separations, Photoshop prints a separate sheet, or *plate*, for each ink. For a CMYK image, it prints four plates, one for each process color. In this exercise, you'll print color separations.

1 With the 14Working.eps image open from the previous exercise, choose File > Print.

By default, Photoshop prints any document as a composite image. To print this file as separations, you need to explicitly instruct Photoshop in the Print dialog box.

2 In the Print dialog box, do the following:

  • In the Color Management area, choose Separations from the Color Handling menu.

  • Click Print.

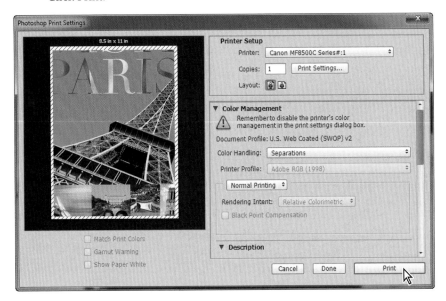

This lesson has provided an introduction to printing and producing consistent color from Photoshop. If you're printing on a desktop printer, you can experiment with different settings to find the best color and print settings for your system. If you're preparing images for professional printing, consult with your print service provider to determine the best settings to use. For more information about color management, printing options, and color separations, see Photoshop Help.

Extra Credit

Sharing your work on Behance

Integrated into Creative Cloud, Behance is the leading online platform for showcasing and discovering creative work. Photoshop makes it easy to upload and post files to your own portfolio on Behance.

1   Open the 14Working.eps file in Photoshop, if it isn't already open.

2   Choose File > Share On Behance.

The Share On Behance dialog box opens.

3   If you have a Behance portfolio, you may need to sign in; if you're already signed in, you'll see a preview of your working file. If you don't have a Behance portfolio, click Start Your Public Portfolio.

4   In the Upload A Work In Progress window, type **Visit Paris** for the title.

5   Type **paris, travel, eiffel tower, collage** for the tags.

6   Choose Private from the Visible To menu if you want to control who sees the image. Choose Everyone if you want it to be publicly available.

7   Click Continue.

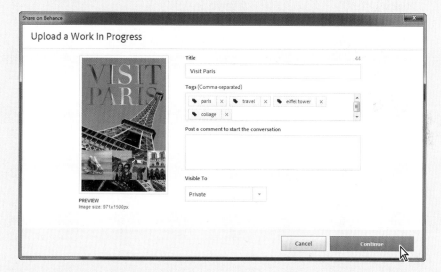

The dialog box displays a link to your artwork. You can share the link on social media or paste it into email or a blog post. You can also click View And Share On Behance to sync to social networks such as Twitter, Facebook, and LinkedIn.

8   Click Close.

Close the file without saving. Your work of art is available to be admired on Behance.

Continues on next page

Extra credit (continued)

With cutting-edge and traditional designers alike sharing their work, Behance is a great source of inspiration. You can browse as wide or narrow a group of works as you like, with filters for popular images, fields of interest, and countries of origin. Or you can enter your own search term. And when you find contributors you like, you can follow them to keep up with their latest work.

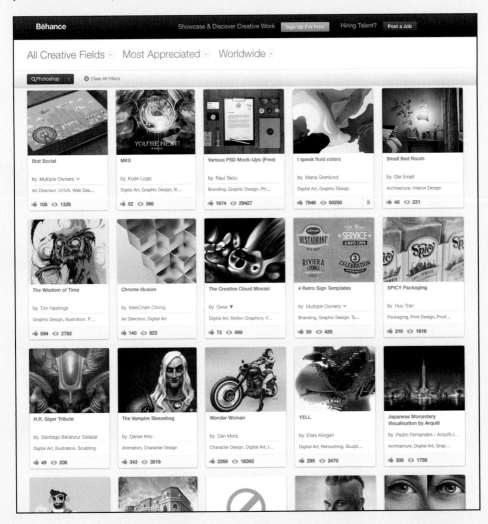

Review questions

1 What steps should you follow to reproduce color accurately?

2 What is a gamut?

3 What is a color profile?

4 What are color separations?

Review answers

1 To reproduce color accurately, first calibrate your monitor, and then use the Color Settings dialog box to specify which color spaces to use. For example, you can specify which RGB color space to use for online images, and which CMYK color space to use for images that will be printed. You can then proof the image, check for out-of-gamut colors, adjust colors as needed, and—for printed images—create color separations.

2 A gamut is the range of colors that can be reproduced by a color model or device. For example, the RGB and CMYK color models have different gamuts, as do any two RGB scanners.

3 A color profile is a description of a device's color space, such as the CMYK color space of a particular printer. Applications such as Photoshop can interpret color profiles in an image to maintain consistent color across different applications, platforms, and devices.

4 Color separations are separate plates for each ink used in a document. Often, you'll print color separations for the cyan, magenta, yellow, and black (CMYK) inks.

15 PRINTING 3D FILES

Lesson overview

In this lesson, you'll learn how to do the following:

- Create a simple 3D object using a mesh preset.

- Use 3D tools in Photoshop.

- Manipulate 3D objects.

- Adjust the camera view.

- Prepare 3D files for printing.

- Export a file for remote printing.

This lesson will take about 30 minutes to complete. Download the Lesson15 project files from the Lesson & Update Files tab on your Account page at www.peachpit.com, if you haven't already done so. As you work on this lesson, you'll preserve the start files. If you need to restore the start files, download them from your Account page.

PROJECT: 3D LUGGAGE TAG

You can print 3D objects directly from Photoshop. If you have a 3D printer on-site, you can print locally. Otherwise, you can export your file for printing by an online vendor.

Getting started

● **Note:** Features covered in this lesson require Mac OS 10.7 or later, or Windows 7 or later, and at least 512MB VRAM. For more complete Photoshop system requirements, visit www.adobe.com/ products/photoshop/ tech-specs.html.

This lesson explores 3D features, which are available only if your video card has at least 512MB of dedicated vRAM and supports OpenGL 2.0, and if OpenGL 2.0 is enabled on your computer. To learn about your video card, choose Edit > Preferences > Performance (Windows) or Photoshop > Preferences > Performance (Mac OS). Information about your video card is in the Graphics Processor Settings area of the dialog box.

In this lesson, you'll create a three-dimensional luggage tag. First, you'll view the finished tag.

1   Start Photoshop, and then immediately hold down Ctrl+Alt+Shift (Windows) or Command+Option+Shift (Mac OS) to restore the default preferences. (See "Restoring default preferences" on page 4.)

2   When prompted, click Yes to delete the Adobe Photoshop Settings file.

3   Choose File > Browse In Bridge to open Adobe Bridge.

4   In Bridge, click Lessons in the Favorites panel. Double-click the Lesson 15 folder in the Content panel.

5   View the 15End.psd file in Bridge.

The 15End.psd file contains a 3D rendering of a luggage tag. In this lesson, you'll combine elements to create the luggage tag, and then prepare it for printing. If you want to, you can print it locally to a 3D printer or export it to an online vendor for printing. (You'll see estimated costs before placing the order.)

Before you create the luggage tag, you'll play with the 3D tools to become familiar with the 3D environment.

6   Return to Photoshop.

Understanding the 3D environment

The advantage to working with 3D objects is, obviously, that you can work with them in three dimensions. You can also return to a 3D layer at any time to change lighting, color, material, or position without having to re-create a lot of the art. Photoshop includes several basic tools that make it easy to rotate, resize, and position 3D objects. The 3D tools in the options bar manipulate the object itself. The Camera widget in the lower left corner of the application window manipulates the camera so you can view a 3D scene from different angles.

You can use the 3D tools whenever a 3D layer is selected in the Layers panel. A 3D layer behaves like any other layer—you can apply layer styles, mask it, and so on. However, a 3D layer can be quite complex.

Unlike a regular layer, a 3D layer contains one or more *meshes*. A mesh defines the 3D object. For example, in the following exercise, the mesh is the cone shape. Each mesh, in turn, includes one or more *materials*—the appearance of a part or all of the mesh. Each material includes one or more *maps*, which are the components of the appearance. There are nine typical maps, and there can be only one of each kind; however, you can also use custom maps. Each map contains one *texture*—the image that defines what the maps and materials look like. The texture may be a simple bitmap graphic or a set of layers. The same texture might be used by many different maps and materials.

In addition to meshes, a 3D layer also includes one or more *lights*, which affect the appearance of 3D objects and remain in a fixed position as you spin or move the object. A 3D layer also includes *cameras*, which are saved views with the objects in a particular position. The *shader* creates the final appearance based on the materials, object properties, and renderer.

That may all sound complicated, but the most important thing to remember is that the 3D tools in the options bar move an object in 3D space and the Camera widget moves the cameras that view the object.

You'll start by creating a simple 3D object from a plain colored layer.

1   In Photoshop, choose File > New. Click OK to accept the default values.

2   Choose Select > All to select the entire background layer.

3   Choose Edit > Fill. In the Fill dialog box, choose Color from the Use menu, and then select a vivid blue color in the Color Picker. Click OK to close the Color Picker, and click OK again to close the Fill dialog box.

4   Choose Select > Deselect.

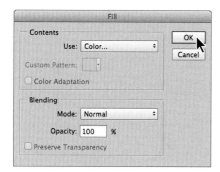

5 Choose 3D > New Mesh From Layer > Mesh Preset > Cone. If you see a message asking whether you want to switch to the 3D workspace, click Yes.

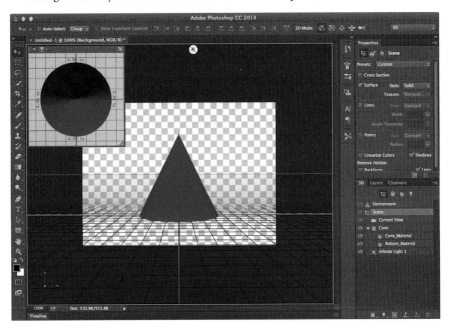

Your blue layer becomes a blue cone. Photoshop displays a grid, a Secondary View window, a Camera widget, and other 3D resources. Now that you have a 3D object, you can use the 3D tools.

6 In the Tools panel, select the Move tool (⤵).

All the 3D capabilities are embedded into the Move tool, which recognizes when a 3D layer is selected and enables the 3D tools.

7 Select the Drag The 3D Object tool (✥) in the 3D Mode area of the options bar.

8 Click the edge of the cone, or just outside it, and drag to move it from side to side or up and down. Return the cone to the center. (If you click the cone itself, Photoshop recognizes the 3D Axis widget, and switches to the tool that corresponds with the active area of the widget, which you'll learn about shortly.)

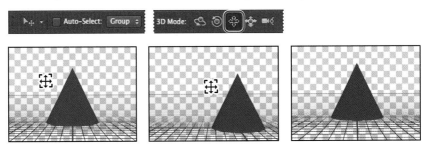

9 Select the Rotate The 3D Object tool () in the options bar, and then click and drag the cone to rotate it.

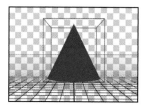

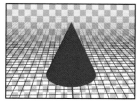 

10 Experiment with the other tools to see how they affect the object.

When you select a 3D object, Photoshop displays the colorful 3D Axis widget, with green, red, and blue representing different axes. Red represents the x axis, green represents the y axis, and blue represents the z axis. (Hint: Think of RGB color to remember the order.)

If you hover the mouse over the center box until it turns yellow, you can click the box and drag to scale the object uniformly. Click an arrow to move the object along that axis; click the curved handle just before the arrow to rotate on that axis; click the smaller handle to scale along that axis.

11 Rotate, scale, and move the cone using the widget.

12 Right-click (Windows) or Control-click (Mac OS) the Camera widget in the lower left corner of the application window (it has two axes visible), and choose Top.

▶ **Tip:** As you move the object, the 3D Axis widget shifts, too. For example, the x and y axis arrows may be available, while the z axis is pointing directly into the scene. The yellow center box may also be obscured by an axis.

Options in the Camera menu determine the angle from which you see the object. The camera angle changes, but the object itself does not. Don't be fooled by its relationship to the background; the background is not 3D, so it remains in place when Photoshop moves the camera for the 3D object.

13 Choose other camera views to see how they affect the perspective.

14 When you're done experimenting, close the file. You can save your creation if you want to, or close without saving.

Positioning 3D elements

Now that you've gotten a feel for the 3D tools, you'll use them to position the text on a luggage tag.

1   Choose File > Open, navigate to the Lesson15 folder, and double-click the 15Start.psd file.

The file contains two 3D elements: the text and the tag itself. Currently, the text is in an awkward position, overlapping the tag. You'll start by centering it.

2   Make sure the Move tool is selected in the Tools panel.

3   Click the front of the "Visit Paris" text to activate the 3D Axis widget.

4   Hover the cursor over the tip of the green arrow until the Move On Y Axis tool tip appears.

5   Click the tip of the green arrow, and drag the type down until it's centered vertically on the red tag.

6   Click the tip of the red arrow, and drag the type to the right so that it's horizontally centered on the red tag.

Your tag is ready to print!

7   Choose File > Save As. Navigate to the Lesson15 folder, and save the file as **15Working.psd**. Click OK in the Photoshop Format Options dialog box.

Printing a 3D file

When you think of printing, you usually think of producing a flat page of two-dimensional text and images. They may be high-quality, amazing images, but you can't see them from different angles, and what you hold in your hand remains a piece of paper or other relatively simple media.

3D printers open up a whole new world of printing opportunities. Instead of printing an image of a thing, you can print the *thing* itself. The possibilities are endless, including medical uses, prototyping, and creative enterprises such as making jewelry and one-of-a-kind souvenirs.

3D printers were once the province of well-funded labs, but have recently become much more accessible. In many cities, you can use one at a "maker" or do-it-yourself (DIY) space, a shared workshop area where, for a fee, you can use many advanced resources. If you don't have a 3D printer yourself or easy access to one, you can also send your 3D creations to online vendors who will print them using the material you specify and mail them to you.

You can create 3D objects in Photoshop—or import 3D objects that have been created elsewhere—and print them directly from Photoshop.

Specifying 3D print settings

You don't use the standard Print dialog box to print 3D objects from Photoshop. And before you print, you need to make sure the settings are appropriate.

1   Choose 3D > 3D Print Settings.

The Properties panel displays the 3D print settings, and the image window shows a preview of your 3D object. The preview shows you how it will look when printed, based on the printer you select.

2   Choose Shapeways from the Print To menu in the Properties panel.

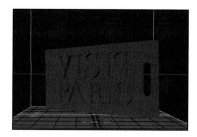

Shapeways is an online vendor that prints 3D objects and mails them to you for a fee. There are other online vendors, but Shapeways is easiest to use because you can choose its printers directly within Photoshop. If you use another vendor, ask them for instructions for printing from Photoshop.

If you own a 3D printer, choose Local from the Print To menu, and then choose your printer from the Printer menu. If your printer isn't listed in the menu, choose Get Latest Printers from the Print To menu, and then download the profiles for all supported printers.

3   Choose Plastic Alumide from the Printer menu. Plastic alumide is a plastic that simulates metal.

When you choose Shapeways from the Print To menu, the Printer menu lists dozens of material options. The material you select affects the appearance and cost of the object you print.

The preview of the 3D object changes in the image window to reflect the choices you've made. When you choose Plastic Alumide, the preview shows a silver-gray tag with extruded text.

4   Make sure Inches is selected in the Printer Volume menu to specify how printer volume should be measured.

3D printers have different capacities, and it's important to consider whether your object will fit within the printer's volume. The Printer Volume values are dimmed, because you can't change them; they describe the volume for the printer you've chosen. The Scene Volume values reflect the size of your 3D scene (in this case, a single object). If Show Printer Volume Overlay is selected, the preview shows a cube outline to represent the printer volume that the scene lies within.

If the scene volume is larger than the printer volume, click Scale To Print Volume in the Properties panel to reduce its size so that your printer can print it. In this case, the scene volume is comfortably smaller than the printer volume.

▶ **Tip:** You can learn more about the materials available through Shapeways, and compare costs of various options, by visiting http://www.shapeways.com/materials.

5 Choose Medium from the Detail Level menu. This option determines how detailed the preview image is.

The Surface Detail options preserve bump maps, other texture, and opacity settings when you print. You can leave those selected, though there are no bump maps or opacity settings in this object.

You're ready to print.

Exporting a 3D object

Printing a 3D object is a little more complicated than printing a two-dimensional image. It's not that much more challenging for the person doing the printing, but Photoshop has to do a lot of behind-the-scenes calculations.

3D printers build objects from the bottom. If you're printing a cube, for example, or another object with a significant base, the printer can create it without further support. However, many 3D objects are irregularly shaped, and the bottom of the object may actually be a set of disconnected surfaces. For example, think of a model of an animal. The bottom of the animal is composed of the four separate feet. In order to print such an object, the printer requires a support structure. That structure typically includes a *raft*, which provides a base to print from, and *scaffolding*, which supports portions of the object so they don't collapse while the rest of the object is being printed.

When you choose 3D Print, Photoshop prepares the object for printing, and calculates any necessary raft and scaffolding as well.

1 Choose 3D > 3D Print, or click the Start Print button at the bottom of the Properties panel.

Photoshop displays a progress bar as it prepares the print job.

2 Click OK in the dialog box that informs you that the estimated price may differ from the final purchase price.

3 In the Photoshop 3D Print Settings dialog box, review the estimated price and print size.

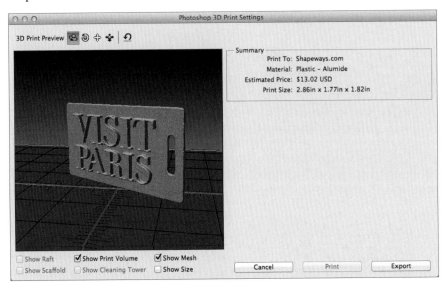

Click options in the Preview area of the dialog box to see the size, shadows, raft, scaffolding, and other aspects of the job. This object requires no raft or scaffolding, so those options are dimmed.

Use the 3D tools at the top of the dialog box to see your object from different angles.

Printing prices vary dramatically depending on the material you choose. You can click Cancel, choose a different printer, and then let Photoshop calculate the price again. You've made no commitments at this point in the process.

4 Click Export.

5 Click Save in the Save dialog box.

Photoshop saves the 3D print file information in the 15Working.psd file.

6 When you're prompted to upload your file to the Shapeways site for printing, click Yes to continue to the site, or click Cancel to stop the process.

7 If you continue to the Shapeways site, sign in if you have an account, or create one if you don't. (Creating an account is free.)

8 When prompted, select the file you just saved. It will be in the Lesson15 folder, called 15Working.stl.zip. Then click Upload.

Shapeways uploads and unzips the file. It displays the object and lists possible materials and their prices.

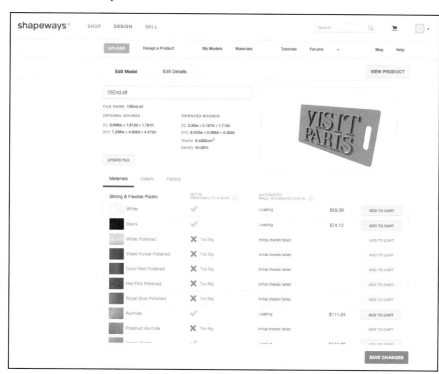

Note: You are not committed to a purchase until you check out and pay for the object.

9 Click Add To Cart next to the material you want to print, and then follow the onscreen instructions to place your order. The printed object will be shipped to you.

Review questions

1 How does a 3D layer differ from other layers in Photoshop?

2 How can you change the camera view?

3 Which color represents each axis on the 3D Axis widget?

4 How do you print a 3D object?

Review answers

1 A 3D layer behaves like any other layer—you can apply layer styles, mask it, and so on. However, unlike a regular layer, a 3D layer also contains one or more meshes, which define 3D objects. You can work with meshes and the materials, maps, and textures they contain. You can also adjust the lighting for a 3D layer.

2 To change the camera view, you can move the Camera widget, or right-click (Windows) or Control-click (Mac OS) the widget to choose a camera view preset.

3 In the 3D Axis widget, the red arrow represents the X axis; the green arrow represents the Y axis, and the blue arrow represents the Z axis.

4 To print a 3D object from Photoshop, first choose 3D > 3D Print Settings, and set up your printer options. Then choose 3D > 3D Print, or click the Start Print button at the bottom of the Properties panel.

Appendix: Tools Panel Overview

Photoshop CC Tools panel

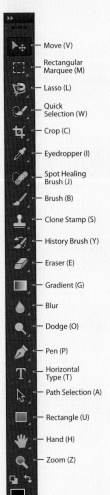

- Move (V)
- Rectangular Marquee (M)
- Lasso (L)
- Quick Selection (W)
- Crop (C)
- Eyedropper (I)
- Spot Healing Brush (J)
- Brush (B)
- Clone Stamp (S)
- History Brush (Y)
- Eraser (E)
- Gradient (G)
- Blur
- Dodge (O)
- Pen (P)
- Horizontal Type (T)
- Path Selection (A)
- Rectangle (U)
- Hand (H)
- Zoom (Z)

The Move tool moves selections, layers, and guides.

The marquee tools make rectangular, elliptical, single row, and single column selections.

The lasso tools make free-hand, polygonal (straight-edged), and magnetic (snap-to) selections.

The Quick Selection tool lets you quickly "paint" a selection using an adjust-able round brush tip.

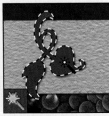

The Magic Wand tool selects similarly colored areas.

The crop tools trim, straighten, and change the perspective of images.

The Eyedropper tool samples colors in an image.

The 3D Material Eyedropper tool loads selected material from a 3D object.

The Color Sampler tool samples up to four areas of the image.

The Ruler tool measures distances, locations, and angles.

The Note tool makes notes that can be attached to an image.

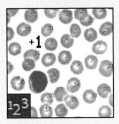

The Count tool counts objects in an image.

The Slice tool creates slices.

The Slice Select tool selects slices.

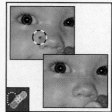

The Spot Healing Brush tool quickly removes blemishes and imperfections from photographs with a uniform background.

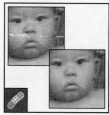

The Healing Brush tool paints with a sample or pattern to repair imperfections in an image.

The Patch tool repairs imperfections in a selected area of an image using a sample or pattern.

The Content-Aware Move tool recomposes and blends pixels to accommodate a moved object.

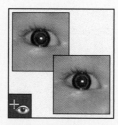

The Red Eye tool removes red eye in flash photos with one click.

The Brush tool paints brush strokes.

The Pencil tool paints hard-edged strokes.

The Color Replacement tool substitutes one color for another.

The Mixer Brush tool blends a sampled color with an existing color.

The Clone Stamp tool paints with a sample of an image.

Continues on next page

Appendix: Tools Panel Overview (continued)

The Pattern Stamp tool paints with a part of an image as a pattern.

The History Brush tool paints a copy of the selected state or snapshot into the current image window.

The Art History Brush tool paints stylized strokes that simulate the look of different paint styles, using a selected state or snapshot.

The Eraser tool erases pixels and restores parts of an image to a previously saved state.

The Background Eraser tool erases areas to transparency by dragging.

The Magic Eraser tool erases solid-colored areas to transparency with a single click.

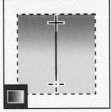

The Gradient tool creates straight-line, radial, angle, reflected, and diamond blends between colors.

The Paint Bucket tool fills similarly colored areas with the foreground color.

The 3D Material Drop tool drops the material loaded in the 3D Material Eyedropper tool onto the targeted area of a 3D object.

The Blur tool blurs hard edges in an image.

The Sharpen tool sharpens soft edges in an image.

The Smudge tool smudges data in an image.

The Dodge tool lightens areas in an image.

The Burn tool darkens areas in an image.

The Sponge tool changes the color saturation of an area.

The pen tools draw smooth-edged paths.

The type tools create type on an image.

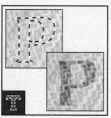

The type mask tools create a selection in the shape of type.

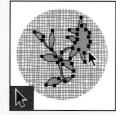

The path selection tools make shape or segment selections showing anchor points, direction lines, and direction points.

The shape tools and Line tool draw shapes and lines in a normal layer or shape layer.

The Custom Shape tool makes customized shapes selected from a custom shape list.

The Hand tool moves an image within its window.

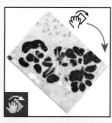

The Rotate View tool nondestructively rotates the canvas.

The Zoom tool magnifies and reduces the view of an image.

Appendix: Keyboard shortcuts

Most tools and commands in Photoshop can be accessed through keyboard shortcuts. As you grow more comfortable with the software, learning shortcuts for tools and commands you use most often can save you time.

Tools *Each group of tools in the Tools panel shares a shortcut. Press Shift+ the letter key repeatedly to cycle through hidden tools.*

Move tool	V
Rectangular Marquee tool	M
Elliptical Marquee tool	M
Lasso tool	L
Polygonal Lasso tool	L
Magnetic Lasso tool	L
Quick Selection tool	W
Magic Wand tool	W
Eyedropper tool	I
3D Material Eyedropper tool	I
Color Sampler tool	I
Ruler tool	I
Note tool	I
Count tool	I
Crop tool	C
Perspective Crop tool	C
Slice tool	C
Slice Select tool	C
Spot Healing Brush tool	J
Healing Brush tool	J
Patch tool	J
Content-Aware Move tool	J
Red Eye tool	J
Brush tool	B
Pencil tool	B
Color Replacement tool	B
Mixer Brush tool	B
Clone Stamp tool	S
Pattern Stamp tool	S
History Brush tool	Y
Art History Brush tool	Y
Eraser tool	E
Background Eraser tool	E
Magic Eraser tool	E
Gradient tool	G

Paint Bucket tool	G
3D Material Drop tool	G
Dodge tool	O
Burn tool	O
Sponge tool	O
Pen tool	P
Freeform Pen tool	P
Horizontal Type tool	T
Vertical Type tool	T
Horizontal Type Mask tool	T
Vertical Type Mask tool	T
Path Selection tool	A
Direct Selection tool	A
Rectangle tool	U
Rounded Rectangle tool	U
Ellipse tool	U
Polygon tool	U
Line tool	U
Custom Shape tool	U
Hand tool	H
Rotate View tool	R
Zoom tool	Z
Default Foreground/Background Colors	D
Switch Foreground/Background Colors	X
Toggle Standard/Quick Mask Modes	Q
Toggle Screen Modes	F
Toggle Preserve Transparency	/
Decrease Brush Size	[
Increase Brush Size	]
Decrease Brush Hardness	{
Increase Brush Hardness	}
Previous Brush	,
Next Brush	.
First Brush	<
Last Brush	>

Application Menus *These shortcuts are for Windows. For Mac OS, substitute Command for Ctrl and Option for Alt.*

File

New . . . . **Ctrl+N**
Open . . . . **Ctrl+O**
Browse in Bridge . . . . **Alt+Ctrl+O** or **Shift+Ctrl+O**
Open As . . . . **Alt+Shift+Ctrl+O**
Close . . . . **Ctrl+W**
Close All . . . . **Alt+Ctrl+W**
Close and Go to Bridge . . . . **Shift+Ctrl+W**
Save . . . . **Ctrl+S**
Save As . . . . **Shift+Ctrl+S** or **Alt+Ctrl+**S
Save for Web . . . . **Alt+Shift+Ctrl+S**
Revert **F12**
File Info . . . . **Alt+Shift+Ctrl+I**
Print . . . . **Ctrl+P**
Print One Copy . . . . **Alt+Shift+Ctrl+P**
Exit . . . . **Ctrl+Q**

Edit

Undo/Redo . . . . **Ctrl+Z**
Step Forward . . . . **Shift+Ctrl+Z**
Step Backward . . . . **Alt+Ctrl+Z**
Fade . . . . **Shift+Ctrl+F**
Cut . . . . **Ctrl+X** or **F2**
Copy . . . . **Ctrl+C** or **F3**
Copy Merged . . . . **Shift+Ctrl+C**
Paste . . . . **Ctrl+V F4**
Paste Special > Paste in Place . . . . **Shift+Ctrl+V**
Paste Special > Paste Into . . . . **Alt+Shift+Ctrl+V**
Fill . . . . **Shift+F5**
Content-Aware Scale . . . . **Alt+Shift+Ctrl+C**
Free Transform . . . . **Ctrl+T**
Transform > Again . . . . **Shift+Ctrl+T**
Color Settings . . . . **Shift+Ctrl+K**
Keyboard Shortcuts . . . . **Alt+Shift+Ctrl+K**
Menus . . . . **Alt+Shift+Ctrl+M**
Preferences > General . . . . **Ctrl+K**

Image

Adjustments >
    Levels . . . . **Ctrl+L**
    Curves . . . . **Ctrl+M**
    Hue/Saturation . . . . **Ctrl+U**
    Color Balance . . . . **Ctrl+B**
    Black & White . . . . **Alt+Shift+Ctrl+B**
    Invert . . . . **Ctrl+I**
Desaturate . . . . **Shift+Ctrl+U**
Auto Tone . . . . **Shift+Ctrl+L**
Auto Contrast . . . . **Alt+Shift+Ctrl+L**
Auto Color . . . . **Shift+Ctrl+B**
Image Size . . . . **Alt+Ctrl+I**
Canvas Size... . . . . **Alt+Ctrl+C**

Layer

New > Layer . . . . **Shift+Ctrl+N**
New > Layer via Copy . . . . **Ctrl+J**
New > Layer via Cut . . . . **Shift+Ctrl+J**
Create/Release Clipping Mask . . . . **Alt+Ctrl+G**

Group Layers

Group Layers . . . . **Ctrl+G**
Ungroup Layers . . . . **Shift+Ctrl+G**
Arrange >
    Bring to Front . . . . **Shift+Ctrl+]**
    Bring Forward . . . . **Ctrl+]**
    Send Backward . . . . **Ctrl+[**
    Send to Back . . . . **Shift+Ctrl+[**
Merge Layers . . . . **Ctrl+E**
Merge Visible . . . . **Shift+Ctrl+E**

Select

All . . . . **Ctrl+A**
Deselect . . . . **Ctrl+D**
Reselect . . . . **Shift+Ctrl+D**
Inverse . . . . **Shift+Ctrl+I** or **Shift+F7**
All Layers . . . . **Alt+Ctrl+A**
Find Layers . . . . **Alt+Shift+Ctrl+F**
Refine Edge . . . . **Alt+Ctrl+R**
Modify > Feather . . . . **Shift+F6**

Filter

Last Filter . . . . **Ctrl+F**
Adaptive Wide Angle . . . . **Alt+Shift+Ctrl+A**
Camera Raw Filter . . . . **Shift+Ctrl+A**
Lens Correction . . . . **Shift+Ctrl+R**
Liquify . . . . **Shift+Ctrl+X**
Vanishing Point . . . . **Alt+Ctrl+V**

3D

Show/Hide Polygons > Within Selection . . . . **Alt+Ctrl+X**
Show/Hide Polygons > Reveal All . . . . **Alt+Shift+Ctrl+X**
Render . . . . **Alt+Shift+Ctrl+R**

View

Proof Colors . . . . **Ctrl+Y**
Gamut Warning . . . . **Shift+Ctrl+Y**
Zoom In . . . . **Ctrl++ Ctrl+=**
Zoom Out . . . . **Ctrl+-**
Fit on Screen . . . . **Ctrl+0**
100% . . . . **Ctrl+1** or **Alt+Ctrl+0**
Extras . . . . **Ctrl+H**
Show > Target Path . . . . **Shift+Ctrl+H**
Show > Grid . . . . **Ctrl+'**
Show > Guides . . . . **Ctrl+;**
Rulers . . . . **Ctrl+R**
Snap . . . . **Shift+Ctrl+;**
Lock Guides . . . . **Alt+Ctrl+;**

Window

Actions . . . . **Alt+F9** or **F9**
Brush **F5**
Color **F6**
Info **F8**
Layers **F7**

Help

Photoshop Help **F1**

INDEX

R

S

Production Notes

Adobe Photoshop CC Classroom in a Book (2014 release) was created electronically using Adobe InDesign CC. Art was produced using Adobe InDesign, Adobe Illustrator, and Adobe Photoshop. The Myriad Pro and Warnock Pro OpenType families of typefaces were used throughout this book. For information about OpenType and Adobe fonts, visit www.adobe.com/type/opentype/.

References to company names in the lessons are for demonstration purposes only and are not intended to refer to any actual organization or person.

Images

Photographic images and illustrations are intended for use with the tutorials.

Lesson 4 pineapple and flower photography © Image Source, www.imagesource.com

Lesson 6 and 7 model photography © Image Source, www.imagesource.com

Team credits

The following individuals contributed to the development of *Adobe Photoshop CC Classroom in a Book (2014 release)*:

Project Manager: Denise Thompson

Writer: Brie Gyncild

Illustrator and Compositor: Lisa Fridsma

Copyeditor and Proofreader: Wendy Katz

Indexer: Brie Gyncild

Technical Reviewer: Lisa Fridsma

Keystroker: Megan Ahearn

Cover design: Eddie Yuen

Interior design: Mimi Heft

Art Director: Andrew Faulkner

Designers: Jeff Brown and Lauren Donohue

Adobe Press Executive Editor: Victor Gavenda

Adobe Press Project Editor: Connie Jeung-Mills

Adobe Press Production Editor: Tracey Croom

Contributors

Jay Graham began his career designing and building custom homes. He has been a professional photographer for more than 22 years, with clients in the advertising, architectural, editorial, and travel industries. He contributed the "Pro Photo Workflow" tips in Lesson 5. www.jaygraham.com

Lisa Farrer is a photographer based in Marin County, CA. She contributed photography for Lesson 5. www.lisafarrerphoto.com

Gawain Weaver has conserved and restored original works by artists ranging from Eadward Muybridge to Man Ray, and from Ansel Adams to Cindy Sherman. He contributed to "Real World Photo Restoration" in Lesson 2. www.gawainweaver.com

Special Thanks

We offer our sincere thanks to Christine Yarrow, Daniel Presedo, Pete Falco, Stephen Nielson, Russell Brown, and Zorana Gee for their support and help with this project. We couldn't have done it without you!